Equality in Law between Men and Women
in the European Community

Ireland

Equality in Law between Men and Women in the European Community

---

Series Editors

MICHEL VERWILGHEN
Professeur ordinaire à la Faculté de Droit
Université catholique de Louvain

FERDINAND VON PRONDZYNSKI
Professor of Law and Dean of the Law School
University of Hull

European Commission

Equality in Law
between Men and Women
in the European Community

Ireland

by

ROSHEEN CALLENDER
B.A. (Econ.)
Dublin University

FRANCES MEENAN
B. Comm., M.B.S. (N.U.I.)
Solicitor

MARTINUS NIJHOFF PUBLISHERS
DORDRECHT/BOSTON/LONDON

OFFICE FOR OFFICIAL PUBLICATIONS OF THE EUROPEAN COMMUNITIES
LUXEMBOURG

A C.I.P. Catalogue record for this book is available from the Library of Congress.

ISBN (this volume)   0-7923-1834-X (Martinus Nijhoff Publishers)
                     92-826-4468-5 (Office for Official Publications of the EC)

This study was commissioned by the Equal Opportunities Unit of Directorate-General V
(Employment, Industrial Relations and Social Affairs) of the European Commission. It
does not, however, express the Commission's official views. The responsibility for the
views expressed lies with the authors.

A French version of this text has been published by the Office for Official Publications of
the European Communities and Les Editions Juridiques Bruylant, Brussels.

Published by
Office for Official Publications of the European Communities, L-2985 Luxembourg
ISBN (this volume) 92-826-4468-5   Catalogue number CE-97-92-007-EN-C
and
Martinus Nijhoff Publishers,
P.O. Box 163, 3300 AD Dordrecht, The Netherlands
ISBN (series) 0-7923-1842-0   ISBN (this volume) 0-7923-1834-X

Sold and distributed for the Office for Official Publications of the European Communities
by the distributors listed on the inside back cover.

Kluwer Academic Publishers incorporates the publishing programmes of D. Reidel,
Martinus Nijhoff, Dr W. Junk and MTP Press.

Sold and distributed in the USA and Canada
by Kluwer Academic Publishers,
101 Philip Drive, Norwell, MA 02061, U.S.A.

In all other countries sold and distributed
by Kluwer Academic Publishers Group,
P.O. Box 322, 3300 AH Dordrecht, The Netherlands

TABLE OF CONTENTS

COMMENTARY ON EQUALITY LAW

SOURCES OF EQUALITY LAW

FOREWORD

Since the Second World War several international organizations have been endeavouring to promote the principle of equal opportunities between women and men, in law as well as in practice. This objective has also been pursued in a number of countries within the framework of domestic law. The intention has been to pursue a social objective and to achieve a change in the patterns of social conduct. In this context it has been felt that where the law visibly adopts the principle of equality this may contribute to the transformation of attitudes.

It has generally been accepted that equal opportunities ought to be pursued in the working environment in particular. In part this is because employment equality is a concept which can be more easily addressed by legal means than can other aspects of equality, but it is also true that a better distribution of wealth and income between the sexes and the abandonment of separate gender roles in the labour market can provide a powerful impetus to the realization of equal opportunities in society more generally.

To some extent these initiatives have been successful. Progress has been made in a relatively short space of time, although perhaps in limited areas of the equal opportunities agenda. But the impact has been restricted, and much effort still needs to be made in order to improve both law and social practice.

* * *

Within the European Community also there has been a steady growth of interest in the issue of equality between women and men. Article 119 of the Treaty instituting the European Economic Community, signed in Rome on 25 March 1957, provides for equal pay for women and men workers who perform equal work. The main Directive advancing the idea of equal pay, Directive 75/117/EEC, will soon be celebrating its twentieth birthday.

But it is not enough to enact Directives. It is also necessary to analyse and control the implementation of these texts in the Member States of the European Community. The Commission of the European Communities has obviously understood this, since in its Action Programme for 1982-1985 it placed particular emphasis on the need to follow up the implementation of the Equality Directives. In pursuit of this the Commission established a number of expert networks to consider the equality agenda from a variety of viewpoints. One of these networks was the Network of Experts on the Implementation of the Equality Directives, consisting of experts from each of the Member States of the Community.

These experts have drawn up a series of reports on various aspects of their remit, and have been able to offer advice to the Commission on desirable courses of action to be followed. The network has also met regularly to discuss the reports and to update the Commission and each other on important developments in each of the Member States. Some of the network's consolidated reports have been published by the European Commission, and indeed the information contained in network documentation has been used in conferences of legal practitioners and other interested persons organized under the auspices of the Commission. However, the national reports written by network members remain unpublished and are unavailable to the general public.

In fact these reports form an excellent source of legislative and jurisprudential information from the Member States in matters of equality. They shed light on the progress made and the work which remains to be done if we are to achieve equality both in law and in practice. The experts therefore expressed the desire to see their work published and widely disseminated in the European Community and internationally, so that it can be used to assist not only legal practitioners but also other groups and persons seeking to achieve the objective of equal opportunities.

However, the reports drawn up for the network could not necessarily have been published in the form in which they were produced. Their authors had drawn up working documents, rather than studies designed for publication. Furthermore network members were, at any rate initially, given significant discretion as to how the work should be produced. From 1986 onwards a common format based on agreed schemas was devised to give network reports greater homogeneity, and this also prompted a growing desire to produce a more extensive collection of knowledge in this field.

The European Commission therefore decided to promote the progressive publication of an encyclopædia on equality in law between women and men in the European Community. This was to consist of volumes which were no longer to be only administrative documents intended for Commission use, but were to present a high level of scientific and formal quality.

There is no need to discuss at length the importance and interest of such a publication, which forms a natural part of the Commission's programme of action regarding the promotion of equality of opportunity. In fact it represents an excellent method of consolidating Community knowledge of existing legal provisions in order to ensure their better implementation. It represents also the desire to extend and develop the traditional means of disseminating information, in such a way as to sensitize the public more effectively.

The plans for such an encyclopædia were formulated by experts attending the Spanish Presidency seminar on equal opportunities in Toledo in April 1989.

It was with much pleasure that the coordinators of this major project have been able to witness the gradual production of the volumes in this collection. Nevertheless, in spite of all the care take by the experts involved in this work, the encyclopædia is neither exhaustive, perfect nor definitive, since the law continues to evolve. However, it is hoped that it will prove useful to all those — judges, tribunal members, lawyers, civil servants, teachers and researchers — who are interested in this subject.

* * *

The present volume, pertaining to Irish law, is an integral part of the encyclopædia. It was therefore prepared on the basis of a structure common to all volumes in the series, in order to allow for a comparative reading of the law in each Member State on equality between women and men.

The first part of the volume — the Commentary — is based on a detailed plan common to all the national volumes, drawn up in such a way as to allow the reader to adopt a comparative approach. This plan draws both on the characteristics of the legal systems in use in the States linked to the Roman-Germanic legal tradition and in those following the common law tradition. One result of this is that certain headings may not be relevant to the position in each Member State.

The rest of the volume contains legislative texts in force in Irish law which implement the principles laid down in the EC Equality Directives, as well as the most significant court and tribunal decisions applying those texts.

Chapters 1 to 6 (the Commentary) state the law as of 1 August 1993; Chapter 8 (Cases) is accurate as of 1 February 1992, with some later additions.

The Irish constitutional and legislative texts reprinted in Chapter 7 are copyright of the Stationery Office, Dublin, and are reproduced by permission of the Controller.

* * *

The coordinators wish to express their gratitude to all those who have lent their assistance and support to the encyclopædia project, and to show particular appreciation to certain of them.

We need to record our gratitude to the authors, without whom this work would not have been produced. The essential quality of the encyclopædia lies in the work of its main authors; they spared no effort in the assembling of the necessary documentation and in drawing up an intelligible and useful commentary.

A particular word of thanks is due to the staff of the Equal Opportunities Unit of DG V of the European Commission. Since the project was discussed in the initial stages a large number of officials have been associated with it and have provided active assistance and support to the coordinators. It has been a pleasure to collaborate with the Unit.

Similarly, the coordinators would like to express their sincere thanks to the officials of the Office for Official Publications of the European Communities, whose patient and expert supervision made it possible to convert the manuscripts into publishable texts of a very high quality.

We express particular gratitude to the publishing houses which accepted the burden of the present work, which is hardly lightweight as it numbers some thirty volumes!

May this work assembled with the active participation of so many eminent and committed collaborators contribute to progress in the law, to the common good and to the promotion of formal and actual equality between the women and men of Europe.

Ferdinand von PRONDZYNSKI   Michel VERWILGHEN
Professor of Law and   Professeur ordinaire
Dean of the Law School   à la Faculté de Droit
University of Hull   Université catholique de Louvain
United Kingdom   Belgium

NOTICE TO THE READER

The editors of the encyclopædia wish to draw the attention of the reader to certain characteristics of the collection.

1. Each volume of the encyclopædia is published in two languages, English and French. The volumes have been edited so as to ensure that they have, as far as possible, the same content and structure in their English and French versions, although the language and terminology may occasionally differ as a result of normal usage in English and French respectively.

2. The authors of the Commentary section of each volume have worked according to a common schema agreed in the European Commission's Network of Experts on the Implementation of the Equality Directives. This allows the collection as a whole to follow a uniform structure. However, the Sources section in each volume is structured according to the domestic law framework, which varies from Member State to Member State.

3. The materials contained in the Sources section of each volume have (except where the original language is English or French) been translated into the two languages of the encyclopædia. These translations are not official, though every effort has been made to provide translated versions which are of high quality and accuracy. In the event of any doubt, it will be necessary for the reader to refer to legal sources in the original language; these are the only sources of guaranteed accuracy.

4. Equality in law between women and men within the European Community is a subject affected by rapid change, in EC law as well as in the law of each Member State. The formal sources evolve so quickly that information supplied in these volumes may have to be updated from that contained in the published encyclopædia. As far as possible major legislative and jurisprudential changes which occurred during the preparation of the volumes have been indicated in footnotes. The editors hope to be able to produce regular updates at a later stage.

5. References to laws, regulations and judicial decisions follow the normal usage of the Member State from which they originate.

ABBREVIATIONS

AG	Attorney General
art.(s)	article(s)
ASTMS	Association of Scientific, Technical and Managerial Staffs
ATGWU	Amalgamated Transport and General Workers' Union
CJ	Chief Justice
CMLR	Common Market Law Reports
DEE	Determinations on employment equality (Labour Court)
DEP	Determinations on equal pay (Labour Court)
DULJ	Dublin University Law Journal
EAT	Employment Appeals Tribunal
EC	European Community/ies
ECHR	European Convention of Human Rights, or European Court of Human Rights (Strasbourg)
ECJ	European Court of Justice (Luxembourg)
ECR	European Court Reports
EE	Recommendation on employment equality (Equality Officer)
EEA	Employment Equality Agency
EEC	European Economic Community
EEO	Employment Equality Order
ELR	Employment Law Reports
EP	Recommendation on equal pay (Equality Officer)
HC	High Court
IBEC	Irish Business and Employers' Confederation
ICTU	Irish Congress of Trade Unions
ILO	International Labour Organization.
ILRM	Irish Law Reports Monthly
IR	Irish Reports
ITGWU	Irish Transport and General Workers' Union
J	Justice (judge)
JISLL	Journal of the Irish Society for Labour Law
Ltd	Limited (liability company)
OJ C	Official Journal of the European Communities, C Series (Information and Notices)
OJ L	Official Journal of the European Communities, L Series (Legislation)
para.(s)	paragraph(s)
plc	public limited company
Pt	Part
reg.(s)	regulation(s)
s./ss	section/sections
SC	Supreme Court
Sch.	Schedule
SI	Statutory Instrument
subs./ss	subsection/s
UN	United Nations

TABLE OF LEGISLATION ETC.

[Numbers in bold type refer to pages at which provisions are printed verbatim]

Treaties

European Communities Secondary Legislation

Irish Constitution

Statutes

---

1   The text of the Anti-Discrimination (Pay) Act is printed in full on pp 143-151 and its provisions can be consulted there. Page references to specific provisions in this table relate to the Commentary (Chapters 1-6) and Cases (Chapter 8) sections only.

2   The text of the Employment Equality Act is printed in full on pp 152-177 and its provisions can be consulted there. Page references to specific provisions in this table relate to the Commentary (Chapters 1-6) and Cases (Chapter 8) sections only.

---

1   The text of the Social Welfare (No 2) Act 1986 is printed in full on pp 178-189 and its provisions can be consulted there. Page references to specific provisions in this table relate to the Commentary (Chapters 1-6) and Cases (Chapter 8) sections only.

Statutory Instruments

Code of Practice

TABLE OF CASES

[Numbers in bold type refer to pages at which extracts are printed verbatim]

Numerical Table of Cases
before the Court of Justice of the European Communities

Alphabetical Table of Cases

COMMENTARY ON

EQUALITY LAW

1. GENERAL

1.1   INTRODUCTION

1.1.1   INTRODUCTION TO NATIONAL LEGAL SYSTEM

When Ireland became independent in 1922, all existing British legislation was carried into Irish law; but since then, much of it has been replaced by Irish legislation. Present-day Irish law consists of a written Constitution[1] (adopted in 1937 and, by 1993, amended on thirteen occasions), post-1922 Irish legislation, some pre-1922 British legislation and a substantial body of case law. A special position in law is given to Ireland's obligations as a Member State of the European Community, and this is reflected in the provisions of the Constitution.[2]

As in most Western European States, government in Ireland is divided between a legislature, executive and judiciary. Under the 1937 Constitution,[3] the national legislature (the Oireachtas) comprises a President and two Houses: Dáil Éireann (which currently has 166 members, elected by universal suffrage) and Seanad Éireann (with 60 members). The executive powers of the State are exercised by a Government comprising at least seven, but not more than fifteen, members of the Oireachtas. They are assisted by a maximum of fifteen Ministers of State, and are advised, in matters of law and legal opinion, by an Attorney General (who need not be a member of either of the Houses of the Oireachtas).

The present judiciary, as envisaged in arts 34 to 37 of the Constitution, and established by the Courts (Establishment and Constitution) Act 1961, consists of courts of first instance and a court of final appeal.[4] The courts of first instance include a High Court (with a President, 15 other judges, the Chief Justice and the President of the Circuit Court); a Circuit Court (with a President and 15 judges); and a District Court (with a President, 39 District Justices and five temporary District Justices). The court of final appeal is the Supreme Court, which is made up of the Chief Justice, five other judges and the President of the High Court. There are also the criminal courts — namely the Central Criminal Court, a Special Criminal Court, and a Court of Criminal Appeal.

---

1   Bunreacht na hÉireann (Constitution of Ireland), 1937.
2   Article 29.4.3.
3   *Ibid.*, arts 16.2 and 18.1.
4   A Court and Court Officers Bill, which was originally expected in early 1992, was also expected to include the provision of a new Court of Civil Appeal, to which civil matters could be appealed from the High Court; as of mid-1993 the Bill has still not been published.

Most disputes connected with employment-related matters are dealt with
by institutions specifically designed for the purpose: the Labour Relations
Commission (LRC) established under the Industrial Relations Act 1990,[1]
(which, *inter alia*, provides a conciliation service, an industrial relations
advisory service and a monitoring and research service, as well as having
responsibility for appointing Equality Officers and Rights Commissioners);
the Employment Appeals Tribunal (which adjudicates on unfair dismissal,
redundancy payments, minimum notice, payment of wages, maternity and
insolvency cases); Rights Commissioners of the LRC (who may hear
maternity, payment of wages and unfair dismissals cases under the relevant
legislation, as well as mediating in individual grievances under the Industrial
Relations Act 1969); Equality Officers (who are officers of the LRC and
make recommendations on equality cases — recommendations which may
be appealed to the Labour Court); and the Labour Court itself.

The Labour Court was established by the Industrial Relations Act 1946[2]
to help resolve industrial disputes and uphold good standards in industrial
relations; despite its name, in its original functions it was not a court of law.
It began its work in 1946, and in the 1970s additional functions, this time of
an adjudicatory nature, were given to it under the equality legislation.[3]
Members of the Court are appointed by the Minister for Enterprise and
Employment following nominations by the main trade union and employer
organizations, the Irish Congress of Trade Unions (ICTU) and the Irish
Business and Employers' Confederation (IBEC). The ICTU nominees are
known as 'worker members' and the IBEC nominees as 'employer members';
there is also a Chair and Deputy Chair (who may be either 'worker members',
or 'employer members', or neither). The Court works in divisions, with each
division comprising a Chair (or Deputy Chair), a worker member and an
employer member. None of the members of the Court is a lawyer, but the
Court has a legally qualified Registrar who advises on legal issues. It can
also call on the services of other specialists as and when required.

In the first instance, therefore, a dispute arising under Irish equality law
will be generally referred to an Equality Officer of the LRC, who will issue a
recommendation on the matter.[4] The recommendation may then be appealed
to the Labour Court, which will issue a determination on it; this is legally
binding and may only be appealed on a point of law to the civil courts. Such
an appeal may be made to the High Court, whose judgment may, in turn, be
appealed to the Supreme Court.

---

1   Industrial Relations Act 1990 (No 19).
2   Industrial Relations Act 1946 (No 26), as amended by the Acts of 1969 (No 14) and
     1990 (No 19).
3   Anti-Discrimination (Pay) Act 1974 and Employment Equality Act 1977.
4   See, however, the details of these procedures in Chapter 6.

1.1.2   ECONOMIC AND SOCIAL CONTEXT

The population of Ireland was just over 3.5 million in 1991.[1] At that time, its labour force, at 1.33 million, was only 37 per cent of the population,[2] indicating a high dependency ratio with large proportions of people unable to work for age and other reasons. At the end of 1992, nearly 20 per cent of the labour force was unemployed, the highest proportion in the EC, excluding Spain.[3]

The number of women in Ireland who work outside the home increased substantially (by nearly 40 per cent) in the 20 years to 1991. This compared with an increase of only 10 per cent in the number of men in the labour force over the same period.[4] Nevertheless, as a proportion of all women aged between 15 and 64, the number of women in the labour force is still relatively low. It increased from 24 per cent in 1970 to 37.5 per cent in 1991.[5] However, this was still the lowest rate of female labour force participation in the entire Organization for Economic Cooperation and Development (OECD). Also, the number of women in the labour force, as a percentage of the total labour force, remains very low, at 32 per cent. Seven out of every ten workers in Ireland are men.

In 1991, over half the labour force at work in Ireland (58 per cent) worked in the services sector; while 28 per cent worked in industry and 14 per cent in agriculture. During the 1980s, these proportions had altered significantly: industry and agriculture (where most men were employed) had both declined; while services (where most women work) had increased substantially. An occupational breakdown of the labour force also showed a preponderance of women in the few areas of employment which had been growing rather than declining, such as professional and technical work, service work and clerical work.[6]

The increase which has taken place in women's employment has, for the most part, occurred in expanding sectors of the economy. Parallel increases in the average earnings of women, relative to those of men, might therefore have been expected. However, for the most part these have not occurred. In the twenty years from 1967 to 1987, the average weekly earnings of women in manufacturing rose from 50 per cent to 60 per cent of men's (in round figures); while their hourly earnings increased from 58 per cent to 68 per cent of men's hourly earnings. In view of the major social and legal changes

1   Census of Population, 1991, Final Results Summary, Central Statistics Office, Dublin, March 1993.
2   Labour Force Survey, 1991, Central Statistics Office, Dublin, June 1992.
3   Central Statistics Office, Dublin, April 1993.
4   Labour Force Surveys, 1971 and 1991, Central Statistics Office, Dublin.
5   *Ibid.*
6   *Ibid.*

in those two decades, this was hardly a dramatic improvement: an average of only half a percentage point per annum. Worse still, in the following five years, the average annual amount by which the difference narrowed was even less than this, so that by 1992 women's weekly earnings were still only about 60 per cent of men's and their hourly earnings were still only 68.6 per cent of men's hourly earnings.[1]

The reasons for women's low relative earnings and low participation rates are historical, social, industrial and economic. Fertility rates, while falling, are still the highest in the EC. Unemployment is exceptionally high and there is a general lack of job opportunities for men and women alike. Continuing sex discrimination, both direct and indirect, as well as sex segregation in the labour market and the failure to put men and women on a genuinely equal footing in the workplace (e.g. through provision of childcare facilities, parental leave etc.), have also served to depress women's earnings and economic status.

Progress towards equality must involve more effective outlawing of discriminatory practices in employment, together with positive action to ensure women's full and equal participation at all levels of economic and social life. To date the overall impact of European equality legislation in assisting this process has been limited. In the 17 years from the enactment of equal pay legislation until the end of 1992, some 437 claims, involving fewer than 10,000 workers (only about 2 per cent of the female workforce), were the subject of Equality Officer recommendations. Over the entire period, a majority of these claimants were successful in establishing their entitlement to equal pay; but in recent years both the number of claims and the proportion of successful ones have been falling.

Claims under the equal opportunities legislation have been even smaller in number: between 1978 and 1992 only 254 claims came to the Equality Officers for recommendation[2] and only about 500 workers were successful in establishing an entitlement to equal treatment. Yet potentially this is the legislation which should have the most positive implications for women at work, by outlawing many forms of discrimination in employment and encouraging the entry of more women to traditionally sex-segregated industries, occupations and grading structures.

In Ireland, the small number of equality claims, relative to the extent of inequality in employment, has been a source of some concern. However, from an EC perspective, the body of case-law which has developed is relatively substantial, by comparison with that in other Member States, and a

---

1   Industrial Earnings and Hours Worked, 1967, 1987 and 1992; Central Statistics Office, Dublin.
2   *Ibid.*

number of issues have been raised and explored which have not arisen often, or even at all, in other countries.

1.2 SOURCES

1.2.1 INTERNATIONAL STANDARDS

Ireland became a member of the EC, as from 1 January 1973, by the Act of Accession which was signed in Brussels on 22 January 1972. Membership involved a significant diminution of the legislative authority of national institutions and necessitated constitutional change (the Third and Tenth Amendments, now incorporated into art. 29.4.3) to give EC legislation the force of law in Ireland. The European Communities Act 1972 also provided for EC law to become part of Irish law and to be fully effective in, and binding on, the Irish courts.

Apart from the 1972 Act, Ireland has no national legislation specifically approving international treaties on equality matters. However, it has acceded to the UN Covenant on Civil and Political Rights and the UN Convention on the Elimination of All Forms of Discrimination against Women (with some reservations); it has ratified a number of ILO Conventions; and is a signatory to the Council of Europe's European Social Charter, as well as the European Convention on Human Rights.

1.2.1.1 Human rights

As noted above, Ireland has ratified the UN Covenant on Civil and Political Rights, which was originally adopted by the UN General Assembly in 1966 and came into force in 1976. Ireland is also a signatory to the Council of Europe's European Convention on Human Rights.

1.2.1.2 Treaties on special questions

In December 1985, Ireland acceded to the UN Convention on the Elimination of All Forms of Discrimination against Women, entering a number of reservations. Two of these were withdrawn in 1986 and one of the remaining reservations (relating to art. 13) was the subject of draft legislation at that time (the Equal Status Bill). The latter subsequently lapsed, but in early 1993 the newly elected Government stated its intention to introduce similar legislation as soon as possible.

The reservations which remain relate to art. 13(b) and (c) (concerning access to financial credit and other services, as well as to recreational facilities); art. 15 (concerning the validity of certain contracts and other private instruments); art. 16(1)(d) and (f) (extending to men rights identical to those of women in relation to the guardianship, adoption and custody of children born out of wedlock); and art. 11(b), (c) and (d). The last-mentioned

concerns equal employment opportunities and pay, and the measures taken to
implement Directives 75/117/EEC and 76/207/EEC are regarded as
sufficient implementation of this article.[1]

Ireland has ratified the International Labour Organization (ILO)
Convention on Equal Remuneration, 1951 (No 100), and part of the
Convention on Equality of Treatment (Social Security), 1962 (No 118). ILO
Conventions on Night Work and Underground Work, which were originally
ratified, have since been denounced; and a number of other Conventions
concerned with women's rights have not been ratified.

Ireland is also a signatory to the European Social Charter of the Council
of Europe (though not to its Protocol). The Charter complements the
Convention on Human Rights, which covers civil and political rights: it is the
counterpart of the Convention, in the sphere of economic and social rights.
The original Social Charter was signed by Ireland in 1961; a revised version
was ratified in 1964; and it came into force in 1965. In 1988 nine Member
States of the Council of Europe, excluding Ireland, signed the Protocol to the
Charter. However, the reason why Ireland did not sign the Protocol was
because of the latter's references to workers' rights to information and
consultation, rather than because of references to equal treatment and equal
opportunities.

1.2.2   EUROPEAN COMMUNITY LAW

Ireland's membership of the EC was effected through an Act of
Accession, two Constitutional amendments and the European Communities
Act 1972.[2] The 1972 Act was amended on several occasions between 1973
and 1986.

Directive 75/117/EEC was implemented in Ireland by the Anti-
Discrimination (Pay) Act 1974, which came into force on 31 December
1975. Directive 76/207/EEC was implemented by the Employment Equality
Act 1977, which came into force on 1 July 1977 and was amended by
subsequent Regulations in 1982 and 1985. Directive 79/7/EEC was
implemented by the Social Welfare (No 2) Act 1985, which became law in
July 1985, although none of its provisions was activated until 1986. It was
amended by the Social Welfare (No 2) Act 1989. Directive 86/378/EEC was
implemented by Part VII of the Pensions Act 1990. The Act was passed in
July 1990 but although most of its other provisions were made effective by
Regulations on 1 January 1991, the implementation of Part VII, on equal

---

1   For further details of these reservations see §7.2.2 below.
2   The Act of Accession was signed on 22 January 1972; the Third and Tenth
    amendments to the Constitution were incorporated in art. 29.4.3; and the final legal
    formality for joining the European Communities was the enactment of the European
    Communities Act 1972.

treatment in occupational social security schemes, was deferred until 1 January 1993.

1.2.2.1 Direct effect of Community law

Section 2 of the European Communities Act 1972 provides that the treaties and laws of the EC 'shall be binding on the State and shall be part of the domestic law thereof under the conditions laid down in those treaties'.

Article 119 has both 'vertical' and 'horizontal' direct effect in Ireland; that is, it imposes directly effective ('vertical') obligations on the State, both as legislator and as employer. It also imposes obligations on individuals in relation to each other ('horizontal' direct effect). Following *Marshall* v. *Southampton and SW Hampshire Area Health Authority*,[1] Directives should also be seen as having vertical direct effect, which may be significant in view of the relatively large public sector in Ireland.

To date, no equal pay or equal treatment cases involving the direct effect principle have been brought against either public or private sector employers. However, the State, as legislator, has been involved in a number of 'direct effect' cases: first, in relation to the introduction of the equal pay legislation; and, more recently, in relation to the implementation of Directive 79/7/EEC on statutory social security.

1.2.2.2 Retrospective implementation

Ireland became a member of the EC on 1 January 1973 and its equal pay legislation, implementing Directive 75/117/EEC, came into effect on 31 December 1975. Application of the 'direct effect' principle would have meant, therefore, that some claimants might have sought retrospective entitlements, for up to three years, in respect of the period 1 January 1973 to 31 December 1975. The estimated financial and economic costs of such retrospection led the Irish Government to make submissions to the European Court of Justice (ECJ) in relation to the second *Defrenne* case (concerning backdated equal pay and pension entitlements).[2] Although the Court upheld the principle of 'direct effect', it concluded by limiting its scope to periods after 8 April 1976 (the date of the judgment), except where legal proceedings had already been initiated.

Section 8(5) of the Anti-Discrimination (Pay) Act 1974 restricts the period of retrospection for arrears of equal pay to a maximum of three years before the date on which the dispute was referred to an Equality Officer; and in practice no arrears have been permitted in respect of periods prior to 31

---

1   Case 152/84, [1986] ECR 723, [1986] CMLR 688 (ECJ).
2   *Defrenne* v. *SA Belge de Navigation Aérienne Sabena*, Case 43/75, [1976] ECR 455, [1976] 2 CMLR 98 (ECJ).

December 1975 (when the 1974 Act came into effect). Thus the three-year maximum did not become payable until 31 December 1978. This leaves open the question of whether s. 8(5) of the 1974 Act is in conflict with the ECJ's interpretation of the date from which the principle of direct effect should apply, as indicated in the ruling on the second *Defrenne* case. It would appear that any attempt to impose the three-year limitation after 8 April 1979 could be successfully challenged by reference to *Defrenne*; however, this issue has not been tested.

More recently, similar issues arose following Ireland's implementation of Directive 79/7/EEC, some 17 months after the specified date of 23 December 1984. In *McDermott and Cotter* v. *Minister for Social Welfare*,[1] where arrears of unemployment benefit (arising from this 17-month delay) were claimed, Hamilton J referred the issue to the ECJ for a preliminary ruling on whether the Directive should be seen as having had direct effect since 23 December 1984. The ECJ, following earlier decisions, confirmed that it should. However, when the *McDermott and Cotter* case returned to the Irish High Court after the ECJ's preliminary ruling, Hamilton J decided to limit the claims, relying on the 'direct effect' principle, to periods after that ruling and to proceedings initiated before that date (i.e. 24 March 1987). This was appealed to the Supreme Court, where it was argued that concession of the claim would offend against a principle of national law which prohibited 'unjust enrichment'. The Supreme Court was uncertain as to whether this latter principle could override the 'direct effect' of EC law and specifically art. 4(1) of Directive 79/7/EEC. It therefore referred two questions which raised this issue to the ECJ.

In the meantime, another case arose in the High Court involving the question of retrospection.[2] Here, Barron J found in favour of the applicant's claim for arrears of a social welfare payment, stating that since the judgment of Hamilton J in *McDermott and Cotter*, the law had been altered by two ECJ decisions.[3] He noted that in the *Barra* case the ECJ had said it was for the Court alone to decide on any time limitations on the principle of 'direct effect'; and that no such limitation had been laid down by it in the *McDermott and Cotter* case. There was therefore no need to refer the case to the ECJ: the claimants were, in the judge's view, 'entitled to rely retrospectively' on the *Barra* and *Gravier* rulings.

By 1991, some 3,000 women had initiated proceedings for retrospective payment of social welfare benefits. Many others had written directly to the

---

1   *McDermott and Cotter* v. *Minister for Social Welfare* Case 286/85, [1987] ECR 1453, [1987] 2 CMLR 607, [1987] ILRM 324, (ECJ); *Cotter and McDermott* v. *Minister for Social Welfare* Case 377/89 [1991] ECR I-1155 (ECJ).

2   *Carberry* v. *Minister for Social Welfare*, 28 April 1989 (HC).

3   *Barra* v. *Belgium* Case 309/85, [1988] ECR 355, [1988] 2 CMLR 409 (ECJ); and *Gravier* v. *City of Liège*, Case 293/83, [1985] ECR 593, [1985] 3 CMLR 1 (ECJ).

Department of Social Welfare claiming adjustments. All the individual and group claims were frozen pending the outcome of the second *McDermott and Cotter* reference to the ECJ, as well as another case, *Emmott* v. *Minister for Social Welfare*,[1] in which retrospective payments were being withheld on the grounds that the claim was 'out of time'.

1991 was the year in which clarification of the major outstanding issues finally emerged. In March the ECJ ruled in favour of McDermott and Cotter,[2] stating that Directive 79/7/EEC required the payment of dependants' allowances to married women on the same basis as to married men, even if this resulted in some double-payments; similarly, transitional payments which had been paid to certain married men following implementation of the Directive should be paid to married women in similar family circumstances, even if this infringed the prohibition of 'unjust enrichment' in national law. In June the Irish Supreme Court was told that the outstanding issues in this case had been settled between the parties, without admission of liability, on terms which included payments to Ms Cotter and Ms McDermott. Then in July the ECJ ruled in favour of Ms Emmott,[3] stating that the Irish Government was not entitled to impose time-limits on claims for social welfare arrears relating to its own non-implementation of Directive 79/7/EEC. As long as a Member State had not properly transposed the Directive into its own legal system, it could not rely on national procedural rules about time-limits to prevent individuals from taking proceedings of this kind.

These two 1991 ECJ judgments appeared to clarify all major outstanding matters relating to retrospection and time-limits. At the end of 1991 no claimants (other than Ms Cotter and Ms McDermott) had actually been paid arrears; but in January 1992 it was announced that the Government intended to make appropriate retrospective payments during 1992, 1993 and 1994 and had set aside IR£22m for the first of these payments to be made in 1992. A special Equal Treatment Arrears Section was set up in the Department of Social Welfare, records were trawled for the names and addresses of potential claimants and over 100,000 forms were sent out, with explanatory letters, to women who had been in receipt of certain payments during the relevant 17-month period in 1984-86.

Unfortunately, however, this was still not the end of the story. When the Regulations[4] were issued, providing for the payment of the 1984-86 arrears (the unemployment assistance which should have been payable to some married women at that time, and certain dependants' allowances) it was evident that a number of legal difficulties remained. Specifically: (a) in

---

1   *Emmott* v. *Minister for Social Welfare*, Case C-208/90, [1991] ECR I-4269 (ECJ).

2   *Cotter and McDermott* v. *Minister for Social Welfare* Case C-377/89, [1991] ECR I-1155 (ECJ).

3   See footnote 1 above.

4   European Communities (Social Welfare) Regulations 1992 (SI No 152 of 1992).

relation to the arrears payable during 1992, these were to be paid in 1984-86 values, with no account being taken of losses in purchasing power in the intervening period; (b) in relation to the dependants' allowance payable during 1993-94, in respect of the 1984-86 period, this was to be paid on the basis of an 'actual dependency' test (which had not been applied to men at that time) despite the ECJ's ruling in *Cotter and McDermott,* wherein the court specifically stated that the 1984-86 rules should apply; and (c) instead of extending to women certain post-1986 'transitional' payments that had only been paid to men (again, as clearly indicated by the ECJ in *Cotter and McDermott*) the Regulations provided for their termination, for men, from July 1992.

In early 1993, therefore, new litigation had commenced on issues (a) and (c) above, and full resolution seemed unlikely before 1994 at the earliest.

1.2.3   CONSTITUTIONAL LAW

The 1937 Irish Constitution forbids any exclusions, by reason of sex, from Irish nationality and citizenship, from eligibility for membership of the Oireachtas and from voting for members of the Oireachtas; it also forbids the enactment of laws preventing such eligibility or voting.[1]

Articles 40, 41 and 45 are, however, the most significant ones in relation to the status of women in Irish society. Article 40 states that 'all citizens shall, as human persons, be held equal before the law', but then goes on to allow the State, in its enactments, to 'have due regard to differences of capacity, physical and moral, and of social function'. The 'social function' of women is clearly stated as follows in art. 41.2.1: '... that by her life within the home, woman gives to the State a support without which the common good cannot be achieved'. Furthermore, art. 41.2.2 provides that the State should 'endeavour to ensure that mothers shall not be obliged by economic necessity to engage in labour to the neglect of their duties in the home'.

On the other hand, art. 45 says that all citizens, 'men and women equally', have 'the right to an adequate means of livelihood'; and directs the State to ensure that they may 'through their occupations find the means of making reasonable provision for their domestic needs'. It also pledges the State to safeguard 'the economic interests of the weaker sections of the community' and where necessary contribute to their support; and provides that 'citizens shall not be forced by economic necessity to enter vocations unsuited to their sex, age or strength'.

Over the years, arts 40, 41 and 45 have been cited in a number of constitutional cases concerning women's rights, in such areas as employment, taxation, social security and family/property law.

---

1   Articles 9 and 16.

An attempt to deprive women of employment, purely on grounds of sex, has been deemed unconstitutional.[1] The exclusion of women from jury service has also been found to contravene the Constitution.[2] Taxation rules which treated married couples less favourably than their single counterparts were considered to be an attack on the institution of marriage and hence unconstitutional (with favourable financial consequences for married couples);[3] but when the same principle was followed in relation to social welfare,[4] the outcome was a 'levelling-down' of cohabitees' entitlements to the level of their married counterparts, rather than increasing the benefits payable to married people.

A man claiming 'deserted wife's benefit' (a payment made only to married women raising children alone) was unsuccessful because it was considered that the Constitution specifically and exclusively protected women in this regard.[5] However, a couple who claimed that State support for single mothers was an unconstitutional 'attack on the institution of marriage' had their action dismissed on the basis that such support was child-centred and in accordance with the Constitution.[6]

A number of principles have therefore been clearly established; others remain unclear. For example, discrimination against married couples *vis-à-vis* unmarried cohabiting couples is seen as unconstitutional; but the question of whether discrimination against married women who work outside the home can be defended by reference to the Constitution is unclear: it has not been tested as such, but the Constitution itself implies the permissibility of unequal treatment of men and women in certain respects, and one judgment has confirmed this.[7] Neither has the interpretation of art. 41.2.2 been tested fully, in relation to the level of income support provided by the State for mothers who work in the home. The property rights of such women were defined in a 1988 High Court case as ownership of up to half of the family property,[8] but this was overruled by the Supreme Court in 1991 on the basis that the establishment of 'a brand new right' of this kind was the job of the legislature rather than the courts. The Matrimonial Home Bill 1993, which is intended to give spouses equal rights to ownership of the family home and its contents, was published in mid-1993.

---

1 *Murtagh Properties Ltd* v. *Cleary* [1972] IR 330 (SC).
2 *De Burca* v. *AG* [1976] IR 38 (SC).
3 *Murphy* v. *AG* [1982] IR 241 (SC).
4 *Hyland* v. *Minister for Social Welfare* [1989] ILRM 196 (HC); [1990] ILRM 213 (SC).
5 *Dennehy* v. *Minister for Social Welfare,* 26 July 1984, unreported (HC).
6 *MacMathuna* v. *Ireland,* 1989, unreported (HC).
7 See *Murphy* v. *AG* [1982] IR 241.
8 *BL* v. *ML,* 1988, unreported (HC); 1991, unreported (SC).

As regards fathers who work in the home, the idea of equal treatment
with women following desertion by a spouse was rejected by the High Court
in 1984.[1] In 1989 the Government decided to introduce equal treatment in
respect of certain social welfare payments to lone parents; and in the same
year new proceedings were instituted by a man claiming 'deserted wife's
benefit', which was still payable only to women; however by early 1993 the
case of Anthony Lowth had not been heard.

In summary, the Irish Constitution does not clearly rule out
discrimination against women who work outside the home, especially if
married; the extent of the State's 'protection' to women working at home has
not been fully defined (although the High Court has attempted to do so in
relation to property); and the idea of 'protecting' men who perform non-
traditional 'social functions' in the home has been rejected in law (although it
has since been partially recognized in practice and was likely to be tested
again in the courts in 1993). The issue of whether indirect discrimination, or
discrimination by impact, contravenes the Constitution, is also unresolved.

A number of important issues are therefore outstanding as regards the
extent to which the Irish Constitution guarantees equal treatment between the
sexes, and whether it conforms fully with EC equality laws.

1.2.4   LEGISLATION

1.2.4.1   Prior legislation

Prior to the EC-inspired equality legislation (see §1.2.2 above), Irish
employment law contained no specific provisions relating to sex discrimination. A number of Acts were considered to have contained discriminatory
provisions; and in some cases, these were wholly or partly amended.

1.2.4.2   Present legislation

Two main statutes are of relevance, in addition to the equality
legislation deriving from EC Directives (see §1.2.2 above). These are
designed to provide maternity protection for women in employment, and to
protect certain part-time workers.

The Maternity (Protection of Employees) Act 1981 came into operation
on 6 April 1981. This Act gives working mothers the right to maternity leave
from their employment, as well as the right to return to work after their
confinement. Generally speaking, payment during maternity leave is by the
Department of Social Welfare rather than by employers, and this has been

---

[1]   See *Hyland* v. *Minister for Social Welfare*, 1988, above.

governed by social welfare legislation enacted in 1981 and amended in subsequent years.[1]

The Worker Protection (Regular Part-Time Employees) Act 1991, which became effective on 6 April 1991 (except for certain provisions on redundancy and insolvency rights, which became effective on 17 June 1991), is designed to extend the benefits of the maternity, holidays, redundancy, unfair dismissals and insolvency protection to 'regular part-time workers'. The latter are defined as those who have worked continuously for the employer for at least 13 weeks and are normally expected to work at least eight hours a week. Separate regulations extended full social insurance cover to all workers whose weekly earnings (from one or more employer) exceeded £25 (irrespective of hours worked).[2] This meant that from 6 April 1991 the majority of part-time workers also began to build up social insurance entitlements. However, by the time the first of these workers started to qualify for benefits such as Unemployment and Disability Benefit, i.e. in January 1993, further regulations had been introduced restricting the amounts of benefit payable to people earning less than £70 a week and substantially reducing the amount of any adult dependant allowance payable to such persons.[3]

The Irish Government was committed, under a three-year national 'Programme for Economic and Social Progress' agreed with trade unions and employers in January 1991, to introducing a Bill to amend the 1974 and 1977 Acts before the end of 1991. This commitment was not honoured, but it was understood throughout 1992 that a draft Bill was being finalized and was about to be published. This did not, however, happen before the fall of the Government in late 1992. However, the newly-elected Government promised early action on the matter in Spring 1993.

---

[1]   Social Welfare (Amendment) Act 1981 (and subsequent Social Welfare Acts).
[2]   Social Welfare (Subsidiary Employments) Regulations 1991 (SI No 73 of 1991).
[3]   Social Welfare (Miscellaneous Social Insurance Provisions) (No 2) Regulations 1992 (SI No 448 of 1992).

2. BASIC CONCEPTS

2.1 EQUALITY AND DISCRIMINATION

The Anti-Discrimination (Pay) Act 1974 (the 1974 Act) does not give a precise definition of either 'equality' or 'discrimination'. It provides for equality of 'remuneration' where two persons of the opposite sex are engaged in 'like work' for the same (or an associated) employer, in the 'same place'. Its purpose is to equalize pay in circumstances where 'all other things' can be shown to be equal, unless it can also be shown that the pay differences are 'objectively justified' by reference to reasons which are unrelated to sex. By implication, therefore, sex discrimination is seen as occurring where, in such circumstances, differences in remuneration exist and cannot be 'objectively justified'.

The Employment Equality Act 1977 (the 1977 Act) is more direct and explicit. Its stated purpose is to ensure equal treatment, in relation to particular, employment-related matters, by making unlawful 'certain kinds of discrimination on grounds of sex or marital status'.[1] Section 2 then defines 'discrimination', both 'direct' and 'indirect'.[2] It also outlaws victimization, which in this context means penalizing someone who has opposed sex discrimination or who has assisted in litigation brought in relation to conduct which is wrongful under the 1974 and 1977 Acts.

Section 56(2) of the 1977 Act provides that both the 1974 and 1977 Acts 'shall be construed together as one Act'. This has been taken to mean that such practices as indirect discrimination, and discrimination on grounds of marital status, which were not expressly prohibited by the 1974 Act are now also prohibited in the context of remuneration.[3] Thus certain omissions or imprecisions in the 1974 Act may be seen as being remedied by the 1977 Act.

In contrast to these earlier Acts, the Social Welfare (No 2) Act 1985, which implemented Directive 79/7/EEC, simply states that its purpose is 'to provide for equal treatment for men and women in matters of social welfare'[4] and proceeds to amend earlier Social Welfare Acts without further definitions of either 'equality' or 'discrimination'. However, the Pensions Act 1990, Part VII, which seeks to implement Directive 86/378/EEC, contains essentially the same detailed definitions of direct and indirect discrimination

---

1   Long title of the Act.
2   See §§2.2 and 2.3 below.
3   This principle was first established in the case of *St Patrick's College, Maynooth* v. *19 Female Employees* EP 4/1984.
4   Long title of Act.

as the 1977 Act with two important differences: one of these relates to the burden of proof; the other adds a prohibition of discrimination based on 'family status' to those based on sex and marital status.

The concept of discrimination which is implicit in all the Irish anti-discrimination law is that of 'less favourable treatment' being accorded to a person of a particular sex (or marital status) than is accorded to a person of the opposite sex (or different marital status). It is not sufficient merely to demonstrate 'unfavourable treatment': certain comparisons must be made, certain facts must be presented, and the effects of the alleged discrimination must be shown. It must also be shown that the 'less favourable treatment' has occurred for reasons that constitute discrimination, namely reasons related to the sex, or marital status (or family status, in the case of pensions etc.), of the person(s) concerned. Nor is it sufficient merely to prove that discrimination of this kind has occurred. It must also be shown that the discriminatory act or practice actually caused detriment to the person concerned, and that such alleged discrimination was the sole or major cause of that detriment. It is not always or automatically accepted that discrimination on grounds of sex or marital status, even when proved, is the main reason for the less favourable treatment of a claimant.

Thus the concepts of equality and discrimination are complex and multi-layered. They involve several 'stages of proof' and provide many opportunities for spurious, as well as legitimate, rebuttals of allegations of discrimination. For claimants to work through all these stages can be tortuous, and it has been argued from the outset that it places an excessively onerous burden of proof on persons who are alleging discrimination.

2.2　DIRECT DISCRIMINATION

2.2.1　DEFINITION

The 1974 Act does not specifically define 'discrimination', either direct or indirect. Rather, it bestows an entitlement to equal 'remuneration' where the work of a claimant is the same as, or similar to, or equal in value to, that of a particular comparator who is employed in the 'same place' by the same employer. However, by virtue of s. 56(2) of the 1977 Act which provides that both the 1974 and 1977 Acts shall be construed as one, the definition of 'discrimination' which is contained in s. 2 of the 1977 Act is now deemed to apply to equal pay cases as well as equal treatment ones. The first two parts of the definition relate to direct discrimination and provide that this will be taken to occur:

> '(a) where by reason of his sex a person is treated less favourably than a person of the other sex; (b) where because of his marital status a person is treated less favourably than another person of the same sex.'

The above definition does not include reference to 'family status', although the definition of equal treatment in art. 2(1) of Directive 76/207/EEC specifically states that ' ... the principle of equal treatment shall mean that there shall be no discrimination whatsoever on grounds of sex either directly or indirectly by reference in particular to marital or family status.' This definition is virtually identical to the one given in art. 5(1) of Directive 86/378/EEC, which will be implemented in 1993 by Part VII of the Pensions Act 1990. Interestingly, s. 67(3) of the 1990 Act states that for purposes of ensuring equal treatment in an occupational benefit scheme, sex discrimination will be deemed to occur:

> (a) where because of a person's sex the person is treated less favourably than a person of the other sex; (b) where a person is treated, by reference to his marital or family status, less favourably than a person of the other sex with the same status;

At first glance, this latter definition might appear to conform more closely to the intent of the Directive by including reference to 'family status', than does the definition in the 1977 Act which omits any mention of 'family status'. However, on closer inspection, it actually narrows the basis for comparisons by demanding that while a comparator may have the same marital or family status as the claimant, she or he must be a member of the opposite sex. Under the 1977 Act by contrast, the comparator may be of the same sex as the claimant, but have a different marital status. Enquiries to the Department of Social Welfare on this matter have revealed that it was the intention of those drafting the 1990 Act to confine the definition of discrimination to discrimination based on sex. However, this would seem to beg the question of why 'marital and family status' were mentioned at all; and, at the time of writing, no answers to this question had been proffered.

2.2.1.1   Reason

Whether alleged discriminatory treatment is intentional or unintentional is of no significance in Irish law. The only exception is where the reason can be shown to be 'objective' and unrelated to the person's sex or marital status (or family status, in the case of occupational benefits such as pensions). These 'objective reasons' do not necessarily have to be fair or reasonable: indeed, over the years, some unusual reasons for unequal treatment have been advanced and some have been accepted as being 'objective', in the context of equality law.

In practice, of course, direct discrimination is often intentional, whereas indirect discrimination may more often be unintentional. Indeed, in cases of alleged indirect discrimination, a lack of intent to discriminate is commonly argued, even where it seems clear that a knowledge of discriminatory consequences, or even a clear intention to discriminate, was involved.

2.2.1.2 Detriment

In addition to demonstrating that discrimination has occurred, it is also necessary in some cases to show that this has actually operated to the detriment of the claimants and that the discrimination was the sole or major reason for their less favourable treatment. For example, in one case concerning access to employment, it was considered that discriminatory questions had been asked at or before interviews, but because it was not established that this had been the reason for the non-appointment of the claimant, the compensation, was awarded for 'distress' rather than for the consequences of discrimination.[1]

2.2.1.3 Comparator

The 1974 Act requires a person who is claiming equal pay to demonstrate that she or he is doing 'like work' with a particular member of the opposite sex who is employed in the 'same place' and by the same employer. The comparator need not be employed contemporaneously with the claimant,[2] but must be, or must have been, an actual person. There is no provision for the use of a hypothetical comparator, or for making comparisons with rates of pay which might have applied if members of the opposite sex had been performing 'like work' to that of the claimant.[3]

The 1977 Act does not require direct comparisons of this kind. A woman claiming equal treatment does not necessarily have to compare her treatment with that of a particular man (or a particular woman of different marital status). However, she would have to demonstrate that, in similar circumstances, she had been treated in a materially different manner from a man (or woman of different marital status). If direct comparisons with particular individuals can be made, this will obviously be helpful in establishing a *prima facie* case, but such comparisons are not always possible and for this reason are not seen as being necessary.

The requirement for a specific comparator has often been cited as a defect of the 1974 Act as it restricts the use of equality legislation in challenging low pay rates in single-sex establishments. However, the interpretation of the term 'equal value' has evolved in such a way as to allow the consideration, in some circumstances, of pay rates which might have applied had claimants been members of the opposite sex: this matter is discussed further in §3.8.1 below.

---

1   *A Prospective Female Employee* v. *A Company* EE 12/1989.
2   See §3.6.2 below.
3   See §3.6.3 below.

2.2.2 EXTENDED DEFINITION

2.2.2.1 Marital status

The 1974 Act contains no specific prohibition of discrimination based on marital status. However, the 1977 Act specifically prohibits employers and prospective employers from discriminating, either directly or indirectly, on the basis of marital status, and the Pensions Act 1990 does likewise in respect of occupational benefit schemes. Since both the 1974 and 1977 Acts must be read as one, discrimination based on marital status is now seen as unlawful in relation to equal pay as well as to equal treatment (and occupational benefits); this was confirmed in *St Patrick's College, Maynooth* v. *ITGWU*.[1]

2.2.2.2 Family status

Neither the 1974 Act nor the 1977 Act specifically prohibits discrimination on the basis of family status; in the case of the latter this appears to contravene the requirements of Directive 76/207/EEC, as noted in §2.2.1 above. By contrast, the Pensions Act 1990 mentions 'family status' both in relation to direct discrimination (see §2.2.1 above) and indirect discrimination (see §2.3.1 below). However, as noted elsewhere, the intention behind the Pensions Act wording is far from clear and its interpretation is unlikely to be clarified until the equal treatment sections come into force in 1993.

In practice, the question of family status can arise under the 1977 Act, and has in fact arisen in a number of cases concerning access to employment. Married women have been asked, at interview, about their childcare and other domestic arrangements, questions which have not been asked of men or indeed single women. This matter is discussed further below, in the context of both recruitment and of indirect discrimination. It is also a major issue in the context of social security and the type of questions which claimants are asked when seeking to establish their 'availability for work', for purposes of securing unemployment benefit or assistance.[2]

In equal pay cases the question of family status has been less of an issue. However, it may be indirectly relevant in relation to part-time workers who do not receive equal hourly rates of pay with comparable full-time workers, since large numbers of women work part-time because of family responsibilities and because of the general absence of employer- or State-funded childcare facilities.

---

1   EP 4/1984; DEP 10/1984.
2   See §5.3 below, and see Chapter 4 on recruitment generally.

2.2.2.3   Pregnancy

The 1974 Act does not specifically prohibit discrimination on grounds of pregnancy. For the most part, pregnancy has not been an issue in relation to pay or other direct forms of remuneration. Difficulties have arisen, however, in a number of sick pay schemes and income continuance arrangements where attempts were made (unsuccessfully) to use pregnancy as a reason for non-payment, or deferral, of a benefit which would otherwise be payable.

Pregnancy has more often been an issue in relation to women's access to employment, and since the 1977 Act contains no specific prohibition of discrimination on grounds of pregnancy, such cases have tended to arise under the heading of indirect discrimination (see §2.3.1.1. below).

2.2.2.4   Sexual harassment

Sexual harassment is not specifically mentioned in the 1977 Act. However, a number of cases concerning alleged sexual harassment have been brought to the Equality Officers and Labour Court: the latter has clearly stated that 'freedom from sexual harassment is a condition of work which an employee of either sex is entitled to expect' and that denial of such freedom contravenes the 1977 Act.[1] Sexual harassment is considered to be direct discrimination. To date, it has only been considered in the context of activity between members of the opposite sex; it is not yet known whether the Act covers harassment of a homosexual nature.

The type of behaviour which has been held to constitute sexual harassment varies widely. It can range from direct, persistent, unwanted physical contact and sexual advances, to unsolicited comments, suggestions, 'jokes' and looks, of a sexual nature. It need not even be physical or verbal: in one case, it was established that sexual harassment may be symbolic in form, and may be a matter of intention and psychological effect. But whatever its form, the activity must be unwanted, unwelcome and unsolicited — consensual relations do not constitute harassment — and it must be such as to create a stressful or intimidating working environment for such employees, or to undermine their job security. In other words, there must be detriment, as well as discriminatory behaviour.

Furthermore, the discrimination and detriment need not be caused directly by the employer concerned. Employers may be vicariously liable for the harassment of employees by other employees, if this occurs within the scope of employment. Indeed, in one case, an employer was held responsible for sexual harassment of an employee by a person who was neither an employer nor another employee, but was regularly on the premises at the

---

[1]   *A Garage Proprietor* v. *A Worker* EE 2/1985.

invitation of the employer.[1] In another case, the alleged harassment had been
by the husband of the company's managing director, who was an independent
contractor and frequently visited the premises.[2]

The first Irish case involved a constructive dismissal where a young
employee resigned from her employment due to alleged sexual harassment.[3]
The definition of constructive dismissal in the 1977 Act includes the
termination by an employee of her or his contract of employment where,
because of the conduct of the employer, it was reasonable for him or her to
do so. In this case, which involved a garage proprietor, the claimant alleged
that during the six-month period of her employment she had been continually
sexually harassed by her employer and that when she described the
harassment to her mother, the latter had insisted that she resign. In this case,
the employee contended that she had been a target of her employer's desires
because she was a woman: no male employee had been treated in the same
way. The employer denied that he had ever physically interfered with her,
but acknowledged that he and his staff had, on occasions, made jokes about
sexual matters. The Labour Court determined that 'inappropriate conduct
took place during the employment of the claimant and that the decision of the
claimant thereby to resign amounted to constructive dismissal'. She was
awarded IR£1,000 compensation on the basis that she had been denied a
condition of work which all employees were entitled to expect, namely
freedom from sexual harassment, and that this had led her to resign.

The employer's responsibility for ensuring that employees enjoy
freedom from sexual harassment was also considered in another case,[4] where
a claimant argued that during the period of her employment, she had been
subjected to continual sexual harassment by the husband of the company's
managing director (the husband was engaged as an independent contractor).
She argued that her dismissal, which had been said to be for reasons of
redundancy, had in reality been directly attributable to this sexual
harassment. In this case, however, the claimant was unable to demonstrate
that her employer had been aware of the alleged harassment, or that this was
the real reason for her dismissal. In fact, she admitted that she had not
informed her employer, or other staff members, about the alleged incidents,
which were categorically denied. Since there was completely contradictory
evidence, the Labour Court dismissed the claim. The case underlined the
importance of employees reporting incidents which, in their view, constitute
sexual harassment, to their employers and/or other staff members and of
using whatever grievance procedures exist in the employment concerned.
This may not always be a simple matter, but certainly employees should

---

1   *A Company* v. *A Female Worker* EEO 3/1991.
2   *A Company* v. *A Worker* DEE 2/1988.
3   *A Garage Proprietor* v. *A Worker* EE 2/1985.
4   DEE 2/1988.

record, raise and report such matters while still in employment, rather than resort to resignation.

2.2.2.5   Physical attributes

The issue of physical attributes, such as a person's height or weight, is considered within the context of indirect, rather than direct discrimination.[1]

2.2.2.6   Dress codes

There have been very few cases in which the matter of different dress codes for men and women has been at issue. In one case, women were not allowed to wear trousers or jeans and this was held to be discriminatory.[2] In another case, however, where women were provided with free uniforms, the non-provision of uniforms to men (or compensation in lieu) was not considered discriminatory. The Equality Officer decided that since it was a condition of the women's employment to wear uniforms or 'appropriate dress', rather than 'consideration' in respect of their employment, the provision or non-provision of uniforms did not in this case fall within the definition of 'remuneration' under the 1974 Act.[3]

2.3   INDIRECT DISCRIMINATION

2.3.1   DEFINITION

Equal pay and equal treatment

The 1974 Act does not mention or define indirect discrimination, but s. 2 of the 1977 Act provides that it occurs:

> (c) where because of his sex or marital status a person is obliged to comply with a requirement, relating to employment or membership of a body referred to in s. 5, which is not an essential requirement for such employment or membership and in respect of which the proportion of persons of the other sex or (as the case may be) of a different marital status but of the same sex able to comply is substantially higher.

The concept of indirect discrimination has also been 'imported' into equal pay cases by virtue of s. 56(2) of the 1977 Act which states that both the 1974 and 1977 Acts 'shall be construed together as one Act'.

This definition of indirect discrimination contains a number of different elements and, for explanatory purposes, it may be useful to divide them into four separate strands, as follows. Indirect discrimination occurs where:

---

1   See §2.3 below.
2   *Norwich Union Insurance* v. *131 Female Clerical Staff* EE 19/1981.
3   *Educational Building Society* v. *Male Employees* EP 9/1987.

(i) because of sex or marital status, a person is obliged to comply with a requirement or condition relating to employment or membership of a professional or other body (this would include a trade union); (ii) a substantially higher proportion of persons of either the opposite sex, or of the same sex but of a different marital status, is able to comply with this requirement; (iii) this requirement is not essential to such employment, or to membership of the particular body, or is not 'objectively justified' as being necessary on grounds other than sex or marital status; and (iv) in the case of equal pay claims, the above factors adversely affect the person's remuneration.

The Equality Officers and the Labour Court have on many occasions considered claims of indirect discrimination. Almost all have been brought under the 1977 Act and have involved the assessment of 'suspect criteria' as discussed at §2.3.1.1 below. Only once have the higher courts considered the matter: this was in *North Western Health Board* v. *Martyn*,[1] where Barron J commented, in relation to the definition of indirect discrimination, that it appeared to be 'too wide' and that 'a condition to offend the provision does not have to refer specifically to sex or marital status. It is sufficient that it is such that as the result of an attribute of a person's sex or the circumstances of a person's marital status, such persons are substantially more affected than persons of the other sex or of a different marital status but of the same sex as the case may be'.

The *Martyn* case concerned the issue of women wishing to return to the workforce and having to comply with an age limit of 27 years. It was argued that such an age limit was too low and that its application was indirectly discriminatory as it affected more married women than single women or men. It adversely affected women who had been obliged to resign on marriage, due to the marriage bar, but who later wanted to return to work; and it did not give women who left work in order to have children sufficient time to rear a family. Barron J overturned the Equality Officer's and the Labour Court's determination that the age limit was discriminatory, stating that there was insufficient statistical evidence of this. His judgment was, in turn, subsequently overturned by the Supreme Court, which stressed, however, that because of the lack of statistical information, its judgment was on the narrow basis of unrefuted allegations and might not apply in every case.

'Suspect criteria', or 'non-essential requirements', have caused considerable difficulty in a number of cases. For example, in *Packard Electric Ireland Ltd* v. *EEA*,[2] there was a requirement for part-time women workers to have been laid off for 26 weeks before they could enter into full-time employment; and this was not considered to be an 'essential require-

---

1   EE 14/1981; DEP 1/1982; [1985] ILRM 226 (HC); [1988] ILRM 519 (SC).
2   EE 14/1985.

ment'. However, in *Our Lady's Hospital for Sick Children* v. *A Worker*,[1] the issue of whether a specific requirement was 'essential', or merely a 'preference', was central. It was considered that a 'preference' for a newly-qualified technician was not an 'essential' requirement and thus no discrimination had occurred.

Sometimes anomalies can arise in considering whether requirements are 'essential' or not. In the case of *CERT Ltd* v. *Landy*,[2] where the employer had a requirement for a particular qualification, the female claimant was not given the job because she did not have the relevant certificate, whereas in fact she had a higher qualification. It was held that she was indirectly discriminated against because women had been specifically excluded from the training course which led to the required certificate.

The Labour Court has also considered that a requirement to hold a union card for a particular post was not based on sex even though the female claimant was not offered the job because the union would not grant her a union card. The union had required that all its other and unemployed members had to be considered first for the position. Furthermore, in relation to this predominantly male craft union, the Labour Court concluded that 'historical circumstances, which have resulted in more men then women in a craft industry, do not lead to the conclusion that the small number of women in the industry is now an attribute of their sex' .[3]

Occupational benefits

The Pensions Act 1990 provides a somewhat different definition of indirect discrimination. Section 67(3)(c) and (d) refer to indirect discrimination as occurring:

(c)   where because of a person's sex the person is unable to comply with a requirement or condition -
    (i)   in respect of which the proportion of persons of the other sex able to comply with such requirement or condition is substantially higher than the proportion of persons of the first mentioned sex so able, and
    (ii)   which is not justifiable irrespective of the sex of the persons to whom it applies,

(d)   where because of a person's marital or family status the person is unable to comply with a requirement or condition -
    (i)   in respect of which the proportion of persons of the other sex with the same status able to comply with such requirement or condition is substantially higher than the proportion of persons of the first mentioned sex so able, and
    (ii)   which is not justifiable irrespective of the sex of the persons to whom it applies.

---

1   EE 25/1985; DEE 4/1985.
2   EE 20/1983; DEE 2/1984.
3   *Bailey Gibson* v. *Nathan*, EE 1/1990, EE 2/1990, [1990] ELR 191 and 210; DEE 1/1991; upheld by Murphy J, 8 October 1992, unreported (HC); under appeal to Supreme Court.

The above definition of indirect discrimination is based on sex, although using different wording, has exactly the same effect as under the 1977 Act. However, the definition of indirect discrimination relating to marital status/family status appears to be narrower than in the 1977 Act. It would allow a married woman with a child, for example, to claim discrimination only if she had to comply with a rule or requirement with which a married man with a child did not have to comply. There does not appear to be a provision for a married woman to compare herself with a single woman (for example), whereas such a comparison is permissible under the 1977 Act.

To date, there has been no judicial interpretation of this definition as this section did not come into force until January 1993. However, enquiries to the Department of Social Welfare have revealed that it was the intention of those drafting the legislation to confine comparisons to persons of the opposite sex. This does not satisfactorily explain the purpose of including references to marital and family status, unless it was considered that these references met the requirements of Directive 86/378/EEC (which is not the view of the authors).

2.3.1.1 Suspect criteria

Breadwinner, head of family

This issue has not arisen in equal pay or employment equality cases, but has done so in relation to social security.[1] Historically, of course, it was often argued that equal pay was inappropriate and that men's pay had to be higher than women's because 'men needed to support their families'; however, this argument has not been specifically advanced to the Equality Officers, Labour Court or higher courts.

Full-time, part-time work

The question of 'inessential requirements' has arisen on a number of occasions in relation to part-time work and the employment of married women. For example, in the *Packard* case[2] and in *Michael O'Neill & Sons Ltd* v. *Two Employees*,[3] part-time married women had difficulties performing full-time work by reason of their home responsibilities. In the latter case, the company had decided to make the part-time workers redundant and retain the full-time workers, arguing that availability for full-time work was 'an essential requirement'. However, the Labour Court considered this to be indirectly discriminatory, as 'a greater proportion of males and single women could comply with the requirement of working full-time'.

---

1   See Chapter 5 below.
2   EE 14/1985.
3   DEE 1/1988.

The *Packard* case concerned a union/management agreement which contained a form of structural discrimination which could only affect married women. The Equality Officer concluded that the offending clause of the agreement was indirectly discriminatory, placing married women (who formed a majority of the part-timers) at a disadvantage by comparison with single women, for reasons that were in no way 'essential'.

Working hours

Apart from the *Packard* case, there have been no instances of working hours being at issue in the context of indirect discrimination. In the case of *University College Dublin* v. *Zeuli*,[1] a female claimant sought flexible working hours in respect of evening duties and the amalgamation of breaks during the day so that she could wean her child, a request which was refused by the College. However, this refusal was seen as directly, rather than indirectly, discriminatory.

Marital status

This point has been considered above, in the context of full-time/part-time working and the employment of married women.

Family status

There are no specific provisions in the 1974 or 1977 Acts which prohibit discrimination based on family status although discrimination against women has often arisen from their traditional family role.

In practice, the issue of family status arises frequently in social security cases, but less often in employment cases. One example of the latter was in the interview case of *University College Dublin* v. *Chaney*,[2] where the claimant was asked about her childminding arrangements and was refused access to permanent employment because she was a married woman with children.

Discrimination based on family status is mentioned in s. 67 of the Pensions Act 1990. However, as noted in §§2.2.1 and 2.3.1 above, the wording of this section gives rise to a major doubt as to its intended application; in early 1993 its interpretation had not yet been tested, as the equal treatment sections of the Act did not become effective until 1 January 1993.

---

[1]   EE 4/1987.
[2]   EE 15/1983.

Pregnancy

Where employers have sought to impose a requirement that employees 'must not be pregnant', this has generally been held to constitute indirect discrimination, since clearly such a requirement affects more women than men (in that it cannot affect men at all) and usually the requirement has been seen as inessential.

In *An Foras Forbartha* v. *Geraghty-Williams*,[1] the withdrawal of an offer of employment because of pregnancy was considered to be indirectly discriminatory on the basis that 100 per cent of men could comply with a requirement not to be pregnant, while the proportion of women was substantially smaller. Similarly, in *Pan American World Airways Inc.* v. *Cassidy*[2] a woman's offer of employment was postponed pending the completion of her pregnancy and this, too, was considered to be indirect discrimination.

On the other hand, in *Power Supermarkets Ltd* v. *Long*[3] a somewhat similar allegation was made by the claimant: she contended that she had been offered employment, but that when her prospective employer was advised by her that she was pregnant, the company allegedly said that it could not guarantee her future employment on a specified date after the baby was born. Here the Labour Court upheld the company's argument that she had not been denied access to employment. However, there was considerable conflict of evidence in this case and it should be noted that no claim of indirect discrimination had been made at this point. Subsequently, following an application to the High Court which remitted the case back to the Equality Officer, the latter considered that there had in fact been indirect discrimination. This was confirmed on appeal by the Labour Court.

Mobility requirement

This issue has arisen only in one case, *A Company* v. *A Prospective Female Employee*,[4] where the claimant considered that she had been discriminated against on the basis of her marital status at an interview for the position of customer service agent. The prospective employer had a condition of employment that employees had to be mobile and capable of being placed outside Dublin, including Great Britain. The Equality Officer considered that there had been discrimination on the basis of marital status at her job interview, and she was awarded compensation for 'distress'. However, this had not been what resulted in her non-selection; the real reason for her non-selection was that she was unable to comply with the

---

1   EE 6/1981; DEE 4/1982.
2   EE 3/1989.
3   EE 5/1988; DEE 1/1990; 1991 unreported (HC); EE 15/1991; DEE 2/1993.
4   EE 12/1989.

mobility requirement. The latter was therefore seen as an 'essential requirement' for the job, which justified the unequal treatment of a married woman in this instance.

Strength

There has been one case in which physical strength was accepted as an 'essential requirement' of a job. This was *Dublin Corporation* v. *Gibney* in which a woman had applied for the position of fire fighter. It was held, however, that there were certain essential physical requirements for the position; the claimant had not made a sufficient *prima facie* case for discrimination and accordingly, her case was dismissed.[1]

Age limits

The key Irish case in relation to age limits is *North Western Health Board* v. *Martyn*, which has already been referred to above.[2] The view taken by the Equality Officer and the Labour Court (i.e. that the imposition of an age limit of 27 was indirectly discriminatory) was overturned by the High Court because of inadequate statistical evidence. Subsequently, the High Court judgment was overturned by the Supreme Court, but the latter was careful to stress that its judgment was made on the narrow basis of unrefuted allegations and might not apply in every case. Meanwhile this matter continues to be a major issue for women, particularly in the public service, although some advertisements for positions in the public service have raised the age limit. In general, however, job advertisements by many employers (including the EC Commission) which specify upper age limits continue to be a source of problems.

Minimum height

The 'test-case' as to whether a specified height was an 'essential requirement' for a particular job arose in relation to bus workers in the state transport company, CIE.[3] The company had laid down a minimum height requirement of 5 feet 5 inches for bus conductors, but the Labour Court held that the claimant 'by the fact of her employment as conductor for six years with Greater Manchester Transport Authority has demonstrated conclusively that she is tall enough to be a conductor'. The requirement therefore that conductors must not be smaller than 5 feet 5 inches was not an essential one. Clearly also, a substantially higher proportion of men was able to comply with the requirement. Accordingly, such a requirement was held to be indirectly discriminatory.

---

1   EE 5/1986.
2   §2.3.1; EE 14/1981; DEP 1/1982; [1985] ILRM 226 (HC); [1988] ILRM 519 (SC).
3   DEE 1/1979.

Seniority

Where seniority is used as a basis for promotion, this may be seen as indirectly discriminatory where women have been specifically deprived of the opportunity to amass as much seniority as men. For example, after the 'marriage bar' (which applied in the public service, and even some private sector organizations) was lifted in 1973, some married women returned to their former posts. In time, their loss of seniority began to operate to their detriment when seeking promotion, as only their post-1973 service was counted for these purposes. The practice of seniority-based promotion was challenged by 35 women telephonists and the Labour Court held that they should have been treated as if their service had not been broken: the practice was indirectly discriminatory and 'the continuing effects of past discrimination should be corrected'.[1]

Similar difficulties exist in respect of loss of pension rights arising from broken service and consequent loss of seniority, also caused by the marriage bar. Many women approaching retirement are becoming aware of 'the continuing effects of past discrimination' in this regard, and are likely to seek redress under the Pensions Act when the equal treatment sections become effective. Given the extent of this problem, and the fact that the 1974 Act has been seen in Ireland as covering pensions, and given that the concept of indirect discrimination is now accepted as applying to 1974 Act cases, it is perhaps surprising that no such attempts have already been made.

Preference for existing employees

To date, there has been no case in which an employer cited a preference for existing employees as a legitimate reason for non-selection of other prospective employees.

2.3.1.2 Disproportionate impact

Statistical evidence

Section 2(c) of the 1977 Act defines indirect discrimination, and by implication imports 'proportionality' into evidence in such cases. Thus claimants must clearly demonstrate, and even prove mathematically, that 'the proportion of persons of the other sex or (as the case may be) of a different marital status but of the same sex able to comply is substantially higher'. They must provide detailed statistical evidence to this effect and the Equality Officer must ask all relevant questions to ascertain the exact position. The question of precisely how large the difference in proportions must be before

---

1   *Department of Posts and Telegraphs* v. *35 Women Telephonists* EE 12/1981;
     DEE 3/1982; EEO 1/1985.

one is seen as 'substantially higher' than the other, has not been settled definitively.

In many cases claimants have not provided, or have not been able to provide, such detailed statistical evidence. The required statistics or proof exist at company level, rather than at national level. There have been few cases where the required statistics were available on a national basis; instead, in some instances, expert witnesses on national statistics have had to be engaged.[1]

In the *Martyn* case, Barron J expressed dissatisfaction with the quality of evidence supplied, stating that at no stage in the case had any real statistical evidence been given, by either party, in respect of the issue involved (age limits). The employer had not countered the claimant's allegations with statistical evidence; and the claimant had merely asserted that an age limit of 28 was too low to allow married women to re-enter the workforce having reared their families. In his view, far more statistical evidence and proof was needed. Barron J explained it as follows:

> 'There must be evidence and generally this evidence will be statistical. For example, if a condition is imposed which makes it difficult for women to comply, then two sets of statistics must be considered:
> 1. the actual statistics of the particular application for employment;
> 2. the actual statistics of an application for similar employment on the same conditions but without the impugned condition.
>   If it is found that the proportion of men to women applicants in the first set of statistics is 80/20 and the second set of statistics 60/40, then as a matter of fact the particular requirement is one which discriminates against women. Obviously, it may be extremely difficult in practice to obtain the latter set of statistics but that does not absolve the tribunal hearing the matter from seeking to obtain evidence which is as near as possible to such statistics.'

In overturning this judgment, and conceding that the imposition of an age limit of 28 constituted indirect discrimination, the Supreme Court did not specifically reject Barron J's interpretation of indirect discrimination and the level of statistical evidence required to prove it. Rather, it stated that its decision had been based on the facts of this particular case and might not, therefore, apply in other, similar cases.

Packard Electric Ireland Ltd v. *EEA* [2] provided a further example of detailed statistical evidence being required in order to prove indirect discrimination. However in this case, the relevant internal company statistics were available for consideration by the Equality Officer, as were certain statistics which had been collected by the claimants. The case concerned part-time women workers who operated a 'twilight' shift and were obliged to

---

1   *Vavasour* v. *Bonnybrook Unemployment Action Group* [1991] ELR 199 (Labour Court).

2   EE14/1985.

comply with the requirements that (a) employees who had been laid off or made redundant were not to have been employed on the 'twilight' shift in the previous 26 weeks, in order to qualify for an offer of further employment, when no part-time work was available; and (b) in order to be eligible for full-time employment, a person must not have been employed on the twilight shift in the previous 26 weeks. In order to assess whether the first requirement was discriminatory, the Equality Officer examined the numbers of single and married women and men who were able to comply with the requirement. She found that out of 122 single women employed by the company, 120 (or 98 per cent) worked full-time and were therefore able to comply. Thus the requirement appeared to constitute discrimination based on marital status. Similarly, the proportion of all women employees, married and single, who were able to comply (41 per cent) was significantly lower than the proportion of all men (96 per cent), so the requirement was also discriminatory on grounds of sex.

In assessing the second requirement, the Equality Officer found it necessary to examine that section of the population who would otherwise be considered for employment, were it not for the restrictions placed by the company. She therefore took into account the 'pool' of persons from which the company normally recruited full-time workers, together with the persons from the 'twilight' shift who wished to work full-time. On the basis of the figures supplied by the company (which differed from those supplied by the Employment Equality Agency, and from others supplied by a shop steward), she concluded that a substantially higher proportion of single women (99 per cent) than married women (81 per cent) who would have otherwise been considered for employment, could comply with the requirement. She therefore found the requirement to be discriminatory on grounds of marital status.

In *Revenue Commissioners* v. *Irish Tax Officials' Union*,[1] the Labour Court used a fairly sophisticated statistical technique to assess the impact of the alleged discrimination, namely the Chi-square test. The reason for doing so was that the Court considered that the outcome of the interviews did not make statistical sense, since although there had been more women applicants than men, the men had been more successful than the women, despite the fact that both sexes were generally seen as being equally intelligent. This particular test was used in order to find out whether the observed frequencies (i.e. of successful applications) differed substantially from the expected frequencies. Predictably, the results showed that under normal circumstances, a higher proportion of women would have been expected to be successful, indicating that other factors, such as discrimination, were likely to have been present.

---

[1]   EE 6/1986; DEE 2/1987.

National unemployment statistics were used in *Central Statistics Office v. O'Shea*,[1] where details of the numbers of persons of each sex who were registered as unemployed were considered, in an attempt to ascertain whether a requirement to have been registered as unemployed and in receipt of unemployment benefit was discriminatory. The requirement was found to be indirectly discriminatory against women due to certain social welfare regulations (since changed) which made it difficult for married women, in particular, to be registered as unemployed.

Statistics on the number of part-time women workers and married women in the national workforce were considered in the *O'Neill* case,[2] where part-time women workers were the first to be considered for redundancy.

Relevant pools

The question of what 'pools' are relevant, when making statistical and other comparisons, has arisen in a number of the cases cited above. In *Vavasour v. Bonnybrook Unemployment Action Group*,[3] it was considered that the appropriate 'pool', for comparative purposes, was 'that section of the population who would be eligible for employment if the requirement to be in receipt of unemployment benefit did not exist', a very difficult 'pool' to measure with precision. Here the Labour Court accepted the use of Labour Force Surveys to determine appropriate figures; in other cases, other national statistics have been used; and in a few cases, statistics compiled by the company itself, and/or the employees, or even the Employment Equality Agency have been used and accepted.

Impact on the individual

The alleged discriminatory requirement must be shown to have an impact on the individual concerned. The latter must show a *prima facie* case of discrimination: the purpose of the statistical evidence is then to show, as far as possible, the exact extent of the disproportionate impact on that individual.

2.3.1.3   Objective justification

Section 4(3) of the 1977 Act provides:

> An equality clause shall not operate in relation to a variation between a person's contract of employment and the contract of employment of the other person if the employer proves that the variation is genuinely a consequence of a material difference (other than the difference of sex) between the two cases.

---

1   EE 7/1987.
2   *Michael O'Neill & Son Ltd* v. *Two Female Employees* DEE 1/1988.
3   [1991] ELR 199 (Labour Court).

In other words, unequal treatment may be permissible if there are genuine, 'objective' reasons for it, reasons which are unrelated to the person's sex or marital status. But it is up to the employer to prove that this is the case: it is not sufficient for him merely to assert a lack of intent to discriminate. He must either demonstrate that there is a 'real need' (e.g. on business grounds) for the requirement, or that it is in some way 'appropriate', or that it is actually 'necessary' (e.g. for legal reasons); and in all cases the reasons must be unrelated to sex or marital status.

Real need

It has rarely been accepted that there is a 'real need' for requirements whose intent or effect is discriminatory. 'Market forces' and business reasons have not been accepted as legitimate in this context, although they have on some occasions been advanced.[1] The Labour Court did however accept, on one occasion, that there was a real need for prospective employees to be 'mobile', which in this case militated against the employment of a married woman.[2]

Appropriate

There do not appear to have been any cases in which it was argued by an employer that unequal treatment was in some way 'appropriate'.

Necessary

There have been instances in which it was accepted that certain requirements were absolutely necessary for the performance of the job, however discriminatory their impact appeared to be. The necessity for physical strength, for example, was considered to be an 'essential requirement' for the job of a fire fighter in Dublin Corporation.[3]

2.4   VICTIMIZATION

The third form of discrimination which these Acts seek to prohibit (i.e. in addition to direct and indirect discrimination) is victimization, which in this context means penalising someone who opposes sex discrimination. Section 2(d) of the 1977 Act describes victimization as occurring where a person is penalized for having 'in good faith', either (i) brought proceedings under the 1974 or 1977 Act; or (ii) given evidence in such proceedings; or (iii) given notice of an intention to do either act (i) or act (ii); or (iv) opposed by lawful means an act which is unlawful under these Acts. Interestingly,

---

1   E.g. *Schiesser International (Ireland) Ltd* v. *ATGWU* EP 11-15/1988; DEP 1/1989.
2   *NIHE* v. *Bolton* EE 7/1984; EE 12/1989.
3   *Dublin Corporation* v. *Gibney* EE 5/1986.

ss 67(e) and 80(1) of the Pensions Act 1990 use virtually the same formulation but omit point (iv). Under section 25 of the 1977 Act dismissal for any of these reasons is seen as a criminal offence, unless the employer can prove that these were not the 'sole or principal' reasons for the dismissal. If no prosecution is brought, the person may refer the matter to the Labour Court, under s. 27 of the Act. Similar remedies are provided under the 1990 Act.

There have been relatively few victimization referrals under the 1977 Act, perhaps because the grounds are much narrower than under the Unfair Dismissals Act 1977. While the latter does not specifically list victimization relating to equality matters as being automatically 'unfair', such victimization, if clearly present, would be very likely to be deemed unfair. Therefore it may appear that a claim of general victimization, which includes victimization on grounds of sex and/or marital status, would be more likely to succeed than a claim that the alleged victimization was purely on grounds of sex and/or marital status.

In one case where victimization was alleged,[1] a temporary worker who had been unsuccessful in her application for a permanent post and had advised her employer of her belief that she had been discriminated against, was told soon afterwards that no more work was available for her. She was then replaced by another temporary worker. She was awarded compensation and reinstated to the list of temporary employees. More recently, in a reference under s. 2(d)(i) of the 1977 Act,[2] a clerical worker in a trade union maintained that she had been denied promotion because of her previous involvement in an equal pay claim. The latter had attracted considerable media attention and had also involved the claimant in heated exchanges, during a public Labour Court hearing, with a union officer who was subsequently on the interview board for the promotional post. In a very lengthy recommendation, the Equality Officer concluded that the claimant had been at least as well qualified for the post as the two successful candidates; and better qualified, in one respect, than one of them. This being the case, there was an onus on the union to give 'a reasonably credible explanation' for the interview board's selection; but this it had failed to do. In her view, the selection had been made on the basis of 'a totally subjective assessment' of the candidates and this made it difficult for the interview board to show that its decision had been unrelated to the claimant's previous involvement in the equal pay case. She therefore found that discrimination had occurred, within the meaning of s. 2(d)(i); and recommended compensation of £3,000 for 'distress and loss of status', as well as the creation of a new, promotional post for the claimant, with payment in full, of

---

1   *University College Dublin* v. *A Female Worker* EEO 5/1983.
2   *SIPTU* v. *Ms Mary Dunne* EE 9/1993.

all salary adjustments and other benefits, from the date on which her two colleagues had been promoted. [1]

---

[1] The claimant had specifically requested that if her claim succeeded, the remedy should not involve moving her colleagues from their existing positions. In acceding to this request, the Equality Officer said that she appreciated the difficulties that her recommendation would create for the union, but nonetheless saw it as 'the only appropriate remedy in this case'.

3. EQUAL PAY

3.1 PRINCIPLE

The Anti-Discrimination (Pay) Act 1974, which became effective on 31 December 1975, provides for the right of men and women to receive the same rate of remuneration if employed on 'like work' by the same (or associated) employer, in the same place.

A man and woman are seen as performing 'like work' where both perform the same duties under the same or similar conditions; where the work performed is of a similar nature, with any differences being infrequent or of small importance in relation to the work as a whole; or where the work is equal in value, judged by the demands it makes in terms of skill, responsibility, working conditions and physical or mental effort. The Act does not, however, preclude the payment of different rates to people doing like work where this is for reasons other than sex. The interpretation of each part of this principle has given rise to a substantial body of case law; and while some parts are now quite clearly established, others are still unclear and some have never been tested.

3.2 EXCEPTIONS AND EXCLUSIONS

The 1974 Act covers all 'employed' persons and, according to s. 1, 'employed' means 'employed under a contract of service or apprenticeship or a contract personally to execute any work or labour'. There are no exclusions, in the Act itself, relating to the matters listed below.

3.2.1 SIZE

There are no exclusions related to the size of the establishment or enterprise in which a claimant is employed.

3.2.2 WORK DONE OUTSIDE THE JURISDICTION

There are no exclusions related to work which is performed outside the jurisdiction. The fact that a comparator must be employed 'in the same place' (see §3.6.1. below) might give rise to difficulties for potential claimants if no comparator(s) were working in the same location; however, this issue does not appear to have arisen in any case.

3.2.3   HEALTH AND SAFETY

There are no exclusions in the Act related to health and safety matters. The continued existence of Regulations[1] which place lower limits on the weights which can be lifted by women than on those which can be lifted by men, has been used as a reason not to employ women in certain jobs.[2] It does not, however, appear to have been cited as an argument to justify different pay rates.

3.2.4   NATIONAL SECURITY

There are no exclusions related to matters of national security.

3.2.5   RELIGION, RELIGIOUS SCHOOLS

There are no exclusions related to religion and religious schools.

3.2.6   RETIREMENT AGE

There are no exceptions related to retirement age.

3.2.7   OTHER EXCEPTIONS

Section 56(2) of the Employment Equality Act 1977 provides that both this Act and the Anti-Discrimination (Pay) Act 1974 should be construed as one. In a case dealing with the question of· whether the definition of employee in the 1977 Act applied to the 1974 Act, Costello J said that this meant:[3]

> ... that every part of each of the two Acts are to be construed as if they were contained in one Act unless there is some manifest discrepancy making it necessary to hold that the later Act has modified something in the earlier Act.

In this and other cases, s. 56(2) of the 1977 Act was used to widen the definition of 'employee' in the 1974 Act to that contained in the 1977 Act. However, to date it has not been used to narrow the scope of the 1974 Act by introducing any of the exclusions contained in the 1977 Act and there is some doubt as to whether it could validly be used in this way. If it were, the various exclusions (described in §§4.2, 4.3 and 4.4 below, including those listed above) could be said to apply in equal pay cases.

---

1   Factories Act 1955 (Manual Labour) (Maximum Weights and Transport) Regulations 1972, SI No 283 of 1972.

2   *Tayto Ltd* v. *O'Keeffe* EE 13/1985.

3   *Bank of Ireland* v. *Kavanagh* (1987) 6 JISLL 192 (HC).

3.3   PERSONAL SCOPE

3.3.1   EMPLOYEES

The definition of 'employment' in the 1974 Act covers all persons, whether working under a contract of service, or an apprenticeship, or a contract for services, provided that they personally execute the work or labour concerned. A member of the national parliament has been seen as an 'employee' under this definition, but a solicitor who turned out to be a partner in a firm was not considered to be an 'employee'.[1]

To date, s. 56(2) of the 1977 Act has been used to widen the definition of 'employee' in the 1974 Act (see §3.2.7 above). However, if by virtue of s. 56(2) the definition of 'employment' in the 1974 Act is modified (which seems unlikely, as stated above) then certain categories of employees may be excluded, e.g. some people who work abroad, certain members of the security services etc. — see §4.2 below.

3.3.2   INDEPENDENT CONTRACTORS

The definition of 'employment' would appear to apply to certain self-employed persons and independent contractors, as long as such persons 'personally execute' the work concerned. The exact meaning of this has not yet been tested, however.

3.3.3   HOME WORKERS

To date there have been no cases involving this type of worker, although they would not necessarily appear to be excluded from the scope of the Act. Whether they are would depend in some measure on whether only employees are covered, and whether, in this context, home workers could be said to be employees in legal terms.

3.3.4   PUBLIC SECTOR

Public sector employees are not excluded from the scope of the 1974 Act and numerous claims have been made by such workers. However, it should be noted that under the 1977 Act the process of selection for appointment to certain civil and public service positions is different from that of other employees (see §4.4.4 below).

---

[1]   FERDINAND VON PRONDZYNSKI, *Employment Law in Ireland*, 1989, 2nd ed., Ch. 6.

3.3.5   DOMESTIC EMPLOYEES

These are not excluded from the scope of the 1974 Act although no claims have yet been made by such workers. If, however, the 1974 and 1977 Acts are to be construed together in this particular context, certain domestic workers might be seen as being excluded by virtue of s. 12 of the 1977 Act. This section originally excluded any employment 'in a private residence or by a close relative', but following an amendment[1] it now excludes employment 'which consists of the performance of services of a personal nature, such as the care of an elderly or incapacitated person in that person's home, where the sex of the employee constitutes a determining factor'. Thus it would appear that even if this modification to the 1974 Act were applied, domestic cleaners, for example, should not be excluded from its scope.

3.3.6   NON-EMPLOYED POPULATION

Most other 'non-employees' would seem to be excluded from the scope of the 1974 Act. The possible exceptions are casual workers and temporary workers, including 'agency temps'. The position of casual workers has not yet been tested under the equality legislation; but the Employment Appeals Tribunal has considered them to be employees for purposes of unfair dismissals legislation and the courts have regarded certain casuals (usually hotel workers) to be employees for redundancy purposes.[2] However, in one case, a football correspondent was considered not to be an employee of the newspaper concerned for purposes of protective legislation.[3]

Agency temps are workers who register with employment agencies whose business it is to enter into contracts with such workers and then make them available to a third party — a hirer — who requires the services of a temporary worker. In a case brought under different legislation (the Holidays (Employees) Act 1973), the High Court decided that such persons were not employees of the hiring company, nor was it considered that they were employees of the agency itself.[4] To date, however, neither agency temps, nor other temporary workers, have tested their eligibility for equal pay claims.

3.4   ACTIVITIES COVERED

There are no exemptions or exclusions based on the activity or nature of business of the employer concerned.

---

1   SI No 331 of 1985.
2   For example, in *Byrne* v. *Gartan Ltd* 1048/1983 (EAT).
3   *Kelly* v. *Irish Press Ltd*, (1986) 5 JISLL 170 (CC).
4   *PMPA Insurance Co. Ltd* v. *Minister for Labour*, (1986) 5 JISLL 215 (HC).

3.5 DEFINITION OF 'REMUNERATION'

3.5.1 ARTICLE 119 OF THE EEC TREATY

The definition of remuneration in the 1974 Act is virtually the same as in art. 119 of the EEC Treaty, in that it '... includes any consideration, whether in cash or in kind, which an employee receives, directly or indirectly, in respect of his employment from his employer'.[1] This has been interpreted widely to include not only basic pay, but accommodation, bonus earnings, commission payments, marriage gratuities, overtime payments, pensions, permanent health insurance, redundancy payments and sickness payments. However, claims that staff uniforms were part of 'remuneration' and that the cost of laundering staff uniforms should be taken into account in determining equality of pay, have been rejected.

3.5.2 FRINGE BENEFITS

As stated above, numerous fringe benefits have now been specifically interpreted as falling within the 1974 Act's definition of 'remuneration', while certain attempts at inclusion have failed. These are shown in alphabetical order below.

Accommodation

In a 1982 case, an Equality Officer held that staff accommodation provided by the employer at a subsidized rate constituted 'remuneration', but this was later overruled by the Labour Court on the grounds that the accommodation was only 'incidentally available'.[2] However, in a number of other cases it has been established that accommodation which is 'part and parcel' of a job should be seen as part of 'remuneration'. The right to equal pay thus includes the right to avail of whatever accommodation is provided to the comparator.[3] By the same token, a woman who was in receipt of free accommodation, but had a lower basic rate of pay than a man performing like work, was denied equality in her basic rate (although it was stressed that should she cease to avail of the accommodation, the rates should be equalised).[4]

Bonus payments

In the first case involving the question of bonus payments, equal pay was seen as including equal bonus earnings for equal levels of output, and

---

1   Anti-Discrimination (Pay) Act 1974, s. 1(1).
2   *Midland Health Board* v. *Stokes* EP 26/1982; DEP 2/1983.
3   *Southern Health Board* v. *Kennedy* EP 26/1984; *Metropole Hotel, Cork* v. *Seven Female Waitresses* EP 19/1986; DEP 4/1987.
4   *CIE* v. *ITGWU* EP 13/1977; DEP 1/1978.

this has been confirmed in subsequent cases.[1] However, in one case of this kind, considerable difficulty was experienced in applying this principle, because the bonus payments of the men and women concerned began at different proportions of standard performance, reached a maximum at different proportions, and were paid at different rates. Thus at certain performance levels the men earned higher percentages of their pay than the women, and vice versa.[2] The claimants were entitled to equal basic pay and the production bonus at the same minimum level of performance.

Commissions

Commission paid to sales assistants was accepted in 1983-84 as an element of remuneration; this has not been challenged since.[3]

Marriage gratuities

Prior to the removal of the 'marriage bar' (which formerly required women employees to resign on marriage), many public and private sector employments paid 'marriage gratuities', based on pay and service, to women resigning for this reason (while generally including male employees in a pension scheme). Following the removal of the 'marriage bar' during the 1970s, many of these employments continued to pay the gratuities in certain circumstances (e.g. to women who had been in the employment prior to the change and still wished to take advantage of the gratuity on marriage). In one case in such an employment, a man who had joined service prior to the change, and resigned after it, claimed payment of the gratuity on the grounds that he was performing like work with a woman in a similar situation. The case ultimately revolved around the issue of whether 'unequal pay' was for reasons other than sex, but the premise that the marriage gratuity was part of remuneration was upheld.[4]

In another case, where the claimant sought payment of a marriage gratuity on the basis that unlike his female counterparts, he had not been given the choice between this and preserved pension benefits, the conclusion was that he should be paid the gratuity.[5] However, because of the particular circumstances, the Court said that this should not be regarded as precedent.

---

1   *Plunder and Pollak* v. *ATGWU* EP 30/1978; DEP 3/1979; followed by *Galway Crystal* v. *ATGWU* EP 22/1978; *Waterford Crystal Ltd* v. *60 Women Canteen Assistants* EP 31/1981; *Polymark (Ireland) Ltd* v. *Breen* EP 15/1984.

2   *Lissadell Towels Ltd* v. *56 Female Employees* EP 10/1986; DEP 2/1987; (1988) 7 JISLL 184 (HC); DEP 3/1989.

3   *Clery (1941) Ltd* v. *25 Female Employees* EP 26/1983; DEP 2/1984.

4   *Bank of Ireland* v. *Kavanagh* EP 11/1985; DEP 10/1985; (1987) 6 JISLL 192 (HC).

5   *Revenue Commissioners* v. *O'Sullivan* EP 10/1983; DEP 7/1983.

Because of the time which has elapsed since the removal of the marriage bar and the regular payment of such gratuities, it seems unlikely that there will be any further cases of this kind.

Overtime payments

Overtime payments have been accepted as amounting to 'remuneration', although the main case involving overtime was lost by the claimants because its non-payment was held to be 'for reasons other than sex'.[1]

Permanent health insurance (PHI)

Membership of permanent health insurance (or income continuance) schemes has also been clearly established as part of 'remuneration'. In the first case involving this question, it was held that the claimants were eligible for benefit under a PHI scheme on the same terms as men and that the practice of excluding them in respect of disabilities arising from pregnancy or childbirth was discriminatory.[2]

In the second case,[3] it was also held that membership of a PHI scheme constituted remuneration and that equality in such remuneration included eligibility for benefit in respect of pregnancy-related disabilities. The company had argued that it was the insurance premium payable in respect of each employee, rather than the potential benefit which might be derived from membership of the scheme, that should be considered; but this argument was rejected.

Redundancy payments

Lump sum redundancy payments, in excess of the statutory amounts, have also been found to be 'remuneration'.[4]

Uniforms

In a case concerning the provision of free uniforms, or compensation in lieu of this, it was held that uniforms did not in the particular instance come within the definition of 'remuneration' because it was a condition of employment that they be worn (rather than being a 'consideration' in respect of their employment).[5] The same logic was followed in a second case of this kind, where uniforms were laundered free of charge for men, but not for women performing like work. The latter maintained that their real

---

1   *Clery & Co. (1941) Ltd* v. *47 Female Sales Assistants* EP 26/1983; DEP 1/1984.
2   *Shield Insurance Co. Ltd* v. *Two Female Employees* EP 8/1984.
3   *McCarren & Co.* v. *Jackson* EP 5/1987.
4   *Grant, Barnett & Co. Ltd* v. *Kiernan* EP 6/1983.
5   *Educational Building Society* v. *Male Employees* EP 9/1987.

remuneration was lower as a result, because of the cost of laundering, but the Court took the attitude that the wearing of laundered uniforms was a condition of employment; accordingly, the provision of such uniforms was not part of any 'consideration' or remuneration.[1]

3.5.3   CONTRIBUTIONS BY EMPLOYER

Contributions made by employers towards pension schemes have been viewed as remuneration (see §3.5.6 below), as have contributions towards permanent health insurance plans and other fringe benefits (see §3.5.2 above).

3.5.4   CONTRIBUTIONS BY EMPLOYEE

The question of whether employee contributions towards pension schemes or other fringe benefits constitute remuneration for purposes of the 1974 Act has not arisen.

3.5.5   POST-EMPLOYMENT BENEFITS

No cases have yet arisen in respect of benefits which continue to be payable after the cessation of employment. However, benefits which start to be paid after employment has ended, i.e. survivors' pensions, have been held to be part of an employee's remuneration (for further details see §3.5.6 below).

3.5.6   PENSIONS

The inclusion of pension arrangements within the scope of 'remuneration' was first established in Ireland in 1977.[2] The same approach was followed in subsequent cases where it was held that membership of a death benefit plan, a non-contributory pension scheme and an income continuance scheme all constituted 'remuneration' (and that the eligibility age for these benefits should be the same for women as for men);[3] and that the non-provision of a widower's pension was discriminatory. In another case, it was held that survivors' benefits were part of an employee's remuneration 'and the fact that they are paid after the death of the employee does not put them outside the scope of the Act'.[4]

The question of survivors' benefits was considered further in later cases. In one of these, an Equality Officer said that although a deceased woman had had an entitlement to a survivor's pension on the same basis as her male

---

1   *British Home Stores (Dublin) Ltd* v. *127 Catering Assistants* EP 1/1988; DEP 5/1988.
2   *Linson Ltd* v. *ASTMS* EP 1/1977; DEP 2/1977.
3   *Clery & Co. (1941) Ltd* v. *O'Brien* EP 17/1984.
4   *Department of Public Service* v. *Robinson* EP 36/1978; DEP 7/1989.

colleagues, her widower could not subsequently claim it because the Act only allowed claims by employees. However, the Labour Court overruled this on the basis that the case had been referred to it by the EEA under s. 7(2) (so that the widower was not in fact the claimant), and that the issue concerned the equal pay entitlements of the former employee.[1]

In the next case of this kind, where a woman teacher had died before the date on which women were admitted to a scheme providing survivors' pensions, the Court also overruled an Equality Officer's recommendation that payment of benefits to her widower was outside the scope of the Act.[2] It determined that survivors' benefits should be paid to the widower in line with the amounts which 'would have been due to him had he been the widow of a male teacher who was in the same circumstances as [the teacher]'. The employer had argued that this outcome would have grave financial consequences, both for the particular pension scheme concerned and for public sector pension schemes generally; it is worth noting that the Court placed no time-limits on its determination in deference to such arguments.[3]

Also noteworthy in relation to EC law is that while pensions have long been seen in Ireland as falling within the scope of art. 119 and Directive 75/117/EEC on equal pay, this view has only been taken relatively recently by the ECJ.[4] In fact the Labour Court has dealt with a number of issues in this area which have still not been fully clarified by the ECJ.

3.5.7   COLLECTIVE AGREEMENTS

Most collective agreements simply describe the employees' rates of pay, hours of work, leave arrangements, fringe benefits, work practices, disciplinary procedures and related matters. While they may detail all the various elements of the employees' remuneration, they will not normally list

---

[1]   *University College Galway* v. *EEA* EP 18/1984; DEP 2/1985.

[2]   *Department of Education* v. *EEA* EP 19/1984; DEP 3/1987 — subsequently withdrawn in accordance with Labour Court Equal Pay Order dated 20 November 1989.

[3]   Significantly, however, this case can no longer be referred to or quoted as precedent. For several years, it was said to be on appeal to the High Court; but in the end no appeal was actually made. Instead, following protracted negotiations between the parties an out-of-court settlement was reached under which the Department of Education is understood to have agreed to withdraw its appeal, and pay Mr Candon the recommended amount, on condition that the Labour Court would 'withdraw' its determination. Thus on 20 November 1989 the Labour Court issued an order stating that '... whereas the parties ... have settled their differences by negotiation and have requested the Labour Court to discharge and set aside ... (DEP 3/87) ... the Labour Court hereby discharges and sets aside DEP 3/87 to the intent that the recommendation of the Equality Officer EP 19/1984 shall stand as if no appeal had been made therefrom'. The validity of this procedure would appear to be questionable, but it has not been challenged to date.

[4]   In its ruling of 13 May 1986 in *Bilka Kaufhaus GmbH* v. *Weber von Hartz,* Case 170/84, [1986] ECR 1607 (ECJ).

the grades or individuals to which each and every benefit applies; and the grading structure itself will not normally reveal the gender breakdown of each grade. Indeed, since the 1974 Act came into force, it has become more difficult to establish whether particular grades are predominantly or exclusively 'male' or 'female', or whether particular benefits are payable wholly or mainly to members of a particular sex, since titles that were seen as reflecting sex discrimination were generally replaced by 'unisex' ones.

Whether for this reason (i.e. because sex discrimination is rarely evident in collective agreements), or because there is no mechanism under the Act for replacing discriminatory clauses in collective agreements, the provision for declaring such agreements 'null and void', i.e. s. 5(1) of the 1974 Act, has never been used.

3.6   COMPARATOR

Section 2(1) of the Act provides that comparators must be employed in the same place, by the same (or associated) employer. This has been taken to mean that a comparator must be a real, rather than a hypothetical, member of the opposite sex, but need not necessarily be employed at the same time, i.e. contemporaneously. However, the 'same place' requirement has given rise to a number of cases whose outcome is far from consistent or conclusive.

3.6.1   SAME PLACE

Several cases have arisen in which comparators were cited who were employed by the same company or organization, but in different locations. No very clear pattern has emerged. In one case, a comparator located 18 miles away was considered to be in the 'same place'.[1] In another case, it was held that since salaries were determined on a national (rather than local or regional) basis in the company concerned, the fact that the comparator was 30 miles away was immaterial; so this comparison too, was valid.[2] However, in the case of another employer whose pay rates were determined nationally, the same argument was rejected on the basis that it implied that the 'same place' could mean the entire state, which would render the Act's mention of 'place' pointless.[3] The locations concerned (Sligo and Portlaoise) were further away from each other than the ones in the successful cases; as, also, were the locations in another unsuccessful case, involving workers in Dublin and Cork.[4] However, in most instances, distance, of itself, does not appear to have been the determining factor.

---

1   *Midland Health Board* v. *Stokes* EP 26/1982.
2   *PMPA Insurance Co. Ltd (Waterford)* v. *Three Women Insurance Officials* EP 29/1981.
3   *North-Western Health Board* v. *Brady* EP 12/1985; DEP 9/1985.
4   *Department of Posts and Telegraphs* v. *Six Employees* EP 9/1983.

In one case, in which the Equality Officer decided that a potential comparator located 75 miles away could not be seen as being in the 'same locality', the question was raised as to whether restricting entitlements under the 1974 Act to people in the 'same place' was in conflict with EC law. It was considered that a decision from the ECJ would be required to clarify this.[1]

One reason for the original inclusion of a 'same place' requirement in the 1974 Act was that regional variations in pay rates were, at that time, commonplace in Irish industry. It seemed necessary, therefore, to specify that comparators should be within the same catchment area for purposes of pay rates that were legally or industrially determined. In the course of the 1970s, however, these 'area differentials' (as the regional variations were known) were largely eliminated. In any event, it can be argued that where people performing like work are paid differently for legitimate, long-standing, regional and industrial reasons, such differences may be validated 'on grounds other than sex'. There is therefore no necessity for a specific 'same place' requirement; indeed, its removal has been suggested in a number of proposals which have been made for reform of the 1974 and 1977 Acts.[2]

3.6.2 CONTEMPORANEOUS EMPLOYMENT

The 1974 Act contains no specific requirement that a comparator must be employed at the same time as a claimant and, in one case in which this issue arose, the Equality Officer concluded that 'nothing in the Act' suggested 'that a woman cannot be entitled to the same rate of pay as a man who had previously performed the same job as her'.[3] Thus it was held that there was no need for the man and woman concerned to be employed contemporaneously. The only exception might be where a comparator was employed, and left the employment, before the Act came into force: this was the reason why one 1982 claim failed,[4] but at this stage such a case is unlikely to recur.

3.6.3 HYPOTHETICAL MALE

In general, s. 2(1) of the Act has been interpreted by claimants and potential claimants as requiring comparisons with actual, rather than hypothetical, members of the opposite sex. The only clear attempt to claim what would have been the 'male rate' for a job, had there been men performing it, was unsuccessful and has not been repeated.[5] However, the

---

1 *Leaf Ltd* v. *49 Female Employees* EP 10/1988; DEP 4/1989; the case was in the end not referred to the ECJ.
2 E.g. Irish Congress of Trade Unions, 1984; Employment Equality Agency, 1985; Department of Labour, 1987.
3 *Champion Fire Defence Ltd* v. *Byrne* EP 8/1985.
4 *Veha* v. *Lipsett* EP 13/1982; DEP 7/1982.
5 *Ostlanna Iompair Éireann Teo.* v. *Nine Female Employees* EP 38/1981.

interpretation of s. 3(c) of the Act on 'work of equal value', has evolved in such a way as to allow consideration, in some circumstances, of pay rates which might have applied had claimants been members of the opposite sex (see §3.8.1 below.)

An amendment to s. 2(1), to allow the use of hypothetical comparators, has long been sought by those seeking to broaden the scope of the Act so as to cover the many women in sex-segregated employment. This is seen as perhaps one of the most crucial amendments required in Ireland in order for the equality legislation to become an effective instrument for tackling the low pay problem which adversely affects the status of a high proportion of women in employment.

3.6.4   DIFFERENT ESTABLISHMENT BUT SAME (OR ASSOCIATED) EMPLOYER

In one case, where a comparator worked in a different hospital from the claimant, but the hospitals were run by the same health board, it was considered that they both had the 'same employer'.[1] However, in another case, where the claimants all worked for the same organization and had their pay rates negotiated nationally, but were located in different parts of the country, an Equality Officer rejected the claim on the grounds that they were not located in the 'same place'.[2] Thus it appears that to have the 'same employer' is not always enough: if people are working in different establishments, these also have to be located in the 'same place'.

3.6.5   CROSS-INDUSTRY COMPARISONS

In theory, it might be possible to make cross-industry comparisons in the very limited circumstances where the same (or associated) employer has employees in different industries, who perform like work, in the same place. However, in practice no such cases have arisen. Thus many local and occupational comparisons are ruled out, e.g. between typists working in the same town, performing very similar work, for employers in different industries.

3.7   WOMAN DOES SAME WORK AS MAN (OR SIMILAR WORK)

3.7.1   IDENTICAL/SAME WORK

In order to qualify as the 'same work', in accordance with s. 3(a) of the 1974 Act, the work actually performed, and the conditions under which it is performed, must be virtually identical. In one case where the employer

---

1   *Clonskeagh Hospital* v. *Two Telephonists* EP 40/1979.
2   *ITGWU* v. *23 Female Employees* EP 19/1983.

argued that a claimant's work was not the same as that of her comparator because the latter had a liability for additional attendance and duties, it was found that in practice the work performed was substantially the same; equal pay was therefore awarded on the basis of the actual work situation, rather than liabilities which rarely materialised.[1]

However, a claim by another woman who appeared to be doing the same work as her male predecessor was rejected, not because he was no longer performing the work, but because it emerged that there were in fact some crucial differences in the work performed by each. All the work performed by the claimant was substantially the same as work her comparator had performed, but she did not have the necessary technical knowledge to perform some additional tasks which had been carried out by him and were a necessary part of the job.[2]

3.7.2   SIMILAR WORK

Section 3(b) of the Act applies where work is broadly similar, where differences occur only infrequently, or where they are of small importance in relation to the work as a whole. This means, effectively, that there can be frequent differences, as long as these remain 'of small importance'. However, even an occasional difference can make the work dissimilar, if the difference is sufficiently 'important in relation to the job as a whole'.

Clearly this leaves a great deal of room for manoeuvre and argument and there has been a large number of references under s. 3(b). In some cases, also, there is scope for overlap with s. 3(c) and many claimants have been uncertain as to whether the reference should be under para. (b) or (c). For example, jobs which are not sufficiently 'similar' to qualify under s. 3(b) might nevertheless qualify as being equal in value, under s. 3(c). In such cases, the reference is usually made under both paragraphs.

The general approach of the Equality Officers and Labour Court to investigating claims of 'similar work' was spelt out in some detail in two cases and has been followed in subsequent claims of this kind.[3] The 'running order' in such investigations is usually that the Equality Officer or Court considers: (i) whether the work actually performed is broadly similar; (ii) whether there are differences between the work; (iii) whether these differences occur infrequently; and (iv) whether the differences are of small importance in relation to the job as a whole.

---

1   *Department of Posts and Telegraphs* v. *Kennefick* EP 9/1979; DEP 2/1980.
2   *Champion Fire Defence* v. *Byrne* EP 8/1985.
3   *Toyota Motor Distributors (Ireland) Ltd* v. *Kavanagh* EP 17/1985; DEP 1/1986; *Dowdall O'Mahony & Co. Ltd* v. *ITGWU* EP 2/1987; DEP 6/1987.

Next, having ascertained the magnitude, frequency and significance of the differences, the question of whether these justify pay differences must be addressed, in the context of the particular employment concerned. The context is vital because, as was pointed out in the one case,[1]

> ... in a company with a large number of job grades, a relatively small difference between two jobs could be sufficient to warrant a difference in pay. In another company, however, one with only a small number of grades each consisting of broadly similar jobs, the same difference might well be considered unimportant and warrant no difference in pay.

Finally, in examining the context of the pay differences, it might be necessary to examine the work of others in the same grade as the comparator, and to see whether there were differences in the demands made on various male workers who were on the same grade. It could well be the case that there were such differences, yet they had not given rise to pay differences between the men. In other words, the grading structure itself might be discriminatory, as in one case, where the Court said it was 'satisfied ... that the difference(s) ... are not of such importance that, if the sex of the worker was not a factor, would justify a different grade and therefore a different rate of pay.'[2] This general approach has been followed in many subsequent cases.

3.7.3   NIGHT-WORK

The principle of considering 'actual performance' has been followed strictly in any cases which have arisen in which the time at which work was performed was at issue. For example, in a case involving female day telephonists and male night telephonists,[3] the Equality Officer concluded that 'the time at which the work is performed should be disregarded in considering whether ... [they] ... are employed on like work'. Thus the basic rates of pay should be equalised; and additional payments made, as appropriate, to those who worked at night.

3.8   EQUAL VALUE

Section 3(c) can be seen as allowing for the possibility of comparisons to be made between jobs which are radically different in content and value to the employer, as long as they are equally demanding for the employee, in terms of skill, responsibility, physical or mental effort and the quality of working conditions, as laid down in the Act.

In practice, however, very few claims have been made comparing jobs which are radically different, either in content or value. Most 's. 3(c) claims' have been extensions of 's. 3(a) claims' and/or 's. 3(b) claims', in the sense

---

1   *Toyota* v. *Kavanagh* above.
2   *Dowdall O'Mahony* v. *ITGWU* above.
3   *Department of Posts and Telegraphs* v. *POWU* EP 4/1979.

that the claimants sought, initially, to show that work concerned was the same or similar; if this failed, they would then seek to demonstrate that it was equal in value. One exception was the case of a seamstress who claimed, unsuccessfully, that her work was equal in value to that of a painter and a carpenter.[1]

3.8.1   JOB EVALUATION

The 1974 Act does not either require or debar the use of formal job evaluation schemes. Such schemes have been considered in a number of cases, but they have not formed the basis of any recommendation or determination. This is because when cited by one party, the other usually claims bias. In one such case,[2] each side produced its own scheme (using different weightings, with different results) to support its case. The Labour Court considered both and found, in this particular instance, that the company had not produced sufficient evidence to warrant upsetting the Equality Officer's recommendation, which had favoured the union; it therefore rejected the company's appeal.

The Court made its attitude to job evaluation clear at a relatively early stage when it said, in effect, that the result of such an exercise would be one of a number of considerations to be borne in mind in evaluating a case, but would not be the determining one: 'The results may or may not contain an element of bias based on sex but they should not be ... ignored'.[3] In other words, a healthy scepticism should be, and generally has been, maintained about the use of job evaluation. This approach, and the fact that on one occasion the Court was extremely critical of the way in which a company was attempting to use job evaluation,[4] may be why it has not often been relied upon in recent claims.

The 1974 Act provides no guidance as to how exactly jobs should be evaluated and compared in terms of the factors mentioned in s. 3(c), i.e. skill, responsibility, physical and mental effort, and quality of working conditions. In practice, therefore, the approach of the Equality Officers and Labour Court has gradually evolved and been refined over the years. What it normally amounts to is a detailed investigation of all the tasks involved, an analysis of the demands each of these tasks makes (in terms of skill, responsibility, etc.), and a 'weighing-up' and 'balancing-out' process to see if the overall value of the work can be said to be equal.

Equality is not seen in strictly mathematical terms:[5]

---

1   *North-Western Health Board* v. *A Seamstress* EP 24/1982.
2   *C H Arthur and Sales Finance Co.* v. *ITGWU* EP 3/1977; DEP 5/1977.
3   *Data Products (Memories) Ltd* v. *Simpson* EP 20/1978; DEP 1/1979.
4   *Toyota Motor Distributors (Ireland) Ltd* v. *Fitzpatrick* EP 10/1987.
5   *Pauwels Trafo (Ireland) Ltd* v. *15 Women Winding Machine Operators* EP 48/1981.

'There is no method by which the Equality Officer nor any assessor can determine with mathematical precision that the woman's work and the man's work comes out exactly the same. The Equality Officer must therefore take a practical approach to the work under examination and determine whether the total package of every individual's work under examination can be reckoned as being of equal value in terms of s. 3(c).

It has also been stated by a High Court judge that the words 'equal in value' 'should not be used so as to require a mathematical exactitude of equality';[1] nor is 'value' usually seen in terms of the financial value of the work to the employer. In one case, the Equality Officer also had to consider the argument, advanced by the company, that since the machine worked by the men was more expensive than the one worked by the women claimants, the men had 'greater responsibility' than the women. 'Responsibility' was thus being seen by the company in financial terms, but the argument was rejected, with the Equality Officer saying that he 'would not accept that it follows that if the machine is more expensive the responsibility is higher'.[2]

On the other hand, the question of potential financial loss to the company (e.g. because of a mistake) was considered relevant in a case where a female confectioner was claiming equal pay with a male baker.[3] The Equality Officer here accepted the employer's argument that since bread was the employer's main money-making commodity, and 'spoiled dough or bread would cost the bakery a lot of money', the baker's 'responsibility' surpassed that of the confectioner (whose work appeared to be more marginal, financially, to the business). On two other occasions,[4] the Equality Officers listed the factors which they had considered in assessing 'responsibility' and specifically included the replacement value of machines used and the financial consequences of workers' mistakes. In most situations, however, no one factor of this kind has been seen as conclusive: 'responsibility' has been judged from a wider perspective, under all of the factors mentioned in the Act.

Frequently, when women's jobs are evaluated and assessed in relation to men's, it emerges that the demands of the women's jobs are greater or equal in terms of skill, responsibility and mental effort; less in terms of physical effort; and less or equal in terms of working conditions. In many such cases, the overall value of the jobs has been seen as being equal.[5]

---

1   *An Bord Telecom Éireann* v. *Murphy* EP 28/1983; DEP 6/84; *Murphy* v. *Bord Telecom Éireann* [1986] ILRM 483 (HC); see §3.8.3 below.

2   *Pauwels Trafo* above.

3   *Haddens Ltd, Cork* v. *Gould* EP 17/1981.

4   *Linson Ltd* v. *27 Stomahesive Operatives* EP 32/1981; *Addis (Ireland) Ltd* v. *19 Female Employees* EP20/1981.

5   For example, *Youghal Carpet (Yarns) Ltd* v. *Canteen Attendants* EP 21/1982; *Harringtons Goodlass Wall Ltd* v. *Five Female Operatives* EP 12/1983; *Eastern Health Board* v. *O'Brien* EP 1/1984 (where the woman had greater demands in terms

It seems clear from a number of cases that all relevant factors, including dexterity, are normally considered in the assessment of jobs. Dexterity was specifically mentioned in one instance when an Equality Officer concluded that on balance, the female claimants' work was equal in value to that of their male comparators: the latter's work 'demands a high level of physical strength and endurance and sometimes is carried out in extremely unpleasant working conditions', while the women's work 'requires a degree of skill, dexterity and concentration which is as demanding as the physical energy required of the male general workers'.[1]

The Labour Court has been very insistent about the need to assess work in detail in this way, by reference to the various demands it makes. In one case where an Equality Officer had taken a different approach, this was firmly overruled.[2] The Equality Officer had made a distinction between 'like work' in s. 3(c) — which meant work that was equal in terms of the demands it made on people — and work that was 'equal in value'. In his view, the latter meant more than simply work which was equally demanding: it meant work which warranted the same rate of remuneration. This was, he believed, consistent with the nature and practice of job evaluation, from which the terminology in s. 3(c) derived, and with the fact that employers usually treated jobs equally, for pay purposes, if they were evaluated as being appropriate to the same grade, even if they were not necessarily equally demanding. Following this line of reasoning, the Equality Officer had concluded that the two different rates of pay were, in reality, different rates for men and women which applied irrespective of differences between the demands of their individual jobs. Therefore, the differing demands were not the reason for the differing pay rates; and did not warrant unequal pay. However, the Labour Court, overturning his recommendation, said that work must be assessed objectively, in terms of the demands it makes. The factors used should generally be the ones which were used in the employment concerned (skill, responsibility etc.), unless of course there was 'an element of bias in the factors themselves'. To do otherwise, and to accept that work which is equal in value is merely work which warrants the same rate of remuneration, 'introduces circularity into the argument'.

This is not to say that having thoroughly assessed the work in relation to the demands it makes, the Labour Court and Equality Officers do not then

of physical effort and the man had less desirable working conditions); *Howmedica International Inc.* v. *Female Pleur-Evac Operators* EP 2/1986; *CMP Dairies Ltd* v. *Eight Female Employees* EP 2/1989; *Ko-Rec-Type (Europe) Ltd* v. *12 Female Operatives* EP 3/1989; *Ko-Rec-Type (Europe) Ltd* v. *Two Supervisors and 30 Operatives (female)* EP 4/1989.

1   *Waterford Glass Ltd* v. *ITGWU* EP 15/1977.
2   *Lissadell Towels Ltd* v. *56 Female Employees* EP 10/1986; DEP 2/1987; but see §3.5.2 above.

consider the value it might have had in the absence of sex discrimination. In several cases they have had to decide, in effect, whether the differences in demands between two jobs would have led the employer to grade them differently if both jobs had been performed exclusively by members of one sex. In one of these, the Court described the 'test' in this way: that it had to decide 'whether or not these differences were of such importance that they would normally be used as the basis for establishing a different grade, salary scale or rate of pay irrespective of the sex of the worker concerned'.[1] Interestingly, this test is comparable to the 'hypothetical man' approach, but allows for the possibility of even wider comparisons. Rather than requiring an actual or notional male comparator, a woman might be able to argue that but for her sex, she would have been paid the same rate as a man. This opens up many new prospects, which have not yet been explored.

3.8.2   JOB CLASSIFICATION

This concept does not apply in the Irish context.

3.8.3   HIGHER VALUE

One unexpected consequence of the wording of s. 3(c) of the 1974 Act was the literal and rigid interpretation of the word 'equal' so as to preclude the equalization of pay rates where a claimant's work was considered higher in value than a comparator's. The test case involved female factory workers who claimed equal pay with a male stores labourer and whose work was assessed as being higher in value than that of the man. In view of this finding, the Equality Officer, the Labour Court and the High Court all found it necessary to take the literal interpretation of s. 3(c) and Keane J referred it to the ECJ. The latter concluded that in such situations, art. 119 of the EEC Treaty must be interpreted as prohibiting pay differences and that 'to adopt a contrary interpretation would be tantamount to rendering the principle of equal pay ineffective and nugatory ...'. Eventually, these claimants were granted equal pay; and a number of other similar claims, which had been awaiting the outcome of the ECJ judgment, began to be heard.[2]

3.8.4   PROPORTIONATE PAY

As with jobs which are 'more than equal', there is no provision in the Act for pay awards in respect of jobs which are 'nearly equal'. Even if it were possible to decide that a claimant's work was equal to say, 80 per cent or 90 per cent of a comparator's work (or indeed 110 per cent or 120 per cent), there is no provision for proportionate payment in this regard. The

---

1   *Dowdall O'Mahony & Co. Ltd* v. *ITGWU* EP 2/1987; DEP 6/1987.
2   *An Bord Telecom Éireann* v. *Murphy* EP 28/1983; DEP 6/1984; *Murphy* v. *Bord Telecom Éireann* [1986] ILRM 483 (HC); Case 157/86, [1988] ECR 673 (ECJ), [1989] ILRM 53 (ECJ and HC); DEP 7/1988.

suggestion that a mechanism to achieve this should be devised has been advanced by some but not yet adopted.

3.9   LEGITIMATE REASON FOR PAY DIFFERENTIAL

Section 2(3) of the Act provides that even in cases of 'like work', pay differentials may be permissible if these are 'on grounds other than sex'. However such grounds are not defined and there is no requirement that they be 'reasonable', so that in theory, at any rate, the grounds could be absurd, but still permissible if not sex-related.

Over a dozen different 'grounds other than sex' have now been advanced as legitimate reasons for pay differentials. Four of them have been ruled out each time they arose: actuarial factors, flexibility, maternity and part-time working. The others have generally received a favourable or mixed response. Most of these are described in §3.9.6. below.

3.9.1   MATERIAL DIFFERENCE

Those 'material differences' not based on sex which have been used by employers to justify discrimination are discussed at §3.9.6 below.

3.9.2   ECONOMIC BENEFITS/MARKET FORCES

There have been no cases in which market forces were cited as an objective justification for different pay rates for men and women. This may be partly because of widespread sex segregation in the labour market and the fact that the absence of male comparators in certain all-female grades and industries precludes claims in the very areas where this argument might be expected to be used.

3.9.3   NIGHT-WORK

Since women are no longer barred from performing night-work, the necessity for such work cannot now be cited as a legitimate reason for pay differentials between men and women. However, in some cases it has been argued that more onerous attendance liabilities, such as the liability to work at night, justified higher pay rates (see §3.9.6 below); and the question of night-work has also been raised in the context of assessing 'like work' (see §3.7.3 above).

3.9.4   PART-TIME WORK

On two occasions, Equality Officers and the Labour Court have held that the payment of lower hourly rates to part-time workers than to full-time workers was indirectly discriminatory and hence unjustified under s. 2(3).[1] Thus payment of a lower hourly rate, on grounds of part-time working, was not accepted as being objectively justified. Interestingly, in these cases, it was held that although the 1974 Act does not itself outlaw indirect discrimination, the fact that the 1977 Act does, and that s. 56(2) of the latter requires that both Acts be construed as one, means that indirect discrimination should also be disallowed in 1974 Act cases.

3.9.5   RED CIRCLES

An employee whose work is deemed to be over-valued, but who is allowed to keep the higher rate of pay on a personal basis, is said to be 'red-circled'. Four cases have arisen in which women have claimed equal pay with a 'red-circled' man. In one, the Equality Officer found it was a genuine case of 'red-circling', so the reason for the pay difference was not sex-related.[2] However, in the second case, the Court found that if the claimant had been a man, she too, like her comparator, would have been 'red-circled'. The reason she was not treated the same way was her sex; so her claim for equal pay succeeded.[3] The third case involved four claimants: it was found that for three of them, the 'red-circling' was a genuine 'reason other than sex' for the difference between their pay and that of the comparators; but for the fourth, the same circumstances applied as in the above case. Had she been a man, she too would have been 'red-circled', so the company's defence under s. 2(3) was not acceptable.[4] The company's defence was also rejected in the fourth case: here the Court said it would have to be satisfied that the existence of a 'red-circling' arrangement was a known and acknowledged fact whereas many of the comparators had made written statements to the effect that they had been quite unaware of any such arrangement.[5]

3.9.6   OTHER REASONS

A number of other reasons have also been advanced as 'objective justification' for pay differentials between men and women. These are listed in alphabetical order below.

Actuarial factors

The argument that the use of sex-differentiated actuarial factors, in the calculation of benefits under an income continuance scheme, constituted a legitimate reason for the payment of lower benefits to women, was rejected

---

1   *Dunnes Stores (Navan) Ltd* v. *Two Female Employees* EP 15/1982; *St Patrick's College, Maynooth* v. *ITGWU* EP 4/1984; DEP 10/1984.

2   *Hanson Ltd* v. *McLoughlin* EP 45/1989.

3   *Data Products (Memories) Ltd* v. *Simpson* EP 20/1978; DEP 1/1979.

4   *Micromotors Groschopp (Ireland) Ltd* v. *ITGWU* EP 18/1986; DEP 5/1987.

5   *Eastern Health Board (St Brendan's Hospital)* v. *Coffey* EP 8/1990; DEP 5/1991.

in a 1984 case.[1] Subsequently, Directive 86/378/EEC, on Equal Treatment in Occupational Social Security, allowed for unequal treatment where this results from the use of such factors. However, the National Pensions Board, in its report to the Irish Government on the implementation of Directive 86/378/EEC, recommended that although the use of actuarial factors must be allowed in the interests of accurate costing of income continuance (and pension) arrangements, and although insurance companies should be permitted to charge different premiums for men and women, this should not result in the payment of different benefits to men and women.[2] In the event, s. 69(1)(b) of the Pensions Act 1990 (of which Part VII implements Directive 86/378/EEC), allows for the citing of actuarial factors as a valid reason for providing different benefit levels for men and women, but only in 'defined contribution' schemes and not in the (more common) 'defined benefit' arrangements to which most pension scheme members in Ireland belong.

Age and/or service

In one early case involving s. 2(3),[3] the Labour Court specifically mentioned 'age or service' as examples of valid 'grounds other than sex'; and in two out of the three cases centring on this issue, such grounds have been accepted as legitimate.[4] In the third instance, however, the Equality Officer concluded that on the facts of the case, the arguments about seniority and service did not stand up: '... it is evident that no matter what her experience or seniority ... [the claimant] ... would never have received the same remuneration as the male', although there was insufficient difference between their jobs to justify the pay differential.[5] From this, it is clear that Equality Officers and the Labour Court must be satisfied, on the facts of every case, that age and/or service are the real and only (or major) reasons for the pay difference.

Attendance liability

There have been several cases in which it was argued that more onerous attendance liabilities, such as the liability to work at night, justified higher pay rates. None of these claims has received full endorsement,[6] although the

---

1   *Shield Insurance Co. Ltd* v. *Two Female Employees* EP 8/1984.
2   *Equal Treatment for Men and Women in Occupational Pension Schemes*, Report of National Pensions Board, Dublin, 1989.
3   *Brooks Thomas Ltd* v. *ASTMS* EP 6/1977.
4   *Irish Plastic Packaging Ltd* v. *ITGWU* EP 25/1978 — '... an age-related wage structure, in itself, does not constitute discrimination ...'; and *Dunnes Stores (Northside) Ltd* v. *Five Female Employees* EP 6/1988; DEP 4/1988.
5   *Inter-Beauty (Ireland) Ltd* v. *Bobbett* EP 41/81.
6   See, for example, *Department of Posts & Telegraphs* v. *POWU* EP 4/1979 and *Navan Carpets Ltd* v. *92 Female Employees* EP 46/1979, which were both rejected on the facts of the case; in the former, however, the idea of more onerous attendance requirements constituting 'grounds other than sex' was implicitly accepted.

principle would appear to have been accepted and in one case it was considered that part of the difference in pay rates was justified as being paid on grounds other than sex, i.e. the more onerous attendance liabilities.[1] Liability to work over a 24-hour period has also been accepted as a legitimate reason for paying an extra allowance in a security company, where this liability is provided for in a registered agreement covering the industry as a whole.[2]

Capacity for extra duties

Under s. 3 of the Act a person's 'actual performance of like work' is deemed to be the correct basis for comparison, but under s. 2(3) there is no such restriction and in several cases it has been argued that people's liability and capacity for performing extra duties is a legitimate reason for higher pay.

In two cases,[3] consideration of 'actual performance' appeared to be the basis of the claimant's success (i.e. the employer's failure to establish 'extra capacity' as 'grounds other than sex'). However, in another case, where the male comparators were found to have actual flexibility and capacity for performing extra duties, the claim for parity failed, as this was seen as a legitimate reason for the pay differential.[4]

Compassion

In a number of instances,[5] it has been accepted that men have been paid higher rates than women 'on compassionate grounds' and that this was legitimate. Generally, they were men who for health reasons were no longer able to perform the full range of duties for which they had been employed, but were allowed to maintain their former rate of pay.

Flexibility

It has been argued, in several cases, that because claimants could not give the same 'flexibility' as their male comparators, their work was not as valuable, economically, to the employer; lower pay rates were therefore justified 'on grounds other than sex'. However, to date, no employer has succeeded with this argument. In one case, it was found that the higher rate for men had not originated because of their greater flexibility.[6] In another,

---

1 *Department of Posts and Telegraphs* v. *POMSA* EP 7/1977.
2 *Group 4 Securitas (Ireland) Ltd* v. *26 Female Store Detectives* EP 3/1991.
3 *Nitrigin Eireann Teo.* v. *ITGWU* EP 49/1979; DEP 16/1980; and *Coombe Lying-in Hospital* v. *Bracken* EP 14/1980.
4 *Dunnes Stores (Parkway) Limerick Ltd* v. *28 Female Employees* EP 6/1987.
5 *Nitrigin Eireann Teo.* v. *ITGWU* EP 2/1977; DEP 4/1977; *Central Bank of Ireland* v. *One Female Cleaner* EP 48/1980; *CIE* v. *Two Female Waiting Room Attendants* EP 46/1981.
6 *Kayfoam Woolfson Ltd* v. *Seven Female Employees* EP 4/1987; DEP 6/1988.

the company argued that the men's work was of higher economic value because they were able to lift heavy weights (which the women were prevented by legislation from doing). However, the Equality Officer found that s. 14 of the 1977 Act (permitting unequal treatment due to compliance with certain protective legislation) did not apply in circumstances such as these, where it was perfectly practicable for the employer to re-organize matters so as to avoid either contravening that legislation or confining the work to men only.[1]

Finally, in a case in which the employer had argued that the male comparators were paid more than the female claimants because they were liable to be transferred to other departments, it emerged that each man had been in his own department for years and had never been asked to transfer elsewhere. Accordingly the employer's argument was rejected.[2]

Former position/personal rate

In several cases, it has been argued that male employees were on higher rates of pay than female claimants because of their former position rather than their present work. For various reasons, they had been allowed to retain a higher rate on a personal basis and this was accepted as legitimate: the difference in pay was therefore for reasons other than sex and women in the same situation would have been treated the same way.[3]

Grading structure

The 'grounds other than sex' which are most commonly cited by employers to justify pay differentials are that claimants occupy a lower position on a grading structure and that the structure is not a discriminatory one. Generally, where an employer can show clearly that a grading structure does not itself discriminate on the basis of sex, or that the work has been evaluated in a non-discriminatory way, or that the pay difference would still exist even if the men were women and *vice versa*, the differences are accepted as legitimate.[4] However, where grading structures look 'suspicious' (e.g. with all-female grades at the lowest levels and all-male ones at the

---

1   *Charles Bell (Ireland) Ltd* v. *Three Female Employees* EP 7/1987.
2   *University College Cork* v. *Two Female Laboratory Aides* EP 4/1988.
3   *Irish Dunlop Ltd* v. *Cronin* EP 39/1978; DEP 4/1979; *Boart Hardmetals Europe Ltd* v. *Three Women Canteen Assistants* EP 64/1980; *Cadbury Ireland Ltd* v. *Eight Female Employees* EP 5/1985; *Cahill May Roberts Ltd* v. *24 Female Employees* EP 7/1987.
4   As, for example, in *Johnson & Johnson (Ireland) Ltd* v. *Kershaw* EP 11/1987; DEP 2/1988; *Department of Justice* v. *186 Court Registrars/Clerks* EP 16/1988; *Meath Hospital* v. *Male Night Porters* EP 12/1986; DEP 9/1986.

highest), or the origins of the grading structure were clearly sex-based, pay differences are more likely to be seen as discriminatory.[1]

Industrial action

On one occasion, prior to the 1977 Act coming into operation, the Labour Court accepted that 'the threat of industrial action' constituted a valid reason for pay differences between men and women, although it was careful to add that s. 9 of the 1977 Act prohibited procuring or attempting to procure discrimination, so that 'the circumstances which give rise to this determination should not be repeated in this company or elsewhere'.[2] Briefly the circumstances were that after fixing pay rates on a new, non-discriminatory basis, the company hired some men to do 'Grade F and G' work. These grades carried an agreed 'unisex' rate, which also applied to women but was lower than the original 'male' rate. The union insisted that the company pay the new entrants the old, higher, 'male' rate and the company agreed; whereupon the women in Grade F and G claimed equal pay with the new male entrants. The Equality Officer had seen the payment of higher rates to the men as an effective re-establishment of sex-differential pay rates, but the Labour Court disagreed and said the extra money had been paid 'on grounds other than sex, i.e. threat of industrial action'.

This case highlights a major weakness in s. 2(3), namely the failure to require that the grounds for pay differentials be in some way reasonable, as it is clearly insufficient that they merely be 'not based on sex'. Such a negative formulation leaves the way open for a bizarre range of possibilities to be devised as 'legitimate' (i.e. non-sex-based) reasons for pay differences between women and men.

Incidentally, in a later case an Equality Officer clearly recognized that the principle of equal pay must be adhered to, even if it meant upsetting traditional pay patterns, disrupting industrial relations and disturbing industrial peace.[3] In other words, industrial expediency was not an acceptable reason for maintaining unequal pay. On the other hand, the Labour Court has also stated that there can be differences in pay arising from the industrial relations process, and that such differences may be justifiable as long as they are not inherently discriminatory.[4]

---

1   As, for example, in *Krups Engineering Ltd* v. *ITGWU* EP 8/1986; *Howmedica International Inc.* v. *Four Pleur-Evac Operators* EP 2/1986; *An Bord Telecom Eireann* v. *29 Female Factory Workers* EP 28/1983; DEP 7/1988; see also § 8.3.8.3.

2   *Brooks Thomas Ltd* v. *ASTMS* EP 6/1977; DEP 7/1977.

3   *Calor Kosangas Ltd* v. *Four Secretaries* EP 19/1979.

4   *Grant, Barnett & Co. Ltd* v. *Kiernan* EP 6/1983.

Juvenile rates

In one case, the Labour Court had to decide whether the practice of paying 'juvenile rates' to young women who performed adult work, was justified 'on grounds other than sex'. When male juveniles performed adult work they received the adult rates. The Court upheld an Equality Officer's recommendation that this was invalid and that the difference in rates was not 'for reasons other than sex'.[1]

Marital status

Two cases involving the issue of marital status have illustrated a major limitation of the 1974 Act, in that it explicitly covers discrimination on grounds of sex, but not on grounds of marital status. Thus it has been possible to argue successfully that a pay difference which was due to a person's marital status was legitimate under s. 2(3), as it was not based on sex.[2] Indeed, the second case of this kind went to the High Court, where it was held that the pay difference in question (involving non-payment of a marriage gratuity) was also based on grounds other than sex, namely marital status and entry to the employment before a certain date.[3]

An extension to the 1974 Act of the provision in the 1977 Act which prohibits discrimination on the basis of marital status has been sought by a number of organizations.

Maternity

As with discrimination on grounds of marital status, discrimination because of maternity is also technically allowable under the very wide umbrella of 'grounds other than sex'. However, in a case heard under the 1977 Act unequal treatment on the basis of the normal incapacities associated with a normal pregnancy was held to be indirectly discriminatory;[4] and interestingly, this approach was followed in subsequent equal pay cases even though the 1974 Act does not itself incorporate the concept of indirect discrimination.

In the first of these, the employer tried to refuse the claimant paid sick leave, since unpaid maternity leave was available to her at the time; but the Equality Officer said that it was indirectly discriminatory since only women could make use of unpaid maternity leave.[5] Although the 1974 Act did not

---

1   *Youghal Carpet (Yarns) Ltd* v. *ITGWU* EP 9/1986; DEP 8/1986.
2   *Eastern Health Board (Cherry Orchard Hospital)* v. *21 Female Hospital Attendants* EP 30/1979.
3   *Bank of Ireland* v. *Kavanagh* EP 11/1985; DEP 10/1985; (1987) 6 JISLL 192 (HC).
4   *An Foras Forbartha* v. *Geraghty-Williams* DEE 4/1982.
5   *North Western Health Board* v. *Brady* EP 12/1985; DEP 9/1985.

outlaw indirect discrimination, the 1977 Act did, and s. 56(2) of the latter required that both Acts be construed as one. Thus indirect discrimination should also be disallowed in 1974 Act cases, and what this meant was disregarding as 'grounds other than sex', under s. 2(3), any grounds whose application naturally resulted in unequal pay and could not be objectively justified.

In a second, equally important, case of this kind, a company argued that its income continuance scheme treated women differently from men for 'reasons other than sex', namely actuarial calculations and the fact that Directive 86/378/EEC on Social Security allowed certain exclusions for actuarial reasons. The Equality Officer decided, however, that the Social Security Directive had no bearing on the interpretation of s. 2(3) and that since the exclusion in the income continuance scheme was indirectly discriminatory on grounds of sex, it could not be justified in terms of 'grounds other than sex'.[1]

Qualifications

In a number of cases, it has been argued that superior qualifications, rather than sex, accounted for the higher pay rates of men than of women. On several occasions this was found to be so.[2] However, in one case it was found that despite the employer's insistence that the pay difference was based on qualifications and employment experience, the claimants were, *inter alia*, on an all-female scale which had originated in 1970 when it was common to pay women less than men. Having regard to all the various factors involved, it therefore appeared that the difference was, in reality, based on sex.[3]

Salary and service

There has been one case in which salary and service were accepted as legitimate reasons for the lower remuneration of a woman than a man. A claimant argued sex discrimination in relation to pension, lump sum and other payments, but it was considered that this was mainly because her salary and service (on which the calculation of these benefits was based) were lower than the comparator's; and this was for reasons other than sex. No discrimination had occurred in the calculation of her salary and service, and hence her pension and other benefits: a man in the same situation would have had equally low entitlements.[4]

---

1   *McCarren & Co. Ltd* v. *Jackson* EP 5/1987.
2   *Department of Agriculture* v. *Instructors in Farm Home Management and in Poultry Keeping* EP 23/1978; DEP 10/1979; *John Murphy & Sons Ltd* v. *One Female Employee* EP 11/1986.
3   *ACOT* v. *IAAO* EP 13/1984; DEP 8/1985; 13 April 1989, unreported (HC); DEP 3/1991.
4   *Bord Telecom Éireann* v. *Ní Oireachtaigh* EP 9/1988.

3.10   LEVELLING UP/DOWN

To our knowledge, there have been no cases in which a levelling-down of wages or salaries was at issue in an equal pay claim. Levelling-up has been the norm where such claims succeed.

4. EQUAL TREATMENT

4.1 PRINCIPLE

The long title of the Employment Equality Act 1977 provides that it is 'an Act to make unlawful in relation to employment certain kinds of discrimination on grounds of sex or marital status, to establish a body to be known as the Employment Equality Agency, ... and to provide for other matters related to the aforesaid matter'. The Act came into force on 1 July 1977. The Act makes unlawful various forms of discriminatory conduct in relation to employment, including direct and indirect discrimination and victimization. It also imports an equality clause into all contracts of employment even where such a clause is not expressly provided.

4.2 EXCEPTIONS

The Act provides for certain exceptions or defences to equality claims. It specifically excludes matters in respect of pay and occupational pension schemes. So far as occupational pension schemes are concerned, however, it may be arguable that certain conditions in respect of such schemes fall within the scope of this legislation; in particular, conditions of entry to pension schemes and retirement ages, although retirement age and pension age are not synonymous in Irish law.

The Act regulates discrimination, both direct and indirect, but only in respect of sex or marital status. It does not refer to family status and does not, therefore, necessarily cover such groups as unmarried mothers or other lone parents. In order to bring a claim under the legislation, such persons would have to show that they were discriminated against on grounds of sex or marital status. However, as discussed in §2.3.1.1 above, some of the cases on access to employment suggest that family status is on occasion a factor when discrimination is alleged.

4.2.1 EXCLUSIONS

4.2.1.1 Size

There are no exclusions related to the size of the particular employment or enterprise in which the claimant works, nor is the 'place' relevant (in contrast to the position under the 1974 Act).[1] The reason for this is that employees do not, under the 1977 Act, normally have to provide comparators in making their claim. However, in relation to certain conditions of

---

[1] See §3.6.1 above.

employment, a woman would have to show that she is being treated in a materially different fashion from a male employee or a prospective male employee.

4.2.1.2   Work done outside the jurisdiction

The Act provides for an exclusion in respect of the performance of duties outside the State where there are laws and customs allowing a person of only one sex to do the duties concerned.[1] Such an exception might arise in respect of women working in certain Islamic countries, but to date the Regulations do not appear to have been specifically invoked by any employer.

4.2.1.3   Health and safety

Under s. 14 of the 1977 Act an employer is not seen as unlawfully discriminating against an employee if she or he is specifically complying with the Conditions of Employment Acts 1936 to 1944, or the Safety in Industry Acts 1955 and 1980. The latter contain specific reference to the maximum weights which may be lifted: namely 16 kilos for an adult woman.[2]

In *Tayto Ltd* v. *O'Keeffe*,[3] the Equality Officer accepted the company's argument in relation to weight lifting maxima. However, the Equality Officer also commented that an employer must take reasonable steps to provide for the employment of persons of either sex without being in breach of any requirement of such safety legislation.

Certain other provisions which may be seen as having a discriminatory effect are still in force, including: (a) the prohibition on women working with lead as provided in the Factories Act 1955; (b) special seating arrangements for women as provided in the Shops (Conditions of Employment) Act 1938; and (c) the prohibition of the employment of women below ground at a mine and the employment of women at a mine as provided in the Mines and Quarries Act 1965. In 1985, the Mines and Quarries Act was amended by the Employment Equality Act 1977 (Employment of Females in Mines) Order 1985,[4] which provided for the employment of women in mines in certain capacities, e.g. non-manual management functions, health and welfare services, and necessary underground training as part of a training course.

---

1   Section 17(2)(d), as amended by the European Communities (Employment Equality) Regulations 1985, SI No 331 of 1985.
2   Regulation 2 of the Factories Act 1955 (Manual Labour)(Maximum Weights and Transport) Regulations 1972, SI No 283 of 1972.
3   EE 13/1985.
4   SI No 176 of 1985.

4.2.1.4 National security

The Act does not apply to employment in the Defence Forces.[1]

4.2.1.5 Religion, religious schools

There are no specific exclusions in the Act in respect of religion and religious schools. Although discrimination is not permitted in respect of vocational training,[2] this is generally interpreted as referring to people's access to such training, rather than the manner of its provision. In practice, many single-sex religious schools and education or training establishments exist in Ireland.

4.2.1.6 Retirement age

There is no specific provision in respect of retirement age. There are no upper age limits excluding access to the provisions of this Act.

4.2.2 SEX AS A DETERMINING FACTOR

In certain situations, particularly in the context of recruitment, the sex of the employee or the prospective employee may be a key factor. Sections 12 and 17 of the Act (as amended) provide for various arguments which an employer may raise to justify sex as a determining factor. However, these have not been raised in very many cases.

In *Galway Social Services Council* v. *EEA*,[3] the Council specifically advertized for a male employee in its hostel for homeless men. The Council argued that it did not have separate facilities, due to lack of space, for accommodation and sanitary facilities for women. The Equality Officer did not accept the Council's arguments and recommended that the Council should not make an appointment consequent upon the discriminatory advertisement.

In *Parents Alone Resource Centre* v. *Fozzard*,[4] the Equality Officer considered that the Centre discriminated against the claimant in the recruitment process by specifically stating that 'it would have doubts about the usefulness of having a male worker working with women parents'. The Centre was for one-parent families and for those parenting alone because of marital difficulties.

---

[1] Section 12(1)(a) as substituted by the European Communities (Employment Equality) Regulations 1985, SI No 331 of 1985.
[2] Section 6 of the 1977 Act applies to training over the age of 16 years.
[3] EE 13/1983.
[4] EE 2/1988.

Finally in *Beit (Alfred) Foundation* v. *Gahan*,[1] the Equality Officer considered that marital status was not an 'occupational qualification'. The Foundation had advertised for an administrator but at interview had stated that it wanted a married man.

4.2.2.1   Lists

Section 17 of the 1977 Act contains the comprehensive list of jobs for which sex may be a determining factor, or job attributes which may contribute to that.[2] These are: (a) physiology or authenticity; (b) duties involving personal services; (c) work in an establishment or institution confined to persons of one sex requiring special care, supervision or treatment; (d) privacy or decency; (e) sleeping or sanitary accommodation provided on a communal basis; and (f) the performance of duties outside the State in a place where they can only be performed by members of one sex.

4.2.2.2   Genuine occupational qualification

As stated above, s. 17 provides for certain circumstances where sex may be taken as a genuine occupational qualification for the position. Such areas of employment include modelling, acting, the provision of personal services, the prison service where there is direct supervision of prisoners in relation to dressing and undressing and the carrying out of personal searches, and the Garda Siochana (the police) where for example there is a requirement for an employee of a particular sex on grounds of decency, or to perform personal searches, or the interviewing of persons in relation to sexual offences.

4.2.2.3   Authenticity

Under s. 17(2)(a) sex may be an occupational qualification where 'authenticity for the purpose of a form of entertainment' is claimed. This would include some acting, modelling or singing roles (e.g. a female soprano, or a male model) where it would be necessary, for the purposes of authenticity, to have the work carried out by a person of a particular sex. The Act also allows for physiology to be an occupational qualification, where authenticity is required, but here it specifically excludes any requirements for strength or stamina.

4.2.2.4   Security

The European Communities (Employment Equality) Regulations 1985 amended s. 17 by providing for certain limited exclusions in respect of employment in the prison service and the Garda Siochána (police force). In the Garda Siochána the Act does not apply to a position the duties of which

---

1   EE 18/1983.
2   Amended by SI No 331 of 1985.

include 'disarming, controlling, arresting or escorting violent persons, quelling riots or violent disturbances, controlling or dispersing violent crowds or effecting the rescue of hostages or kidnap victims'. However, such exclusions are only permitted, in relation to the filling of a post, where the Garda Siochána do not already have sufficient persons to carry out these particular duties.[1] In the prison service, exclusions are permitted in respect of appointments where the duties of the post include 'guarding, escorting or controlling violent persons, or quelling riots or violent disturbances', although the same rule applies about the filling of such post as in relation to the Garda Siochána.

The Defence Forces are excluded from the Act under s. 12(1)(a). Fire fighters are included within the scope of the Act in the normal way.[2]

4.2.2.5   Religion

There is no specific reference to religion in the legislation. Individuals who are members of religious orders would not be deemed to be 'in the employment' of the order; accordingly, the Act would not apply. However, there would be various schools and hospitals run by religious orders, which are single sex, and in respect of employment the Act would be applicable to such employment.

4.2.2.6   Decency and privacy

Physical education teachers

There are no specific references to such positions in the legislation; therefore, it appears that sex is not a determining factor for such positions. There have been no cases in respect of any such posts.

Hospitals

Certain positions in hospitals, in particular nursing services, would appear to be covered by the wording of s. 17(2)(b), which refers to duties involving 'personal services' of a kind making it 'necessary to have persons of both sexes engaged in such duties'. There have been no specific cases on this point in relation to hospitals or homes for the sick. Nursing is, of course, a predominantly female profession.

---

[1]   Section 17A, inserted by SI.No 331 of 1985.
[2]   See *Dublin Corporation* v *Gibney* EE 5/1986

Midwives

The same provisions as those referred to in relation to hospitals apply. However, s. 11 of the 1977 Act was amended so that men could train as midwives.[1]

4.2.2.7 Single-sex establishments

In Ireland, by tradition, a considerable number of schools (mainly post primary) are single-sex establishments. However, there are no exclusions from the legislation which would allow school management, for example, to deny access to employment to male teachers in a girls' school. There are a number of single-sex establishments looking after the elderly, for example. Again, the same provisions as apply to single-sex schools would apply except where personal services are provided and the 'occupational qualification' principle could be said to apply.

4.3   TERRITORIAL SCOPE

The performance of duties abroad for an Irish employer may fall within s. 17(2)(f). This section qualifies the protection of the Act in circumstances where the post involves work in countries in which there are particular customs and practices which could preclude the employment of an employee of a particular sex. .

4.4   PERSONAL SCOPE

4.4.1   EMPLOYEES

The term 'employee' has a wide definition in s. 1 of the 1977 Act. It provides that an employee is:

> a person who has entered into or works under ... a contract of employment with an employer, whether the contract is (or was) for manual labour, clerical work or otherwise, is (or was) express or implied, oral or in writing, and whether it is (or was) a contract of service or apprenticeship or otherwise.

All employees fall within the scope of the Act; there are no restrictions in respect of length of service, hours of work, place of employment etc.[2]

---

1   SI No 331 of 1985.
2   See FRANCES MEENAN, 'Temporary and Part-time Employees', *Gazette of the Incorporated Law Society of Ireland*, July/August 1987, and MARY REDMOND, 'Beyond the Net - Protecting the Individual Worker' (1983) 2 JISLL 1.

4.4.2   INDEPENDENT CONTRACTORS

The position of independent contractors is unclear and there has been no litigation in this area. An independent contractor is a person who works under a contract for services as opposed to working under a contract of employment. The wording 'or otherwise' in the definition of employee (see §4.4.1 above) would suggest that persons working under contracts for services may possibly fall within the scope of the legislation. Section 3 also provides that where employers use independent contractors, then the employees of the independent contractors fall within the scope of the Act.

4.4.3   HOME WORKERS

Home workers fall within the scope of the Act, provided that they are employees within the terms of the definition discussed at §4.4.1 above. However, in the absence of any cases in Ireland on this point it is not clear how they would be seen. The position may depend on the particular circumstances of each group of home workers, and on the extent, for example, to which they are integrated into the employer's organization.[1]

4.4.4   PUBLIC SECTOR

The 1977 Act specifically includes public service employees, in that the definition of 'employee' includes:

> a civil servant of the State or of the Government, and an officer or servant of a local authority within the meaning of the Local Government Act 1941, an officer or servant of a harbour authority, health board, vocational education committee or committee of agriculture.

The only area in which certain public servants are treated differently is in the recruitment (including promotion) process.[2] This means that persons in senior grades of the civil service, local authorities, health boards, vocational education committees and other bodies may not refer disputes concerning the process of selection to an Equality Officer; they may not, therefore, appeal to the Labour Court against an Equality Officer's recommendation; they may not have cases investigated by the EEA (see §6.3 below); and do not have the same rights as other employees to information about the reason for the alleged discrimination. The Civil Service and Local Appointments Commissioners, who are responsible for such appointments, maintain that no difficulties have arisen from the above provision. However, there are very few women on their interview panels and the vast majority of senior civil service and public service positions continue to be held by men. The EEA

---

1   See F. VON PRONDZYNSKI, *op.cit.*, pp 37-40.
2   See s. 12(3) of the Act.

has recorded a number of complaints in connection with senior appointments but was precluded by the legislation from investigating them.

4.4.5   DOMESTIC EMPLOYEES

Section 17 of the Act provides for the exclusion of work which consists of the performance of services of a personal nature where the sex of the employee constitutes a determining factor. There have been no cases on this point but it is not considered that the exclusion would apply to cleaning, cooking and general domestic duties. It should be noted that s. 12(1)(d) formerly excluded 'employment in a private residence or by a close relative', but this has been repealed.

4.4.6   PERSONS WITHOUT A CONTRACT OF EMPLOYMENT

It has already been noted that the Act applies only to persons who are 'employees', and that in the ordinary course of events this will mean that it is restricted to those with contracts of employment. The only persons covered who do not have contracts of employment would be those who are included in the definition of 'employee', including those working under a contract of apprenticeship or in the public service.

It may also be useful to draw attention to the position of temporary workers supplied by employment agencies, whose status may be such that they do not have contracts of employment which are readily identifiable. Section 7 of the Act prohibits discrimination by employment agencies, and this may protect the workers concerned even though they cannot point to a contract of employment either with the organization where they work or with the agency.

4.4.7   OTHERS

Apart from the categories of persons mentioned above, no others are covered by the Act.

4.5   ACTIVITIES COVERED

Section 3 provides a wide range of contexts in respect of which discrimination may arise and is prohibited. These include access to employment, conditions of employment, training or experience for or in relation to employment, promotion or re-grading in employment or classification of posts in employment. Conditions of employment, provisions in relation to shift work, short-time, lay-off, redundancies, dismissal and disciplinary measures must not be discriminatory. Opportunities and facilities for training and promotion must not discriminate on grounds of sex or marital status.

4.6   COMPARATOR

The 1977 Act does not impose any specific requirement for claimants to compare themselves with named comparators of the opposite sex, and married claimants do not have to name unmarried comparators. While the Anti-Discrimination (Pay) Act 1974 demands an actual comparator, the 1977 Act merely provides that the claimant must show a *prima facie* case that there was discrimination on grounds of sex or marital status, i.e. that the treatment accorded them was materially different from that which was, or would have been, accorded to a member of the opposite sex or a person of a different marital status.[1]

4.7   HIRING

4.7.1   RECRUITMENT METHODS

There are various different forms of recruitment ranging from press advertisements to 'head hunting'. Section 3 of the 1977 Act provides that a prospective employer may not discriminate either directly or indirectly against a prospective employee in relation to access to employment, classification of posts in employment, arrangements for recruitment, or have entry requirements for employment which could discriminate against a prospective employee or a group of employees.

Some time ago, the EEA raised the issue of the permissibility, in job application forms and interviews, of questions on marital status, numbers of children and other family and personal matters. The EEA has taken the view that questions regarding marital status, ages and number of children and childcare arrangements were valid only when the person has already received the job offer, because such questions may be relevant for personnel records or pension entitlements.[2] The EEA has also argued that since the 1977 Act outlaws discrimination on the basis of sex or marital status in relation to access to employment, not only is there no need or right to ask for this information, but also no other means of obtaining such information should be used. If prospective employers insisted on obtaining the information prior to making a decision to recruit, then, in the event of a subsequent claim of discrimination, such employers should have to show that the information had not been used when making the decision to recruit.

---

1   See e.g. *The Medical Council* v. *Barrington* EE 9/1988 and *Revenue Commissioners* v. *Irish Tax Officials' Union* EE 6/1986; DEE 2/1987.
2   See RTE radio interview, January 1989, with the Chief Executive of the EEA.

4.7.2   ADVERTISEMENTS

Section 8 of the 1977 Act prohibits discriminatory advertising, and this is defined as including newspaper, radio and television advertising.[1] Furthermore, the advertisement may not define or describe a position on the basis of gender; also, if the previous holders of a position were of one sex, it must be made clear that the position is open to both sexes.[2]

The impact of this section is broad and affects not only the prospective employer placing the advertisement, but also the publisher (e.g. newspapers) and, if applicable, any advertising agency involved. In general, the recruitment pages in the daily newspapers tend to state that the positions advertized are open to both male and female candidates, married and single. A person who contravenes s. 8 of the Act is guilty of an offence and liable on summary conviction to a fine of up to £200. Advertisements imposing age limits (e.g. stating that the candidate must be under 35 years) are, however, still common and may constitute indirect discrimination against the prospective employee.[3]

In one case the EEA referred the employer's advertisement for male staff only, for its hostel for destitute men, to an Equality Officer.[4] The advertisement was held to be discriminatory. Similarly, an advertisement which read 'lady required for canteen work' was considered discriminatory.[5] More recently, an advertisement looking for both full and part-time store detectives was considered discriminatory as there was a statement in the advertisement which read 'this may be of particular interest to married women'.[6]

4.7.3   JOB TITLE

Section 8(2) of the Act provides that if there is a job description or job title which implies that the applicant should be of a particular sex, or which implies that in the past the job was mainly carried out by a person of one sex (e.g. 'foreman'), the advertisement must contain an indication that the position is open to members of both sexes.

There have been a number of cases concerning job titles in advertisements including, for example, an advertisement for a 'Head Waiter/Manager'. The EEA referred this advertisement in the *Sunday Independent* (newspaper) to the Labour Court which in turn referred the

---

1   Section 1 of the Act.
2   Section 8(2) of the Act.
3   See §2.3.1.1 above.
4   *Galway Social Services Council* EE 13/1983.
5   *Power Supermarkets* v. *Bradley* EE 1/1981.
6   *EEA* v. *Independent Newspapers (Ireland) Ltd* EE 19/1991; DEE 1/1993.

matter to an Equality Officer. The EEA considered that the job title in the advertisement denoted a particular sex and that the advertisement therefore indicated an intention, or might reasonably be understood as indicating an intention, to discriminate contrary to s. 8 (1)and (2) of the Act. The Equality Officer agreed that the job title denoted a reference to a particular sex and that the prospective employer and the newspaper were therefore in breach of s. 8.[1] The remedy in this case included the newspaper placing a banner across the advertisement pages emphasising equality of opportunity; this was understood to be a permanent banner. On appeal, the Labour Court considered this to be unreasonable and the newspaper therefore only had to carry the banner twice. Furthermore, a notice totalling 24 column inches had to be placed, with the following suggested wording:

> In accordance with the Employment Equality Act 1977, the *Sunday Independent* is committed to ensuring that recruitment advertisements do not give the impression of a preference to candidates of one sex or marital status rather than the other.

Other cases where both the prospective employer and a newspaper were found to be in breach of the Act included advertisements for 'a female supervisor in a health and fitness clinic',[2] and for 'floor/counter waitresses'.[3]

4.7.4   JOB DESCRIPTION

Generally, it is the job title which is discriminatory rather than the job description. However, in one particular case an employer stated that a married man was required for the position. This was held to be discriminatory.[4]

4.7.5   SELECTION ARRANGEMENTS

There has been a large number of cases relating to access to employment and selection arrangements. The first key case was *University College Dublin* v. *Chaney*,[5] where the claimant alleged that the College had refused her access to employment because she was married and had children. She maintained that the College had asked at interview how many children she had and what childcare arrangements she proposed to use. Apparently these questions were not asked of male candidates. The Equality Officer considered that the questions were reasonable only if asked of both male and female candidates. It was reasonable to require prospective employees to be in a position to take up employment; but if employers assumed such availability, in the case of men, without enquiring about their domestic

---

1   *Sunday Independent* v. *EEA* EE 17/1991; DEE 3/1993.
2   *Cork Examiner Publications* v. *EEA* EE 13/1991.
3   *Cork Examiner Publications Ltd* v. *EEA* EE 10/1991.
4   *Alfred Beit Foundation* v. *Gahan* EE 18/1983.
5   EE 15/1983.

arrangements, they should assume likewise in the case of women. Therefore the different treatment accorded to Ms Chaney had constituted discrimination.

Interestingly, there can be some situations where a prospective employer can ask questions about marital status. In *Coombe Lying-in Hospital* v. *Tuite*,[1] a prospective trainee midwife who was a qualified nurse was asked whether she was married and how long she had been married. She had applied for the position in her married name yet all her official certificates and registration with An Bord Altranais (the Nursing Board) were in her maiden name. The claimant maintained that she had been asked discriminatory questions at interview; she alleged that, in addition to the questions about her date of marriage, she was also asked such questions as how her husband felt about her studying again, whether she had any children and whether she would be able to study and be a housewife at the same time. The Equality Officer considered that an unfair onus had been placed upon her; she had been treated less favourably than unmarried female candidates, who had had no such onus placed upon them.

The issue of application forms and alleged discrimination at interview was highlighted in the case of *Medical Council* v. *Barrington*.[2] The claimant had applied for the position of assistant administrative officer. She maintained that when the interviewer discovered certain details on her application form, including her marital status, she was asked if she was thinking of getting married. She said that she replied 'no', that the interviewer allegedly stated 'so you are not thinking of getting married?' and then remarked that '1988 was a leap year and that she could ask someone'. The claimant also maintained that the interviewer had informed her that a woman whom he had previously hired married shortly after taking up the post and subsequently left. The claimant maintained that these remarks had been objectionable, distasteful and embarrassing, but that she had tried to continue with a normal interview. The Medical Council denied that such questions had been asked or statements made; it had simply considered that she did not have the relevant experience for the job. The Equality Officer considered, however, that her non-appointment had been discriminatory.

Where a disproportionate amount of time is spent at an interview on questions relating to marital status, children and family commitments, this may suggest discrimination.[3] It may appear reasonable for employers to request such details as marital status and ages of children on application forms and at interview should they so wish; however, where this is the case, such information should be requested of all candidates and the intention must be clearly related to establishing facts for purposes unrelated to

---

1   EE 17/1985.
2   EE 9/1988.
3   *Southern Health Board* v. *O'Connor* EE 8/1984; DEE 4/1984.

discrimination. Where the information has been requested and the prospective employee is either not called to interview, or is unsuccessful in obtaining the job, there must be a valid, non-discriminatory reason for the employer's decision.

If prospective employees cannot take up a job offer, they may still be successful in their claim if they have been asked discriminatory questions. In *A Company* v. *A Prospective Female Employee*,[1] a female candidate for the position of customer sales agent with an airline was awarded £500 for 'distress' even though she would not have been in a position to take up the position as the job was located abroad.

The Act contains an exclusion in respect of certain public service appointments. Persons applying for certain higher grade posts in the public service have no recourse to the Equality Officers or the Labour Court, and no right to information about the reasons for any alleged discrimination in relation to the selection process.[2] Section 39(4) also prohibits the EEA from conducting investigations into such public service appointments.

4.7.6   TERMS ON WHICH A JOB IS OFFERED

It can be extremely difficult to prove that a job offer is discriminatory and there have been very few cases on this specific point.

4.8   WORKING CONDITIONS

In Ireland, the term 'working conditions' generally refers to the conditions in which people work (e.g. their office accommodation or industrial environment); however, if one considers also conditions of employment, then the 1977 Act provides that there must be no discrimination regarding such matters as overtime and access to overtime and rostering arrangements,[3] internal transfers,[4] work breaks,[5] adoptive leave,[6] allocation of duties so that an employee may gain experience,[7] disciplinary measures,[8] and dress.[9]

---

1   EE 12/1989.
2   See §4.4.4.
3   *Cork Corporation* v. *Four Pool Attendants* EE 17/1984; DEE 1/1985; 2 May 1987, unreported (HC).
4   *National Institute for Higher Education* v. *Bolton* EE 7/1984; EE 12/1989.
5   *University College Dublin* v. *Zeuli* EE 4/1987.
6   *Aer Rianta* v. *37 Male Employees* EE 11/1987; [1990] ILRM 193 (HC); DEE 3/1990.
7   *St. Brigid's Boys NS Foxrock, Co. Dublin* v. *McGuinness* EE 3/1979.
8   *Rank Xerox (Ireland) Ltd* v. *Molloy* EE 3/1983.
9   *Norwich Union Insurance Co. Ltd* v. *131 Female Clerical Staff* EE 19/1981; *Educational Building Society* v. *Male Employees* EP 9/1987; *BHS (Dublin) Ltd* v *127 Catering Assistants* EP 1/1988; DEP 5/1988.

4.8.1   RELATION TO PAY

Remuneration (including any benefits payable under an occupational pension scheme) is specifically excluded from the scope of the 1977 Act. However, certain discriminatory conditions of employment may affect an employee's pay. In *North Western Health Board* v. *Brady*,[1] the claimant argued that the Board's refusal to pay salary in respect of sick leave, where an entitlement to unpaid maternity leave existed, was indirectly discriminatory. In another case, there was a staff loan scheme and it was recommended that the terms of the scheme be amended to give the same benefits to both male and female staff.[2]

4.8.2   EDUCATION AND TRAINING

Section 6 provides that no vocational education body shall discriminate in respect of courses offered (including the terms on which courses are offered, access to the courses and the manner in which they are offered) against persons over the statutory school leaving age, i.e. 16 years.

The case of *Trinity College Dublin* v. *McGhee* [3] concerned an alleged discriminatory interview experienced by the claimant during her audition for a place on the College's course leading to a Diploma in Theatre Studies. She was denied access to the course and the Equality Officer considered that there had been discriminatory questions in relation to her marital status. Another case concerned the School of Physiotherapy in University College Dublin, which used to admit female students only. In *University College Dublin* v. *Corrigan* [4] the male claimant was denied access to such training; the Labour Court determined that the claimant should be accepted for the course in the next academic year.

Generally, there is little discrimination in relation to access to education and training; training courses which once catered only for members of one sex now cater for both.

4.8.3   ACCESS TO BENEFITS, FACILITIES, SERVICES, PROMOTION

The question of access to benefits, facilities and services is usually considered under the 1974 Act, rather than the 1977 Act. However, the equal access to financial and credit institutions was considered in the Equal Status Bill 1991 which was subsequently withdrawn. Many private sports clubs, e.g. golf and tennis clubs, only accept male members, and a few public

---

1   EE 9/1985; DEE 9/1985.
2   *Central Bank of Ireland* v. *ASTMS* EE 4/1980; DEE 7/1980.
3   EE 1/1989.
4   EE 13/1979; DEE 6/1980.

houses still have men-only bars. This difficult issue under Irish law has also been considered by the Commission on the Status of Women.[1]

The question of access to promotion, however, has given rise to a considerable number of cases where discrimination has been alleged. In *Model School, Limerick* v. *Culloo*,[2] Ms Culloo, the claimant, was denied the position of principal following the amalgamation of the boys' school and the girls' school. The interview board was unable to provide objective reasons for her non-appointment. Subsequently, a board member said to the claimant: 'It seems an injustice has been done but we've never thought of women for these positions before'.

Seniority-based promotions have also caused difficulties for women where they had previously been obliged to resign on marriage. If they were then re-employed, previous service was excluded for promotion and other purposes.[3] One of the more interesting cases in this regard was the claim against the Revenue Commissioners where, following recruitment for tax officers, a low proportion of the successful applicants was female. The Labour Court commented that, all other things being equal, there should have been proportionately more women appointed to the panel of successful applicants.[4]

4.9   EXCLUSION, DISMISSAL OR OTHER DETRIMENT

There have been relatively few cases of employees claiming retaliatory or discriminatory dismissal, constructive or otherwise. In the early years of the equality legislation a number of these cases arose concerning persons in the catering industry who had less than one year's service and thus could not bring a claim under the Unfair Dismissals Act 1977.[5] Generally, however, employees will bring their claims under that legislation as they may well also have been dismissed for substantial reasons other than sex or marital status. An employee is not entitled to receive redress for dismissal under both these Acts, but only under one or the other.[6]

A significant case was *Irish TV Rentals* v. *Brady*,[7] in which the claimant, who had previously been made redundant, was dismissed from temporary employment as the company had a preference for a male employee. She was awarded £4,000, which to date has been the highest award in any such dismissal case. The case of *University College Dublin* v.

---

1   Second Commission on the Status of Women, *Report to Government*, January 1993.
2   EE 8/1987; (1989) 8 JISLL 119 (HC).
3   *Aer Lingus Teo.* v. *Labour Court* [1990] ELR 113.
4   *Revenue Commissioners* v. *Irish Tax Officials' Union* EE 6/1986; DEE 2/1987.
5   See e.g. *Hunting Lodges Ltd* v. *A Worker* DEE 3/1980.
6   See s. 15 of the Unfair Dismissals Act 1977.
7   EE 5/1985; DEE 8/1985.

Chaney[1] concerned an alleged retaliatory dismissal. Ms Chaney, who had been employed on a temporary basis, had advised her employer that she thought that she had been discriminated against in respect of her job application for a full-time position. She alleged that after advising the employer of her view that discrimination had occurred, she was advised that there was no further work for her. She was successful in her dismissal claim and was awarded £750 and reinstatement to the list of temporary employees.

4.10 INSTRUCTIONS TO DISCRIMINATE

Section 9 of the Act provides that 'a person shall not procure or attempt to procure another person to do in relation to employment anything which constitutes discrimination'. In no case has it been established that persons deliberately set out to procure, or attempted to procure, discrimination. Such procurement was alleged in the *Packard* case,[2] but the allegation was not upheld. In an earlier equal pay case, in which it appeared that procurement had occurred, the threat of industrial action was cited as 'objective justification' for the procurement. The Labour Court referred specifically to s. 9 of the 1977 Act and said that the circumstances of this case should not recur.[3]

More recently, the Minister for Finance, in the capacity of being in a supervisory role over the public service, was considered to have been in breach of s. 9 as a result of certain rules concerning the re-employment of married women subsequent to their resignation arising from the now abolished marriage bar.[4]

4.11 PRESSURE TO DISCRIMINATE

There have been no cases concerning alleged pressure to discriminate, other than those cited in §4.10 above. Where procurement of discrimination was an issue, it was not clear whether this took the form of issuing definite 'instructions', or merely exerting 'pressure' of an unspecified nature.

4.12 DISCRIMINATION BY AN EMPLOYEE OR A TRADE UNION

In the vast majority of cases, what has been in issue was the employer's decision to discriminate, whether deliberately or inadvertently. However, the question of discrimination by employees and/or trade unions has, on occasion, arisen where there were collective agreements to which both the employers and the trade unions (on behalf of their members) were parties

---

1   EE 15/1983.
2   EE 14/1985.
3   *Brooks Thomas Ltd* v. *ASTMS* EP 6/1977.
4   *Minister for Finance* v. *EEA* EE 21/1991; DEE 5/1993.

and where such agreements contained a discriminatory practice (usually indirectly discriminatory).[1] Examples of such practices have been selection of part-time employees first in a redundancy situation,[2] and internal union rules concerning the granting of union cards.[3] Usually, in such cases, the discriminatory practice involves a degree of collusion between employers and employees/unions. The exception was the *Brooks Thomas* case cited above,[4] where the main pressure to discriminate appeared to have come from the employees.

4.13 DISCRIMINATORY PRACTICES

See §§4.10, 4.11 and 4.12 above.

4.14 SPECIAL TREATMENT

4.14.1 PROTECTIVE LEGISLATION

4.14.1.1 Pregnancy and maternity

Pregnancy

Section 6(2)(f) of the Unfair Dismissals Act 1977, as amended in 1991,[5] provides that a dismissal which results wholly or partly from 'the pregnancy of the employee or matters connected therewith' is unfair. There is a qualification to this, namely that if the employee is unable to do the work for which she is employed and if there is no suitable alternative employment, then the protection of the Act does not apply. Since 1991, regular part-time employees who work at least eight hours a week have also been within the scope of this Act. There is no service requirement for a full-time employee if she maintains that she was dismissed by reason of pregnancy; however, if she is a regular part-time employee she must have at least 13 weeks' continuous service.

Maternity

The Maternity Protection of Employees Act 1981, as also amended in 1991,[6] provides for paid maternity leave of 14 weeks; if there is a late birth, this may be extended by a further four weeks. The leave may be extended by a further four weeks on an unpaid basis. There is also provision for unpaid time-off for ante- and post-natal care. Entitlement to payment during the 14

---

1   *Packard Electric Ireland Ltd* v. *EEA* EE 14/1985.
2   *Michael O'Neill & Sons Ltd* v. *Two Female Employees* DEE 1/1988.
3   *Bailey Gibson* v. *Nathan* EE 2/1990.
4   *Brooks Thomas Ltd* v. *ASTMS* EP 6/1977; see §4.10 above.
5   Worker Protection (Regular Part-time Employees) Act 1991.
6   Worker Protection (Regular Part-time Employees) Act 1991.

weeks of paid leave is based on the requisite social welfare contributions having been made at the full ('class A') rate. All employees earning at least £25 per week have fallen within the scope of the maternity legislation since 17 June 1991,[1] and all such employees have been liable for 'Class A' social insurance contributions since April 1991. Thus all regular part-time employees who earn at least £25 per week and have completed 13 weeks' continuous service are entitled to the benefits of the maternity and social welfare legislation in this regard.

The Maternity Act has, however, given rise to certain technical difficulties for both employers and employees. Major problems have been caused by the very complicated notification procedures surrounding employees' entitlement to take leave and, in particular, the mandatory written notification requirement concerning the right to return to work. In a number of cases the employee has lost her right to return to work for not fully or punctually complying with this provision. There has been considerable legal debate on the effect of non-notification by the employee, particularly as to whether the contract of employment terminates by operation of law or whether it is a dismissal by the employer when the employee is not allowed to return to work. The High Court held in *Ivory* v. *Skyline Ltd*[2] that, if an employee fails to give the four-week written notification of her return to work, then that is a fair reason for her dismissal by the employer.

Interestingly, there is no evidence of claimants bringing cases under the equality legislation when they have failed under the dismissals/maternity legislation.

There is no legal obligation on the employer to advise the employee of her rights under the Maternity Act or indeed to advise her of the strict notification requirements. In a number of cases where employees have not complied with the various notification requirements, employers have waived their rights and have allowed employees contractual leave.

4.14.1.2　Parental leave and similar measures

There is no statutory provision for paternity leave; however, many large employers provide fathers with a few days paid leave on the birth of a child. Furthermore, there is no statutory provision for adoptive leave, although the Minister for Finance indicated in his January 1992 Budget speech that the Government was considering the introduction of a 10-week period of statutory leave later in the year. Many employers provide leave for adoptive mothers on the same terms as maternity leave; however, in such cases, there is of course no State benefit. Therefore, unless the employer pays the

---

1 　Social Welfare (Employment of Inconsiderable Extent) Regulations 1991, SI 28 of 1991.
2 　[1988] IR 399.

person's normal salary, or part thereof, the leave is unpaid. Adoptive leave for male employees was considered in one case,[1] in which the male claimants considered that the denial of such leave to male employees was discriminatory. However, the Labour Court considered that it was not discriminatory.

4.14.1.3 Difficult or unpleasant working conditions

There is legislative provision for female employees working in shops, mines and quarries, and also working with lead.[2]

4.14.1.4 Health and safety

Health

When the Department of Enterprise and Employment grants shift work licences in respect of night-work, there is a recommendation attached to the licence that pregnant employees be given the option of transferring from night-work if it is considered medically advisable. No information is available, however, about the extent to which this recommendation is acted upon.

Safety

There is no safety legislation specifically affecting women, other than that which relates to the lifting of weights, the employment of pregnant women at night, and women working with lead.

4.14.2   POSITIVE ACTION

Positive action is not defined in either the 1974 or the 1977 Act. Positive action may be explained in the context that the legislation:

> will not ... adequately eliminate all forms of discrimination as between men and women in the labour market unless parallel measures are taken to counteract or compensate for the impact of existing employment structures on individual behaviour or to redress the effects of previous unequal opportunities.[3]

A number of employers have introduced positive action programmes including RTE (the state broadcasting authority), the Bank of Ireland and the Electricity Supply Board.

Section 15 of the 1977 Act allows an employer, where there have been few or no persons of one sex in a particular type of work for the previous

---

1   *Aer Rianta* v. *37 Male Employees* EE 11/1987; [1990] ILRM 193 (HC); DEE 3/1990.
2   See §4.2.1.3 above.
3   EEA, *Code of Practice on Equality of Opportunity*, 1984, para. 15.1.

12 months, to provide specific training for the minority sex to take advantage of opportunities for doing such work. This is a fairly limited form of statutory positive action, but even so, its use has not been widespread.

In general, the EEA has recommended that employers should design equal opportunities programmes which would identify the organization's requirements, develop employees' career aspirations and equip workers with the necessary skills for advancement within the organization.[1]

There are no statutory provisions for reverse discrimination other than as provided for in s. 15 of the 1977 Act.

4.14.2.1   Areas

Training bodies

Generally, training bodies provide very little in the form of training or positive action programmes. The Irish Management Institute has courses on women in management; University College Dublin has a post-graduate degree programme on Equality Studies; while a number of other colleges and universities hold courses on women's studies which include material on employment equality and positive action at work.

Employers

Generally, it is only the large State-owned and private companies that have positive action programmes, examples being Aer Lingus, the Electricity Supply Board, and the Bank of Ireland. The Irish Business and Employers Confederation (IBEC) has produced a booklet entitled *Guidelines on Equal Opportunities*, which includes references to positive action and was published in December 1990. The IBEC also provides training programmes for employers on equality issues.

Trade unions

The Irish Congress of Trade Unions highlights the importance of equality in the workplace. It employs an Equality Officer and holds annual women's conferences and seminars, as do many of its affiliated unions. Most of the larger unions, such as SIPTU (Services, Industrial, Professional Trade Union, which is the largest union in the country) are active in highlighting equality issues; as are the public service unions and IDATU (the Irish Distributive and Allied Trades Union). In general, these unions are very active in bringing cases on behalf of their members and providing training programmes for them. The vast majority of cases brought under the 1974 Act

---

1   See EEA Code of Practice, paras 15.3 to 15.6; see also EEA, *A Model Equal Opportunities Policy*, 1991.

and a substantial proportion of the 1977 Act cases have been brought by trade unions, rather than by individuals.

4.14.2.2 Means

Measures to correct imbalance

Employers are increasingly conscious of equality requirements but, as stated above, it is only the larger employers who are actively considering and positively redressing any imbalances. More recently there have been requests for childminding facilities from unions and the EEA generally; and a few employers have begun to respond by providing workplace crèches.

Code of Practice

The EEA published its *Code of Practice on Equality of Opportunity in Employment* in 1984. This is a very good explanatory document on the legislation. However, it does not have direct legal force. It contains many recommendations on equality matters which have been used as guidelines by the adjudicating bodies; but such bodies do not specifically refer to the Code, and the Code is not admitted in evidence. It generally has persuasive effect.

Training

See §4.14.2.1 above.

4.14.2.3 Constitutional or legal problems

Positive action may give rise to constitutional difficulties in relation to art. 40 of the Constitution which provides that all citizens are to be held equal before the law, although the State is to have due regard to 'differences of capacity, physical and moral, and of social function'. Furthermore, art. 45 provides (*inter alia*) that all men and women have a right to an adequate means of livelihood. Positive action and its possible legal difficulties have not been raised in the Irish courts.

5. SOCIAL SECURITY/SOCIAL WELFARE

5.1 DEFINITION OF SOCIAL SECURITY

The term 'social security' is rarely used in Ireland. Normally, the term 'social welfare' is used to cover the statutory social security system; while 'occupational social security schemes' (rarely referred to as such) are called by their particular name, e.g. occupational pension schemes, income continuance schemes or sick pay schemes.

5.1.1 STATUTORY SOCIAL SECURITY

Statutory social security, or the social welfare system, encompasses four main areas: social insurance, social assistance, occupational injuries benefits, and various other schemes. Generally, social insurance payments are known as 'benefits' and become payable to people who have made Pay-Related Social Insurance (PRSI) contributions and meet various qualifying conditions. They are financed by contributions from employers, employees and the self-employed, plus an Exchequer (State) subvention. The various occupational injuries benefits are financed wholly by employers. Social assistance payments, on the other hand, may be payable when people have suffered a particular contingency but do not qualify for insurance benefits, as long as they can fulfil a means test. These assistance schemes are financed entirely by the Exchequer, as are the various other miscellaneous schemes.

Examples of social insurance payments are: unemployment benefit, disability benefit (which covers short-term illnesses), invalidity pension (which is the long-term payment for illness or incapacity), maternity benefit, retirement pensions and contributory old-age pensions.

The means-tested, social assistance payments (sometimes called 'non-contributory payments' but usually just 'assistance') include unemployment assistance (the 'dole'), disabled person's maintenance allowance (for the long-term ill or disabled), non-contributory widow's pensions, non-contributory old-age pensions and supplementary welfare allowance.

The various occupational injuries benefits are payable where an illness, injury, disease or death is directly related to the person's occupation. There are no contribution conditions and no means testing for these benefits.

The only universal payment, requiring neither PRSI contributions nor means-testing, is child benefit, which is payable, normally to the mother, in respect of all children under 16 (and some under 18). There are also a number of benefits-in-kind, like fuel and electricity allowances, free television licences and free travel, granted to people who are receiving some cash benefit, like a pension. Finally, in the 'miscellaneous' category, there is a family income supplement, which is payable to low-paid workers whose incomes are below specified levels. The amounts vary according to the number of children in the family.

The scope of the statutory social security system is broad and has been widened in recent years. The majority of public and private sector employees, as well as all self-employed people, must be covered for PRSI once they are over 16 years of age and earn in excess of specified amounts. There are very few exceptions for men, but a few important ones for women (see §5.4 below). Also, many different contribution rates apply, the main distinctions being between private sector employees (usually class 'A'), civil servants (class 'B'), other public servants (classes 'C' and 'D'), self-employed people (class 'S') and various other categories (classes 'E' to 'N').

Until 1991, the majority of part-time workers were insured at a reduced rate. This meant that they qualified for fewer benefits than their full-time counterparts, although, in contrast with most other workers who paid a reduced rate of PRSI (e.g. civil and public servants), the State schemes for which this rendered them ineligible were not mirrored by similar occupational schemes. This was largely remedied by 1991 Regulations (for details see § 5.6 below) which, it was estimated, would bring 90 per cent of part-time workers fully into the scope of the system.

The question of changing the type of social insurance cover provided for public servants has been a subject of much discussion in recent years. Many argue that, in principle, it would be desirable for them to pay social insurance at the 'full', rather than the 'modified' rate; but most agree that in practice this would present many administrative and other difficulties.

5.1.2   OCCUPATIONAL SOCIAL SECURITY

As noted above, this term is not in common usage in Ireland: people regard 'social security' as being synonymous with 'social welfare' (i.e. the statutory system), rather than something connected with employment. Thus the various types of occupational social security schemes are normally known by their individual names, rather than any collective term, although occasionally they may be referred to as 'occupational schemes'.

The most widespread 'occupational schemes' in Ireland, providing social benefits to employees, are pension (or superannuation) schemes, income continuance or permanent health insurance (PHI) schemes, and sick pay schemes. Some employers also arrange free or subsidized health insurance and/or medical benefits (including access to company doctors, cancer-screening, eye-testing etc.).

For private sector employees, these 'occupational schemes' are privately funded, i.e. by employers and/or employees (although in most cases an element of indirect State funding is present by way of tax relief on contributions). However, in the public sector, the State, as employer, is also directly involved in funding the schemes. There is often confusion, therefore, about such terms as 'State pensions', which for private sector employees denote statutory, social welfare pensions, based on PRSI contributions; and for many public sector workers denotes their occupational pensions.

5.1.3   SOCIAL ASSISTANCE

The social assistance schemes are financed entirely by the Exchequer (in contrast with the social insurance schemes, described in §5.1.1 above, which are financed by contributions from employers, employees and the self-employed, plus an Exchequer subvention). To qualify, claimants must satisfy a means test and must also be able to show that a particular contingency (such as old age, desertion or unemployment) has occurred.

The means tests which must be satisfied by people claiming social assistance are seen as fairly stringent and perhaps discriminatory. With minor exceptions, they take into account all household income (not just that of the claimant), including most of a partner's earnings (after deducting a small amount which is deemed to be 'personal' to the partner concerned). They also take into account the yearly value of certain property and, in some cases, the value of free board or lodgings. Details of the assessment of means for the purposes of social assistance schemes are set out in the Social Welfare (Consolidation) Act 1981 and related Regulations. Limited amounts of earnings are disregarded and, confusingly, these 'disregards' vary from scheme to scheme (e.g. in the case of pensioners, it was £6 a week in 1992, plus £2 a week per dependent child, while for widows and lone parents the 'disregard' was £6 a week per dependent child). The capital sums which are disregarded also vary from scheme to scheme, as does the formula used for converting the excess, the amount not disregarded, into weekly 'means'. In 1992, work was in hand in the Department of Social Welfare to devise a standardized means test, which would apply to all schemes, but by Spring 1993 no changes had been made.

5.2   SOCIAL SECURITY DIRECTIVES AND OTHER LEGISLATION

The Irish social welfare system developed at a time when the vast majority of married women worked exclusively in the home. Even at the start of the 1980s, over 90 per cent did so. The assumption that all wives were financially dependent on their husbands, and that all children were financially dependent on their fathers, held true in most cases. Thus dependants' allowances were payable, almost exclusively to men, on the basis of sex rather than any criteria of actual financial dependency. For similar reasons, several insurance benefits were paid at higher rates, and for longer periods, to men and single women than to married women.

As the position of women in the workforce changed, and especially after the 'marriage bar' in the public service was lifted, the assumption of women's automatic dependency became increasingly unrealistic and pressure for equality of treatment began to grow, both from within the State and from without.

During the 1970s and 1980s a number of directly discriminatory provisions were removed from the Irish social welfare code. However, neither art. 119 of the EEC Treaty, nor the first two equality Directives (on equal pay and equal treatment), had any major impact on the social security system. A few minor changes were made prior to the implementation of Directive 79/7/EEC, but the major changes followed implementation of the Directive; and a number of difficulties still remain, especially in relation to provisions which may be seen as indirectly discriminatory.

Directive 79/7/EEC (the only one with direct relevance to social security in Ireland) was to have been operative in national legislation by 23 December 1984. However, the Social Welfare (No 2) Act 1985 was not enacted until July 1985 and even then did not come into effect immediately. Some of the changes (equalising unemployment benefits for men and women) came into effect in May 1986; others (concerning dependants' allowances) were not implemented until November 1986. Both the late implementation, and the nature of the November 1986 changes, gave rise to major difficulties and considerable litigation.[1]

Thus at the time of writing, the position is that a number of provisions remained which could be seen as directly or indirectly discriminatory, and a number of concepts are still viewed as being exceptionally problematic in the context of equal treatment.

5.2.1 ARTICLE 119 OF THE EEC TREATY

This has had no direct impact in the social security area.

5.2.2 DIRECTIVE 75/117/EEC

Neither Directive 75/117/EEC, nor the equal pay legislation which implemented it, has had any direct impact in the social security area.

---

[1] See §§1.2.2.1 (direct effect of EC law) and 1.2.2.2 (retrospective implementation) above; and §5.3.6 (dependants' allowances) below.

5.2.3   DIRECTIVE 76/207/EEC

Neither Directive 76/207/EEC, nor the equal treatment legislation which implemented it, has had any direct impact in the social security area.

5.2.4   DIRECTIVE 79/7/EEC

This Directive was implemented some 17 months after the mandatory date of 23 December 1984. The Social Welfare (No 2) Act 1985 was enacted in July 1985 but did not become effective until the following year. Some of its provisions came into effect in May 1986; the rest in November 1986.

5.2.5   DIRECTIVE 86/613/EEC

The implementation dates for this Directive were 30 June 1989 (for equal treatment and maternity protection for self-employed persons and their spouses) and 30 June 1991 (for any amending legislation required on matrimonial rights and obligations). The latter has been seen as unnecessary in Ireland, since the conditions for the formation of a company between spouses are not more restrictive than the conditions applying to unmarried persons. However, the absence of implementing legislation in respect of the former is more questionable. Self-employed persons and their spouses only have limited access to the Irish social security system, being included (since 1988) for contributory old-age pensions and widow's and children's pensions, but not for invalidity pensions or for maternity benefit or other short-term benefits.

5.3   PROBLEMATIC CONCEPTS

Before dealing with the 'problematic concepts' which exist in Ireland, in common with other EC countries, it must be said that a number of other provisions remain, in the social welfare code, which are seen as either directly or indirectly discriminatory. These are dealt with first.

In the area of direct discrimination, certain difficulties persist in relation to unemployment benefit and death benefits.

Unemployment benefit

One of the most serious and major discriminations against (married) women, the payment of unemployment benefit (UB) at a lower rate and for a shorter duration than for other recipients, was remedied in 1986. Nevertheless, two difficulties remain in this area. One is the problem of retrospection;[1] the other is the issue of 'discriminatory questioning'.

---

[1]   See §1.2.2.2 (retrospective implementation) above.

A major and long-standing grievance of women claiming UB has been the practice of social welfare officials asking married women questions about childcare and domestic arrangements when ascertaining their 'availability for work' (one of the criteria for eligibility for UB). Prior to the implementation of Directive 79/7/EEC, UB, despite being an insurance-based payment, was frequently denied to married women with children, on the grounds that they had failed to provide 'satisfactory' replies to such questions as 'who would mind the children?' and 'who would cook the dinner?' if the claimant went out to work.

Since implementation of the Directive, the Department of Social Welfare has maintained that all its staff have been instructed to direct such questions equally to married men and married women. The argument that such questions should be discontinued in all cases was rejected by the Departments, on the grounds that its officials should be free to ask whatever questions might be required in order to ascertain peoples' real 'availability for work'.

Nevertheless, major reservations in this area remain, since (a) it is not clear whether, in practice, all officials have ceased to ask such questions more frequently of female than of male parents; and (b) it can be argued that even where questions of this kind are asked equally of both sexes, the perceived impact, significance and consequences of the replies may differ substantially as between men and women. The difficulty of proof in such cases has been a major obstacle to resolving this problem: one case in which legal proceedings were initiated was withdrawn when the particular grievance was remedied on an individual basis. No further cases have yet reached the courts, although instances of 'discriminatory questioning' continue, on occasions, to be reported.

Death benefits

Another area in which direct discrimination persists is that of the death benefits which are payable under the occupational injuries scheme.[1] These involve different eligibility conditions for widows and widowers. Also, widows are disqualified if cohabitation occurs, while widowers are not. Although most survivors' benefits are excluded from the scope of Directive 79/7/EEC, the EC Commission has expressed the view[2] that deaths arising from occupational injuries are covered by the Directive.

Indirect discrimination also persists in a number of areas. There are several schemes in which the rules operate in such a way as to preclude more women than men, or more married than single people, from receiving the benefit in question. Also, the treatment of part-time workers continues to

---

1   Social Welfare (Consolidation) Act 1981, Part II, Ch. 5, ss 50 and 51.
2   *Interim Report on the Application of Directive 79/7*, COM (83).

raise questions as regards indirect discrimination. Important changes were made, during 1991, in both employment and social welfare law. These extended the protection of labour legislation and social insurance to the majority of regular, part-time workers. However, some part-timers have remained unprotected, while for many of those enjoying post-1991 protection, difficulties remain because of the continuing effects of lack of protection pre-1991. These matters are discussed further in §5.6 below.

'Adult dependants' allowances', which are now based on financial dependency rather than sex, are still paid mainly to men in respect of 'dependent' women. This is because far more women than men are deemed to be 'financially dependent'. This matter is discussed further in §5.3.6 below.

Another example of indirect discrimination relates to a payment which used to be (and, for a few people, still is) described as a 'prescribed relatives allowance' (PRA). This was an allowance payable in respect of a person who was providing full-time care and attention to someone who was incapacitated. As it was normally payable only to unmarried people, it was considered that the relevant Regulations[1] may have contravened both the Irish Constitution and the Directive. Prior to 1990, about 2,000 people were in receipt of the PRA. A higher and somewhat less restrictive 'Carer's Allowance' was then introduced and the majority of PRA recipients were transferred to the new payment. However, the 500 or so people on the PRA who failed the means test for the carer's allowance have been kept on the PRA, so that the question of possible indirect discrimination remains, although on a much reduced scale.

Means testing

The operation of a means test for purposes of determining entitlement to social assistance payments such as unemployment assistance (UA) and supplementary welfare allowance (SWA) has long been questioned. It was considered to operate to the disadvantage of married couples (*vis-à-vis* cohabiting couples) and was altered in 1991 so as to treat both groups equally (for further details see §5.5 below). However, there is evidence that married women find it more difficult to qualify for UA than married men,[2] and this may leave it open to the charge of indirect discrimination, under Directive 79/7/EEC.

Although the same methods are used for means testing for purposes of ascertaining eligibility for SWA, the permissibility of these arrangements under Directive 79/7/EEC is more complicated to assess. This is because not

---

1   SI No 248 of 1972.
2   Reply by Minister for Social Welfare to parliamentary question by P de Rossa TD, 13 March 1988, which showed that of the 13,751 people who registered as unemployed but received no payment, 76 per cent were women and 24 per cent men.

all SWA claimants are protected by this scheme against the various risks specified under the Directive. Thus some claimants could fail, for technical reasons, to establish discrimination under Directive 79/7/EEC; although, undoubtedly, many more could succeed. However none has so far attempted to establish discrimination.

5.3.1   BREADWINNER

In Ireland, the term 'breadwinner' is often used synonymously with 'head of household' to refer to the person (usually a man) who provides the bulk of the family income, whether from employment, social welfare, or any other source. Sometimes, however, it refers more narrowly to the provision of income solely from employment; whereas the 'head of household' may provide it from any source.

Traditionally, the concept has been problematic because in practice, despite high male unemployment and increasing female labour force participation, the majority of 'breadwinners' were believed to be men and the social welfare system assumed this to be so. Since the implementation of Directive 79/7/EEC, however, equal treatment in respect of social welfare payments to families applies irrespective of whether the 'breadwinner' is a man or a woman. Because of its traditional connotations, it is the term, rather than the concept, which now tends to be problematic and for this reason its use would appear to be declining.

This is not to say, of course, that there are not still major difficulties in relation to the treatment of households in which there may be one or more then one 'breadwinner' (i.e. employed person), by comparison with households in which one or both adults are dependent upon a social welfare payment. Recent attempts to analyse these difficulties, and to suggest improvements in the treatment of such households so as to ensure both equity and equality, are discussed in §5.3.3 below.

5.3.2   SOLE BREADWINNER

Precise statistics are not available on the extent to which Irish households are 'headed' by one, two or more 'breadwinners'. Some 23 per cent of married women work outside the home, while the corresponding rate for married men is 82 per cent.[1]

It is generally considered that families headed by a 'sole breadwinner' whose earnings are above-average are at an advantage by comparison with those in which the same level of income is earned by two or more 'breadwinners'. This is because, following the *Murphy* case,[2] the tax-free

---

[1]   Labour Force Survey, 1991.
[2]   *Murphy* v. *Attorney General* [1982] IR 241.

allowances of a married couple are twice those of a single person, irrespective of whether the second partner is a labour force participant. Thus a family with one relatively high income-earner, and a partner who remains outside the labour force, enjoys the same tax treatment, but incurs none of the additional expenses (such as childminding, travel costs etc.), as a family in which both partners work outside the home in order to secure the same level of income.

Also, the existence of a 'ceiling' for PRSI contributions clearly favours the household headed by a high-income sole breadwinner, by comparison with one in which two or more breadwinners earn a similar income between them. The 1993 'ceiling' of £20,000 per annum means, for example, that a household headed by a sole breadwinner earning £39,000 per annum pays £1,100 per annum in social insurance contributions (5.5 per cent x £20,000), whereas one headed by two adults each earning £18,500 pays £2,035 (5.5 per cent x £18,500 x 2). (The three other levies, for health and employment, which are 1.25 per cent, 1 per cent and 1 per cent, are payable on gross earnings and are omitted from this calculation.)

5.3.3   HEAD OF HOUSEHOLD

The 'head of household' concept is problematic at three levels in Ireland. It was problematic, initially, because of its traditional, sexist connotations, i.e. that the 'head' was, in the past automatically deemed to be the man (if there was a man present); and many people still view the matter in this way. It remains problematic because, even though households nowadays may in theory be 'headed' by a man or a woman, depending on their income and labour force status, in practice the majority of 'heads' are men because the earnings of most men are higher than those of most women. Thus the term may be viewed as indirectly discriminatory against women. It is also seen as outmoded, and unnecessary, to view a household as being 'headed' by one person, where two (or even more) adults may be present, each contributing in some way to the running of the household.

Thirdly, the concept is problematic because of continuing disagreement about the financial relationship, in the social welfare system, between the 'head of household' and other members of the household. In the Irish social welfare system, all other household members are classed as 'dependants' (either 'adult dependants' or 'child dependants') of the 'head' unless they are themselves classed as members of the labour force (i.e. unless they are employed, or have a social welfare entitlement in their own right). Also, the rates of payments of 'dependants' are related to those of their 'head of household', rather than to the needs of the 'dependants' themselves, so that an 'adult dependant' of a pensioner, for example, receives a higher payment, than that of an unemployed person, whatever their relative circumstances. Finally, the financial relationship itself varies, from payment to payment, so that the 'adult dependant's allowance' of a pensioner is not only higher in absolute terms than that of an unemployed person, but is also so in percentage terms.[1]

Although these issues have long been viewed as problematic by certain organizations and individuals (e.g. women's groups, trade unionists, social welfare reform bodies and unemployed groups), it was not until 1989 that official recognition was given to the need for thorough analysis and review of the treatment of different types of households, and different categories of persons within households, by the social welfare system. Following the May 1989 decision of the Supreme Court confirming that the payment of lower rates of unemployment assistance to married couples than to unmarried couples was unconstitutional,[2] the Government decided to reduce the rates for unmarried, cohabiting couples to the same level as those applying to their married counterparts. The changes were announced in May 1989 and enacted in June 1989.[3] In effect, they meant a 'levelling-down' of payments to cohabiting couples by means of a change in the definition of a 'shared household' and an extension of the definition of a 'couple' to include men and women who were not married to each other but were 'cohabiting as man and wife'. Prior to this, cohabitation of this kind was seen as relevant mainly in the case of widows and 'deserted wives', who were liable to lose certain benefits if found to be cohabiting (a rule which had long been the subject of criticism and concern).

The knowledge that these changes would be the cause of dissatisfaction, and the belief that further analysis was required of the composition and definition of 'couples' and 'households', led the Government to announce the setting up of a Review Group on this issue when introducing the new legislation. Under the title 'Review Group on the Structure of Social Welfare Payments to Households', the Group advertised its existence in the national newspapers in July 1989, stating simply that 'the Government has decided to review the system of social welfare payments as it applies to households with a view to ensuring consistent and equitable treatment of households under the system' and seeking submissions from interested persons or organizations by 4 August 1989. Interestingly, there was no reference to the need for equal treatment between men and women.

This advertisement gave little indication of the Review Group's terms of reference, but it was understood that it would deal with such issues as the appropriate level of payments to couples where each partner was a member of the workforce and entitled to an insurance-based benefit in her or his own

---

1   In 1993-94, this meant weekly payments of £49.50 a week and £35.50 a week for pensioners' and long-term unemployed people's dependants, respectively, which in the case of the former was 72 per cent of the full personal rate and in the case of the latter only 64 per cent.

2   *Hyland* v. *Minister for Social Welfare* [1989] ILRM 196 (HC); [1990] ILRM 213 (SC).

3   Social Welfare (No 2) Act 1989.

right; the appropriate level where one partner was a member of the labour force and the other was not; the question of 'equivalence' scales; the definitions of 'couples' and 'dependency', the composition of 'households' and the way in which means testing is carried out.

The Review Group was to report to the Minister for Social Welfare by November 1989 but did not meet this deadline. Throughout 1990, it was expected to finalize and submit its report at an early date but by the end of the year it had not reported publicly. The report was finally made public in mid-1991.[1] Its contents made clear the reasons for the long delay: the Group had not been able to reach a consensus on the main issue of principle which confronted it. Some members had concluded that rules such as the provisions of s. 12 of the Social Welfare (No 2) Act 1989, which had remedied the constitutional defect identified by the Supreme Court in the *Hyland* case, but precluded certain people who satisfied the contingency of unemployment from qualifying for the full personal rate of assistance, were inequitable and should be abolished. This section of the Group maintained that the system was, primarily, contingency-based and that everyone who experienced specific contingencies should be treated identically. The other members of the Group maintained that the main, underlying criterion of the social assistance system was need, which led them to the conclusion that the limitation (which the others wanted to abolish) should in fact be extended to all persons living in common or joint households. This, in their view, would meet the objective in the Review Group's terms of reference which was to ensure that all households with similar needs were treated in a consistent and equitable way.

While the Review Group did not agree on the issue of changing the existing payments structure, it did agree on certain other changes which, in its view, would remove some of the remaining areas of discrimination. The changes it recommended were precisely the changes which were made, earlier that year, in the Social Welfare Act 1991. The latter gave further effect to the 'levelling-down' changes of June 1989. Sections 45 to 48 provided that cohabiting couples would be treated in the same way as married couples with regard to assessment of their means for purposes of supplementary welfare allowance, disabled person's maintenance allowance and family income supplement; and that the same rates of payment would apply, in these cases, to married and cohabiting couples who were deemed to have the same 'means'. The provisions relating to increases for child dependants were also equalized.

The Government's decision to introduce equality in this area by 'levelling-down' the entitlements of unmarried couples, rather than 'levelling-up' those of married couples, was widely criticised. The effect of establishing

---

[1]   *Report of the Review Group on the Treatment of Households in the Social Welfare Code*, Department of Social Welfare, 1991.

the 'Review Group on Payments to Households' had been to diffuse some of the initial dissatisfaction with this in 1989. However, further 'levelling-down' legislation was passed in early 1991, before the Review Group's report had been made publicly available; and by the time the report was finally published in June 1991, the only recommendations on which there had been agreement had been implemented. Its impact, therefore, was less than momentous; indeed, it was largely ignored.

5.3.4   COHABITANT

Traditionally, cohabitation in Ireland was deemed relevant only in the case of widows, deserted wives, unmarried mothers and other women whose social welfare entitlements were predicated on their 'lone' status. The payments of such women were discontinued if cohabitation could be proved; and indeed this is still the case.

Until 1989, cohabitees who were unemployed, and were each entitled to a payment in their own right, were at a slight advantage, financially, over married couples who were similarly unemployed, because (in most cases) the latter would receive one full personal allowance and one 'adult dependant' allowance (rather than two full allowances). This situation was ended by the series of 'levelling-down' measures described in §5.3.3 above. Thus cohabitees are now in all respects treated as 'man and wife' for purposes of social welfare (though not for tax purposes). Apart from the financial loss, this also means that the formerly equal status of cohabitees, i.e. in relation to each other, has now been altered so as to give one person 'head' status and the other that of 'adult dependant'.

5.3.5   LIVING ALONE

Various social welfare payments (such as the lone parent's allowance) are conditional upon the recipient not 'living as man and wife' with another person. Also, additional payments are made to certain claimants (mainly pensioners) who live alone. Thus, in 1993-94, pensioners received an additional £4.70 a week if they lived on their own.

5.3.6   DEPENDANT

Following the implementation of Directive 79/7/EEC, the system of paying 'adult dependants' allowances was altered in an attempt to redefine 'dependency' in financial, rather than sex-based, terms. At the same time, an attempt was made to minimize the financial hardship which would have been caused to many low-income families had all adult dependant allowances been discontinued where a spouse had an independent income, however small. The result was, *inter alia*, the introduction of a £50 a week 'earnings ceiling' (later increased to £55 a week) on the amount which a spouse could earn and still remain classed as a 'dependant'.

The advantage of this, for existing claimants, was that the dependant's spouse, if receiving a social welfare payment, would continue to receive the 'adult dependant' supplement. The disadvantage was that the adult 'dependant' (usually a woman) would not be eligible, in her (or his) own right, for full social insurance cover and hence full social insurance benefits, in the event of unemployment, disability, maternity, retirement, etc. Also, of course, the 'dependant' status of many women was perpetuated, at a time when this was increasingly being questioned. Evidence later emerged[1] to illustrate what was widely predicted, at the time that this 'earnings ceiling' was introduced: namely, that it would operate mainly to the detriment of women, both in the labour market and in relation to social insurance. It was argued that the ceiling would act as a discouragement to full social insurance cover and would form an incentive for employers (and some employees) to keep certain wage rates below the 'earnings ceiling' — and this was precisely what subsequently happened.

This situation was then further complicated by the 1991 Regulations,[2] which extended full social insurance cover to all workers earning over £25 p.w. This meant that workers earning over £25 p.w. but under £55 p.w. would still be seen as 'adult dependants', for social welfare purposes, even though they had become fully insurable, as workers, in their own right.

The payment of 'adult dependant' allowances, which was traditionally made on the basis of entirely sex-based criteria, has now been modified in the manner described above. Nevertheless, because more women remain 'dependant' than men (i.e. not fully independent financially), in practice the vast majority of the recipients are men upon whom a woman is deemed 'dependant'. It is therefore possible that these payments might be said to be indirectly discriminatory. In the *Teuling* case,[3] however, the ECJ held in response to such an argument that similar payments, although clearly impacting differently on women and on men, were 'objectively justified', i.e.

---

[1] For example, in October 1989 the head office of the country's largest trade union, the ITGWU (now SIPTU), received a letter from one of its Cork branches requesting 'urgent action' to secure removal of the £50 earnings ceiling. This was because the union had recently secured wage increases for more than 300 members in the contract cleaning industry (predominantly part-time, women workers); however, because these increases would bring their earnings over the '£50 ceiling', many had responded by either seeking a reduction in their working hours on an individual basis, or asking the union not to process the wage increase. It was considered, therefore, that the ceiling was operating as a disincentive for women to work for better wages and conditions; was making it difficult to regulate work standards and productivity (since many women were retaining their existing workload but reducing their hours); and constituted an 'attack ... on the poorest sector of Irish society'.

[2] Social Welfare (Employment of Inconsiderable Extent) (No 2) Regulations 1991, SI No 72 of 1991.

[3] *Teuling* v. *Bedrijfsvereniging voor de Chemische Industrie*, Case 30/85, [1987] ECR 2497, [1988] 3 CMLR 789 (ECJ).

on grounds other than sex. The grounds were, basically, that the payments alleviated poverty and therefore had a social, rather than a sexual, origin. This line of argument might or might not succeed in Ireland; but so far, it has not been advanced in any case.

In addition to, and arising from, the above-mentioned provisions where direct or indirect discrimination may still be said to exist, are a number of other conceptual problems. One is an extension of the question raised above, of how best to introduce equality in the area of dependants' allowances, a question by no means fully answered by the manner of implementation of Directive 79/7/EEC, or indeed the report of the Review Group on the Treatment of Households (see §5.3.3 above). Another is the outstanding issue of survivors' pensions and other derived rights; and whether payments made exclusively to women on the basis of their generally disadvantaged position should be discontinued, even though most of the disadvantages remain. Finally, there are continuing problems arising from the 'carry-over effect' of past discrimination. Each of these major issues is considered briefly below. The treatment of part-time workers, which despite improvements continues to be problematic, not least in the context of the continuing effects of past discrimination, is considered separately (see §5.6 below).

Survivors' benefits and other derived rights

Most payments under this heading are excluded from the scope of Directive 79/7/EEC. Nevertheless, in Ireland the common practice is that in occupational pension schemes providing survivors' benefits, the provision is non-discriminatory: it applies equally to both widows and widowers. Even in advance of the adoption of Directive 86/378/EEC on occupational social security schemes, the Irish equal pay legislation had been used to secure equal treatment for men and women in relation to survivors' benefits in occupational pension schemes.[1] The non-provision of equal survivors' benefits in the statutory social security area is therefore something of an anomaly in the Irish context, with practice in the statutory schemes lagging well behind private-sector practice in occupational schemes.

Discussion has not yet been widespread on the question of whether the provision of survivors' benefits and other derived rights have a continuing validity, or merely perpetuate the concept of dependency and inhibit progress towards a system of personal, individual rights. A number of organizations[2] now advocate the replacement of most existing social welfare payments by a 'minimum income' (or a 'basic income', or a 'living income') for all individuals, irrespective of sex, marital or family status, or position in the labour force. This view implies an eventual end to the system of 'derived

---

1　See §3.5.6 above.
2　For example: three political parties, the country's largest trade union, the Combat Poverty Agency and the Conference of Major Religious Superiors.

rights' and its replacement by fully individualized rights. Furthermore, the realities of Irish society, which include increased marital breakdown and single parenthood, make it all the more urgent to address this issue, whether or not an EC Directive requires it. This was also recognized by the Second Commission on the Status of Women, which reported in February 1993 and which recommended, *inter alia*, that 'the Government should work towards establishing by 1997 a system of individual rights and payments in the social insurance and social welfare system'.[1]

Payments made exclusively to women

Until recently, a number of payments were made to women who were considered to be particularly disadvantaged by virtue of their economic and/or domestic situation, or some other occurrence. Thus, for example, payments were made to 'unmarried mothers' and 'prisoners' wives'; and until recently a 'single women's allowance' was payable to unmarried women aged between 58 and 66 who, by virtue of domestic or other circumstances (e.g. loss of a job when approaching retirement age, or absence from the labour market to care for an old or incapacitated parent) were unable to find employment.

However, in 1990 a 'lone parent's allowance' was introduced,[2] replacing a number of means-tested payments such as 'unmarried mother's allowance', which were made exclusively to either men or women; both men and women are now eligible for this allowance on the same terms. In 1992, the single woman's allowance was subsumed into a pre-retirement allowance payable to both men and women who are over 58 and are suffering long-term unemployment.[3] Thus by 1993 the only remaining payments being made exclusively to women were deserted wife's benefit (DWB) and widow's pensions. The DWB was payable on the strength of either the woman's own social insurance contributions, or those of her husband; and prior to 1992, it was payable irrespective of the woman's employment status or income. However, in 1992 a fairly low income threshold was introduced for the DWB,[4] presumably as a prelude to extending it eventually to men on similarly low incomes. A claim for payment of DWB to a man was heard by the High Court in 1984;[5] the claimant, who was unsuccessful, intended to appeal the judgment to the Supreme Court but this did not happen, due to his premature death. Subsequently another man initiated similar proceedings: it was expected that the case of this claimant, Anthony Lowth, would be heard in mid-1993.

---

1   *Report of the Second Commission on the Status of Women*, 1993, page 81.
2   Social Welfare Act 1990, ss 12 to 16.
3   Social Welfare Act 1992, s. 37.
4   Social Welfare Act 1992, ss 25 and 26; SI 237 of 1992.
5   *Dennehy* v. *Minister for Social Welfare*, unreported 26 July 1984 (HC).

As regards widows' pensions, it seemed unlikely, in early 1993, that payment of these would be extended to men, on the same basis as to women, because of the cost implications. A forthcoming report by the National Pensions Board was expected to recommend the introduction of restrictions related to income and/or the presence of dependant children;[1] but any adjustment of this kind would be highly sensitive, politically, for any Government to handle and early action therefore seems unlikely.

Effects of past discrimination

If the ECJ's ruling in the *Dik* case[2] were to be applied so as to remove the effects of all old discriminatory rules, and not just the rules themselves, several other issues may arise. For example, married women who had been denied unemployment assistance (UA) purely because of their sex and marital status should perhaps qualify immediately for the 'long-term' rate of UA when they claim, rather than be placed on the lower, initial, 'short-term' rate.

It could also be argued that various government employment schemes and training opportunities which are open only to those who have been on unemployment benefit for 12 months, and UA for at least a week, should not only change their eligibility requirements but should admit such women immediately, rather than impose the normal waiting-period upon them. This argument has been used by the EEA and by trade union representatives since the inception of various schemes designed to allow the long-term unemployed to transfer to social employment and other Government-sponsored work arrangements.

However, to date all attempts to alter the eligibility requirements so as to ensure full equality of access, especially by married women, have been unsuccessful. The length of time which had to be spent on UA was reduced from one year to one week in 1989, but since many women would have as much difficulty securing UA for a week as for a year, this did not alter the situation fundamentally. The test case on this issue was lost by the claimant: the Equality Officer found that the requirement to be on UA for a specified period was an 'essential requirement' of the scheme and the Labour Court upheld this view, stating that there were no alternative criteria capable of objectively identifying the target group for the scheme. The Court said that the evidence submitted did not sustain a finding that a higher proportion of men than of women, or of single women than of married women, would be eligible for employment under the scheme if the criterion of being on UA did

---

1   Fifth Report of National Pensions Board, expected July-August 1993.
2   *Dik* v. *College van Burgemeester en Wethouders Arnhem and Winterswijk,* Case 80/87, [1988] ECR 1601, [1989] 2 CMLR 963 (ECJ).

not exist. It also refused a request to refer the matter to the ECJ, on the basis that this was not necessary for the determination of the issues involved.[1]

The question of the continuing effects of past discrimination against part-time workers, who have only recently become eligible for full social insurance cover, is also an important issue in this context and is discussed further at §5.6 below.

5.4   EXCEPTIONS

Social insurance cover extends to virtually all categories of employed and self-employed people, although the level of that cover varies. However, there are a few important exceptions, and most of them affect women more than men. The main exception is where a person is employed by her or his spouse, or works with a self-employed spouse. Also, certain employed[2] and self-employed women[3] are exempted from liability to pay social insurance contributions. Women workers who perform certain occasional work for the Revenue Commissioners and the Department of Justice are also specifically excluded from insurability.

Thus two broad categories of women in the labour force are specifically excluded from pay-related social insurance (PRSI) cover in a manner which might be seen as directly discriminatory: (i) the Government employees just mentioned; and (ii) widows and deserted wives who are employed or self-employed. The first group is very small, but nevertheless its exclusion appears to constitute an anomaly. The second group is much larger and its position merits further explanation. Unlike the first, this group comprises women who are in receipt of benefits secured on the basis of their husbands' contributions; and these derived benefits are payable irrespective of whether the woman herself is employed or self-employed, although, as mentioned above, an income limit was introduced in 1992.[4] Therefore, if an employed woman is in receipt of a contributory widow's pension (for example), in addition to a salary, and then becomes unemployed, she will continue to receive the widow's pension (£62.60 a week, in 1993) but will not receive unemployment benefit (which in 1993 was £55.60 a week, plus a pay-related supplement of up to £16.80 a week, making a maximum of £72.40 a week altogether, for someone formerly earning £220 a week or more). Until the late 1980s, such a woman would also have received 50 per cent of the

---

1   *FÁS* v. *Vavasour* EE 11/1989; DEE 2/1991.
2   I.e. those in receipt of widow's pensions, deserted wife's benefit or allowance, death benefits (payable by way of widow's pensions), or similar payments from other EC Member States. These exemptions are contained in s. 10(7) of the Social Welfare Consolidation Act 1981.
3   Social Welfare Act 1988, s. 12.
4   Social Welfare Act 1992, ss 25 and 26; SI No 237 of 1992.

relevant unemployment benefit, in addition to her widow's pension, but this was seen as anomalous and was discontinued.

To date it has been considered that since the derived benefit, in such cases, remains payable regardless of the woman's employment status, there would be no merit in requiring her to pay PRSI contributions, since either these contributions would result in a 'double payment' (in the event of illness, unemployment, etc.), or, if no 'second payment' were to be made, this would render the contributions pointless. Clearly the resolution of such difficulties hinges on a resolution of the problem of derived rights and cannot be easily treated in isolation from this.

The lack of full PRSI cover for two other groups in the workforce can be seen as indirectly discriminatory. Firstly, the exclusion from social insurance of persons who are employed by a spouse almost certainly affects more women then men (although no statistics are readily available on this). It also constitutes discrimination on grounds of marital status. Secondly, even after the 1991 Regulations became effective, an estimated 10 per cent of regular part-time workers were still only insurable at a reduced rate, which rendered them ineligible for many important benefits. This could be seen as indirectly discriminatory in view of the fact that the majority of part-time workers are women.[1] Unlike most other workers on 'reduced rate' contributions (e.g. in the public service), part-time workers who are thereby excluded from sickness, maternity and other benefits are rarely covered by occupational schemes providing such benefits.

Another major issue which arises in relation to part-time workers is that of the continuing effects of past discrimination. If the exclusion of part-timers from full social insurance cover is held to be indirectly discriminatory, then questions must be asked about the adequacy of remedying this (for most part-timers) only from 1991. Many part-time workers with pre-1991 service, who were denied the opportunity of full social insurance cover prior to that date, will fail to qualify for certain insurance benefits because of this. In some cases, particularly the retirement and old age pensions (for which at least 10 years' full contributions are required), this failure will be total, if the workers concerned fall into a particular age-group.

The single largest group of persons to be completely excluded from social insurance cover is, of course, those working full-time in the home, i.e. mainly women engaged in childcare and/or the care of old persons. The question of whether this constitutes indirect sex discrimination, or whether 'objective justification' exists for their continued exclusion, has yet to be fully explored in the context of Directive 79/7/EEC. However, a widespread

---

1   In 1991, 78 per cent of all persons working less than nine hours per week, and 79 per cent of all those working less than 19 hours per week, were women; Labour Force Survey, 1991, Central Statistics Office, Dublin, June 1992.

demand exists for an end to the concept of 'adult dependency' and the introduction of independent social insurance cover for all women, whether working inside or outside the home or both. This was noted by the Second Commission on the Status of Women when it stated that 'to judge from many submissions to the Commission both the nomenclature and the concept of dependency is unacceptable to many people'.[1] The Commission recommended, in this regard, that 'the Government should work towards establishing by 1997 a system of individual rights and payments in the social insurance and social welfare system'.[2]

Finally, the question also arises, in relation to the scope of the social insurance system, whether by its very nature the system itself can be said to be indirectly discriminatory. Does it cover and benefit a significantly higher proportion of men than of women and can this be objectively justified? In Ireland, only 32 per cent of those in the labour force are women. Also, as noted above, the various exclusions from the scope of the system operate mainly to the detriment of women. The proportion of women in the labour force who are eligible for full social insurance cover is therefore considerably lower than the proportion of men who are eligible.

No official statistics are available for the gender breakdown of the insured population, or of those included under the various different classes of social insurance. However, unofficial statistics (based on a 10 per cent sample of insured persons) indicated that 58 per cent of all insured persons are men and 42 per cent are women. Since this is a smaller variation than might have been expected, it would seem that other offsetting influences must operate to redress some of the imbalance resulting from the fact that a much lower proportion of women than men in the labour force are eligible for social insurance cover.

Of course, if similar comparisons are made in respect of all persons over the age of 15 (i.e. including those not classed as being 'in the labour force'), this shows an even greater disparity between the sexes. In 1991, some 67 per cent of all men over 15 were covered for some form of social insurance,[3] whereas only 47 per cent of women had any form of cover.[4]

---

1 *Op.cit.*, p. 80.
2 *Ibid.*, p. 81.
3 Including insurance for all benefits, for limited benefits (e.g. civil servants and some part-time workers) and for long-term benefits only (e.g. the self-employed).
4 Derived from population statistics, statistics for insured population (*Statistical Information on Social Welfare Service*, 1990, Department of Social Welfare) and the gender breakdown of the latter.

5.4.1   RETIREMENT AGE

The same retirement ages apply to men and women in the statutory social security schemes. Insured workers who retire from their jobs may apply for a (contributory) retirement pension at age 65. Old-age pensions (both contributory and non-contributory) are payable at age 66, to employees and to the self-employed, provided that the various qualifying conditions are met.

In most occupational pension schemes, equal retirement ages apply for men and women, usually the age of 65. It was estimated in 1991 that about 5 per cent of schemes had different retirement ages for women than for men; this usually meant age 60 for women compared with age 65 for men.[1]

5.4.2   SEX AS A DETERMINING FACTOR

This concept is not applicable in Ireland in the social welfare context.

5.5   LEVELLING UP/DOWN

In 1989, the Government 'levelled-down' the rates of unemployment assistance payable to unmarried, cohabiting couples, following a Supreme Court ruling that it was unconstitutional for married couples to receive lower rates. Subsequently, the Social Welfare Act 1991 extended this 'levelling-down' approach to certain other payments. For further details see §5.3.3 above.

5.6   PART-TIME WORK

The validity of denying equal remuneration to part-time workers on grounds of their reduced working hours has been rejected in Ireland;[2] and pension benefits have been accepted as 'remuneration';[3] so that scope exists for successfully challenging the exclusion of part-time workers from occupational pensions cover. The outcome of the *Bilka Kaufhaus* case,[4] in which the ECJ stated that such exclusions were open to scrutiny under art. 119 of the EEC Treaty, could strengthen any such challenge; as could the ECJ's ruling in *Rinner-Kühn*,[5] which held that the practice of excluding part-

---

1 'The Challenge of Change', Paper presented to 1991 Annual Conference of the Irish Association of Pension Funds, by Anne Maher, Pensions Manager, Irish Life. Figures quoted were based on a survey by Ms Maher of 2,500 schemes administered by Irish Life.

2 For example, in *Dunnes Stores (Navan) Ltd* v. *Two Female Employees* EP 15/1982; and *St Patrick's College, Maynooth* v. *ITGWU* EP 4/1984; DEP 10/1984.

3 *Linson* v. *ASTMS* EP 1/1977; DEP 2/1977.

4 *Bilka Kaufhaus GmbH* v. *Weber von Hartz*, Case 170/84, [1986] ECR 1607 (ECJ).

5 *Rinner-Kühn* v. *FWW Spezial-Gebäudereinigung GmbH & Co. KG*, Case 171/88, [1988] ECR 2743 (ECJ).

time workers from occupational sick pay cover was in contravention of art. 119 unless it could be justified by objective factors unrelated to sex.

The case for including all remaining part-time workers fully within the scope of statutory social insurance might be seen to have been strengthened by the ECJ's judgment in *Ruzius-Wilbrink*,[1] where it was stated that provisions in Danish law, which prevented certain part-time workers from receiving the minimum subsistence income normally payable to insured workers when suffering from incapacity for work, were in contravention of art. 4(1) of Directive 79/7/EEC.

Until 1991, most people working for less than 18 hours a week were excluded from full, 'class A', social insurance cover. Instead they paid a reduced contribution, which only covered them for a very narrow range of benefits. Since a majority of part-time workers were women, this exclusion would appear to have been indirectly discriminatory.

Regulations extending full cover to the majority of part-time workers became effective from 6 April 1991. They repealed earlier Regulations on 'employment of inconsiderable extent' which were the source of the 18-hours-a-week threshold for most 'class A' contributors. From that time, 'employment of inconsiderable extent' (which was still not insurable at the 'class A' rate) was defined as one or more employments where the total amount of reckonable earnings was less than £25 a week. Thus people earning £25 or more a week, from one or more employment, became insurable at the full rate.

While this now meant full social insurance cover for a high proportion of part-time workers, most recent statistics[2] indicate that about 4.5 per cent of all male part-timers (working less than 30 hours a week) worked less than nine hours a week, while the comparable figure for female part-time workers was 6.4 per cent. Comparing all male and female workers, only 16 men out of every 10,000 worked less than nine hours a week, whereas 110 women out of every 10,000 did so. Given the below-average hourly earnings of part-time workers, and the fact that female part-timers were often doubly disadvantaged in this regard, it seemed likely that a substantial majority of workers earning less than £25 a week and who therefore continued to be excluded from full social insurance cover, were part-time women workers. Thus the question of indirect discrimination, albeit on a much smaller scale than before, continued to hang over the new Regulations, as it did over the old ones.

---

1   *Ruzius-Wilbrink* v. *Bestuur van de Bedrijfsvereniging voor Overheidsdiensten*, Case C-102/88, [1989] ECR 4311 (ECJ).
2   Labour Force Survey, 1991, Central Statistics Office, Dublin, June 1992.

6. ENFORCEMENT OF THE PRINCIPLE

6.1   COURT OR TRIBUNAL PROCEDURE

The tribunal of first instance for most equality cases is the Labour Court, and it is worth stating at the outset that the Court is not, in any recognizable sense of the word, a court of law. The Labour Court's main and original functions were to resolve industrial conflict and to make recommendations in respect of industrial disputes.[1] The equality legislation then added a quasi-judicial and appellate role in 1974,[2] which, at the time, seemed novel and somewhat surprising. The Court's procedures were relatively informal; its members were not required to be legally qualified; and a tribunal with legally qualified personnel already existed to adjudicate on other statutory entitlements. This was the Redundancy Appeals Tribunal, which also, at that time, adjudicated on statutory minimum notice claims;[3] it was later re-named the Employment Appeals Tribunal (EAT),[4] just prior to the enactment of the Employment Equality Act 1977.

Initially, the Labour Court had some difficulty adjusting to its new role of resolving disputes by determining legal entitlements rather than by seeking compromise and conciliation. Indeed the Employment Equality Agency (EEA) in 1978 argued that the EAT should take over the jurisdiction in equality matters exercised by the Labour Court. By 1984, however, the EEA advocated retention of the *status quo*, subject to some structural changes and the issuing of procedural guidelines. It suggested that a separate division of the Court should deal with equality cases so that its personnel would gain the necessary expertise.[5]

In the last few years there has been less criticism of the Court's procedures and handling of equality claims: it is generally accepted that it performs its functions in a satisfactory manner and that no major changes are required.

6.1.1   ACQUIRING THE EVIDENCE

As there are different procedures under the 1974 and 1977 Acts, they will be dealt with separately below.

---

1   Industrial Relations Acts, 1946-1990; see also §1.1.1 above.
2   In the Anti-Discrimination (Pay) Act 1974.
3   Redundancy Payments Acts 1967-1991: s. 39 of the 1967 Act; Minimum Notice and Terms of Employment Acts 1973-1991: s. 11 of the 1973 Act.
4   Unfair Dismissals Act 1977, s. 8.
5   See D. CURTIN, *Irish Employment Equality Law*, Round Hall Press, 1989, pp 300-301.

Anti-Discrimination (Pay) Act 1974

Section 7 of the 1974 Act provides that a 'dispute' between employer and employee may be referred to an Equality Officer.[1] The term 'dispute' is not defined in the legislation. Equality Officers to date have taken a very broad view of what constitutes a 'dispute', and have accepted any case in which an employee has made a claim which the employer has rejected. Employers frequently argue that no 'dispute' exists where the employer has not had an opportunity to answer the allegation. In practice a 'dispute' may only come into existence by virtue of an employer's defence at an Equality Officer's hearing. Of course employers cannot argue indefinitely that there is no 'dispute': in other words, they must answer the allegation. The passing of time would weigh in favour of the existence of a 'dispute'.

The EEA can also refer a pay issue to an Equality Officer where it feels 'that an employer had failed to comply with an equal pay clause' even though technically no 'dispute' has arisen, or where it is not feasible for an employee to bring a claim.[2]

Employment Equality Act 1977

The same points as above apply in respect of the meaning of a 'dispute'. However, under this Act a 'dispute' must be referred to the Labour Court itself, which must endeavour to settle the 'dispute' through an Industrial Relations Officer (whose task it is to provide a conciliation service) or refer it to an Equality Officer.[3] In practice the vast majority of cases are referred by the Court to Equality Officers and in recent years disputes have not been referred to Industrial Relations Officers. However, if a dispute has been referred to an Industrial Relations Officer and if she or he fails to settle the 'dispute' the matter can then be referred to an Equality Officer.

The EEA may (acting under s. 20) refer a 'dispute' to the Court where discrimination is being practised generally, where a person cannot make a reference themselves, where a person has procured or attempted to procure discrimination, or where there is alleged discrimination. The matter is treated as if it were a reference under s. 19 and is referred to an Industrial Relations Officer or an Equality Officer in the normal way.

6.1.1.1   Prescribed forms

There are no statutory forms for the reference of a dispute or the initiation of a claim under either Act. However, the Labour Court has issued

---

1   See §6.2.1.1 below.
2   See s. 36(1) of the 1977 Act and s. 7(2) of the 1974 Act.
3   See s. 19 of the 1977 Act.

a document entitled *Procedures of the Labour Court and Equality Officers in relation to the Anti-Discrimination (Pay) Act 1974 and the Employment Equality Act 1977*. The procedures and forms described therein have no statutory basis but came into operation on 1 December 1989 and are constantly up-dated. This document is very useful to all parties involved in claims.

Anti-Discrimination (Pay) Act 1974

It is recommended that a person referring a dispute under this Act write a letter to the Head of the Equality Service (now coming under the Labour Relations Commission) containing the following details: (a) the name and address of the employer; (b) the name of each individual claimant; (c) the name(s) of the comparator(s), where appropriate; and (d) a statement of what is in dispute. This procedure is not applicable in retaliatory dismissal matters where the issue is referred directly to the Labour Court.

Employment Equality Act 1977

It is recommended that a s. 28 form be sent initially to the employer. The purpose of this form/questionnaire is to allow the prospective claimant to outline the grounds of the alleged discrimination and to ask the employer to respond. If the claimant is still dissatisfied with the information provided by the employer, the matter may then be referred to the Labour Court outlining to the Court the reasons why there is a dispute between the parties and the alleged grounds of discrimination.

This procedure is applicable in dismissal cases except where the dismissal arises from retaliatory dismissals or dismissals covered by s. 3(4) of the Act, e.g. unfair selection for redundancy.[1]

6.1.1.2 Obligation to furnish all relevant evidence

If an Equality Officer considers that she or he is not getting all the evidence that is required, she or he has the right of entry on to the employer's premises to inspect employer records and to inspect work in progress. Any person who obstructs or impedes an Equality Officer commits an offence.[2]

The Court has considerable powers under the Industrial Relations Acts 1946-1990 to hear evidence on oath, issue subpoenas to witnesses and require such persons to bring along certain documents.[3]

---

[1] See ss 25, 26 and 27 of the 1977 Act.
[2] See s. 6(4) of the 1974 Act.
[3] Section 21 of the Industrial Relations Act 1946.

6.1.1.3   Annual information to works council

There is no requirement to provide information to employees other than
the disclosure requirements under company law requiring certain companies
to file specified financial statements and accounts with the Registrar of
Companies.[1]

6.1.1.4   Information to trade union for bargaining

There is no statutory provision for information to be given to trade
unions.

6.1.2   BURDEN OF PROOF

Hederman J in the Supreme Court in the case of *North-Western Health
Board* v. *Martyn* held that discrimination must be proved by the person
alleging it.[2] Whilst the above may be the legal position, in practice a
claimant only has to show a *prima facie* case and the employer must defend
his action. In a number of cases involving interview panels the burden of
proof has shifted back to the employer where there is a very strong inference
that there was discrimination.[3]

6.1.3   COSTS

Neither the Equality Officers nor the Labour Court are empowered to
award costs. The courts can award costs in equality matters, more usually to
the successful party.

6.1.4   LEGAL AID

There is no provision for legal aid (i.e. free legal representation) before
Equality Officers or the Labour Court in claims brought under the 1974 or
1977 Acts, or before deciding officers, appeals officers, or other officers of
the Department of Social Welfare, the Department of Health, or the various
health boards in social welfare claims.

Equality Officers and the Labour Court are not empowered to grant
costs. However, the EEA may, in referring a matter under the 1974 or 1977
Acts, provide assistance to a claimant where it considers that an issue of
principle is involved or where the claimant requires such assistance.

---

1   Companies (Amendment) Act 1986.
2   EE 14/1981; DEE 1/1982; [1985] ILRM 226 (HC); [1988] ILRM 519 (SC).
3   See e.g. *Revenue Commissioners* v. *Irish Tax Officials' Union* EE 6/1986; DEE
    2/1987.

Assistance shall be as the EEA deems fit.[1] Technically, under the legislation, the assistance provisions could also extend to employers.

Most claimants are represented by trade unions and most employers by their appropriate employers' organization. Such bodies have experienced staff, legally qualified or otherwise, to advise and represent in such matters.

In respect of appeals and judicial review applications to the higher courts, an individual may apply to the Free Legal Aid Board for legal assistance but the scope of this scheme is limited, and applicants are severely means tested (currently, disposable income must be less than £6,200 per annum for a person to qualify). The scheme is chronically under-staffed (employing only about 30 solicitors for the entire country) and the assistance provided is confined to representation in the civil courts, so that any assistance with cases at Equality Officer, Labour Court, deciding officer, appeals officer or tribunal level is not available. In practice, the vast majority of cases in which legal aid is granted are family law cases and the role of the scheme in relation to EC equality law has been virtually nil.

Of much greater significance, in this context, has been the role of the Free Legal Advice Centres (FLAC), a voluntary legal aid scheme run by lawyers. FLAC provides assistance in areas not covered by the State scheme, especially in the employment and social and social security areas, but due to the lack of resources has been obliged to confine its activities mainly to 'test' cases. It has been involved in all the major claims to date under the 1985 Social Welfare Act and has provided invaluable legal assistance to those concerned who have mainly been women on very low incomes.

Finally, there is one community-based law centre in Ireland, whose continued existence is constantly threatened by lack of funding, and which provides legal aid and advice to people living in the Coolock area of Dublin. The Coolock Community Law Centre (CCLC) has not, however, had the resources to deal with equality cases and generally refers claims under the 1985 Act to FLAC. Both FLAC and the CCLC refer claims under the 1974 and the 1977 Acts to the EEA or to trade unions, where appropriate.

6.1.5   REMEDIES

Anti-Discrimination (Pay) Act 1974

Equal pay may be awarded retrospectively, i.e. for up to three years prior to the date of the reference of the dispute to the Equality Officer for investigation,[2] or for such period as the claimant was performing 'like work' with the comparator, if shorter.

---

1   Section 48 of the 1977 Act.
2   Section 8(5) of 1974 Act.

Where there is a dismissal, the redress available consists of (a) reinstatement; (b) re-engagement; or (c) compensation of up to a maximum of 104 weeks' remuneration.[1]

Employment Equality Act 1977

The Labour Court may, under ss 22 and 23 of the Act, (a) hold that there was or was not discrimination; (b) recommend a specified course of action; (c) award compensation of up to a maximum of 104 weeks' remuneration; or (d) hold that a person did or did not procure or attempt to procure discrimination or that a publication was or was not discriminatory .

In relation to dismissal the same redress as under the 1974 Act may be awarded.[2] However, a claimant may not obtain redress for dismissal under both the equality legislation and the Unfair Dismissals Act 1977.

6.1.5.1   Nullity/annulment

Anti-Discrimination (Pay) Act 1974

This Act provides that a clause in a collective agreement, an Employment Regulation Order or a Registered Employment Agreement (*inter alia*) which provides for the payment of remuneration which is discriminatory on the basis of sex, is null and void.[3] Interestingly, there are no similar provisions in respect of individual contracts of employment even though logically such collective agreements form part of the employee's terms and conditions of employment. Technically, there is no enforcing provision for such nullity, and the concept of 'nullity' is not common in Irish law. In practice an employee who considers she or he is discriminated against must bring an equal pay claim in order to remedy such alleged discrimination.

Employment Equality Act 1977

The anomaly referred to above seems to have been remedied under the 1977 Act because s. 10(2) provides that 'where a contract of employment contains a term (whether express or implied) constituting discrimination that term shall be null and void'. As s. 56(2) of the 1977 Act provides that the two Acts are to be read as one, this provision may be imported into the 1974 Act. Again, however, there are no enforcing provisions other than the remedies provided as the result of a successful claim.

---

1   Sections 9, 30 and 31 of the 1977 Act.
2   Sections 25-27 of the 1977 Act.
3   Section 5 of the 1974 Act.

6.1.5.2   Termination of discriminatory conduct

Section 22(b) of the 1977 Act provides that the Labour Court (including, in practical terms, the Equality Officers) may 'recommend to a person or persons concerned a specified course of action'. To date most successful claimants under this Act have been awarded compensation; in a few cases, the Equality Officer or the Labour Court has recommended a specific course of action, such as recommending the cessation of discrimination in certain recruitment practices, the deletion of an age bar, and more recently the removal of certain application procedures arising from the marriage bar in the public service.[1]

The Equality Officer in the case of *Packard Electric Ireland Ltd* v. *EEA* recommended that certain recruitment practices be discontinued.[2] She further recommended that the next 30 appointments to full-time positions be made from the disadvantaged group of women workers (subject to sufficient applications being received from them and to the Company's normal requirements on suitability for the employment being met). Further, the company was ordered to make these 30 appointments within three months from the date of the recommendation.

Another case which ordered a termination of discriminatory conduct was the case of *North-Western Health Board* v. *Martyn*, where the Supreme Court disallowed an appeal against a Labour Court determination that upper age limits were discriminatory and requested the Board to review its position.[3]

6.1.5.3   Declaration

Where the Labour Court issues a determination, the 1977 Act provides that this determination can do a number of things, one of which is to 'hold that there was or (as the case may be) was not discrimination'.[4] However, such a decision on its own probably provides no redress, and a remedy is awarded only to the extent that the Court also puruse the other options, including the recommending of a specified course of action, or the awarding of compensation.

---

1   *Minister for Finance* v. *EEA* EE 21/91; DEE 5/1993.
2   EE 14/1985.
3   EE 14/1981; DEE 1/1982; [1985] ILRM 226 (HC); [1988] ILRM 519 (SC); however, the Supreme Court stated that the judgment was based on the facts of this specific case and may not apply to all cases.
4   Section 22(a).

6.1.5.4   Compensation

Anti-Discrimination (Pay) Act 1974

The 1974 Act provides that a successful equal pay claimant is entitled to the difference between her or his rate of pay and that of the comparator for the period of three years prior to the reference of the dispute to the Equality Officer.[1] Proceedings under this Act can take some considerable period of time and it has happened in many cases that claimants may be in receipt of many years' back pay as well as the three years' retrospection. More recently, in *Teagasc* v. *105 Female Employees*,[2] it was reported that £2.5 million was pending in respect of back pay.

Compensation awarded under the 1974 Act is in the nature of pay and accordingly must be subject to income tax and pay-related social insurance in the normal way.

Employment Equality Act 1977 and dismissal cases

The 1977 Act does not provide detailed provisions as to how compensation is to be awarded except in relation to dismissals where both Acts provide that if a person has been dismissed she or he must be placed back in a position as if she or he had not been dismissed. In contrast, the Unfair Dismissals Act 1977 lays down a definition of 'remuneration' and what constitutes 'loss'. There are no such definitions in the 1977 Act or the 1974 Act in relation to dismissal.

Generally, neither the Equality Officers nor the Labour Court give their reasoning for the compensation awarded. Up to recently the awards in equal treatment cases have been low because the claimant may not have had a high degree of loss. For example, in cases involving discriminatory interviewing, the claimant may not have had a high degree of loss because they did not lose the job but only the chance of being fairly considered for employment. Such awards have increased from £30 in 1983[3] to £400 in 1988[4] to £500 in 1989.[5] In the last case, which was brought against an airline, the Equality Officer commented that even though there was discriminatory interviewing, the claimant would not have been able to comply with the contract even if selected. In these cases concerning discriminatory interviewing, Equality Officers have commented that such awards are for distress suffered by the claimants, even though there is no mention of the word 'distress' in the

---

1   Section 8(5) of the Act.
2   DEP 3/1991.
3   *University College Dublin* v. *Chaney* EE 15/1983.
4   *Medical Council* v. *Barrington* EE 9/1988.
5   *An Airline* v. *A Worker* EE 12/1989.

legislation, which merely provides that compensation shall be awarded as is 'reasonable having regard to all the circumstances'.

Claims concerning promotion and the non-appointment of an employee arising from pregnancy have provided higher awards. The sum of £11,000 was awarded to the claimant in *The Model School, Limerick* v. *Culloo*,[1] where the claimant, a teacher, was denied promotion to school principal by reason of her sex. She was awarded £11,000 and the Equality Officer gave details of how the award was computed: £10,000 was awarded as being the difference between her salary at the date of discrimination and the principal's salary multiplied by the number of years to her retirement; plus £1,000 for distress. Another case concerned the non-appointment of an employee by the new employer following transfer of the previous employer's business because she could not take up her new position immediately due to pregnancy. She was awarded £5,500 and part-time employment at such time when a suitable vacancy should arise.[2]

6.1.5.5 Recommendation

Disputes under the 1974 Act may be referred to an Equality Officer, who carries out an investigation and issues a recommendation. Under the 1977 Act, however, disputes are referred to the Labour Court and the latter may then refer them either to an Equality Officer or to an Industrial Relations Officer. If the reference is to an Equality Officer, a recommendation will be issued.

Equality Officer recommendations are not legally binding. Both Acts allow them to be appealed, by either party, to the Labour Court. The appeal may be brought by the unsuccessful party against the recommendation itself, or it may be brought by the successful party on the basis that the recommendation has not been implemented. The Labour Court's determination is binding unless appealed, on a point of law, to a higher court.

6.1.5.6 Positive enforcement order

A determination of the Labour Court is enforceable if there is subsequent non-compliance; this enforceability is provided by s. 8(4)(a) of the 1974 Act, or s. 24 of the 1977 Act. The Labour Court makes an order and if this order is not carried out within two months, the person concerned is guilty of an offence and will be liable on summary conviction to a fine not exceeding £100 and, in the case of a continuing offence, a further fine not exceeding £10 per day during which the offence is continued. The sums involved may be too low to act as a serious deterrent.

---

1   EE 8/1987.

2   *Power Supermarkets Ltd v. Long* EE15/1988; DEE 1/1990; 1990, unreported (HC); EE 15/1991; DEE 2/1993.

6.1.5.7   Positive action plan

There is no provision in the legislation for a positive action plan; this is a matter for employers and employees to agree upon.

6.1.5.8   Criminal sanctions

The Anti-Discrimination (Pay) Act 1974 provides for the following penalties.

Obstruction of an Equality Officer

Any person who obstructs or impedes an Equality Officer in the exercise of her or his powers, or does not comply with the requirements of an Equality Officer, is guilty of an offence, and will be liable on summary conviction to a fine not exceeding £100, or, on conviction on indictment, to a fine not exceeding £1,000.[1]

Non-implementation of Labour Court recommendation on equal pay

Where an employee claims to the Labour Court that an employer has failed or neglected to implement a determination of the Labour Court, the Court may make an order directing the employer to implement the determination. If the order is not carried out within two months (or appealed to the High Court), the employer is guilty of an offence and will be liable on summary conviction to a fine not exceeding £100; and in the case of a continuing offence, a further fine not exceeding £10 for every day during which the offence is continued.[2]

Dismissal because of equal pay claim

Where a woman (or a man) claims from her (or his) employer the same rate of remuneration as a man or woman employed by the same employer in the same place on like work, and subsequent to the making of the claim the employer dismisses the employee solely or mainly because she or he has made the claim, the employer is guilty of an offence and will be liable on summary conviction to a fine not exceeding £100, or on conviction on indictment to a fine not exceeding £1,000. This also applies where a person is dismissed for giving evidence in proceedings under the 1974 Act, opposing an act which is unlawful under the 1974 Act, or giving notice of intention of doing any of the above.[3]

---

1   Section 6(4)(b) of 1974 Act.
2   Section 8(4)(b) of the 1974 Act.
3   Section 9(1) of the 1974 Act.

Non-implementation of the dismissal award

Where a dismissal award has been made by the Labour Court, and where the order has not been implemented, the employer is guilty of an offence and liable on summary conviction to a fine not exceeding £100, and in the case of a continuing offence to a further fine not exceeding £10 for every day during which the offence is continued.[1]

The Employment Equality Act 1977 also provides for various penalties, as follows.

False statements when using employment agencies

An employer who, with a view to obtaining the services of an employment agency, knowingly makes a statement contrary to the Act and which is in a material respect false or misleading, is guilty of an offence and liable on summary conviction to a fine not exceeding £200.[2]

Discriminatory advertising

A person may not be involved in discriminatory advertising contrary to the Act. A person who makes a statement which he knows to be false with a view to securing publication, or displays an advertisement in contravention of the Act, is guilty of an offence and liable on summary conviction to a fine not exceeding £200.[3]

Failure to implement Labour Court determination

Where an employer fails to carry out a Labour Court order which requires the implementation of a determination (e.g. to pay compensation), he is guilty of an offence and liable on summary conviction to a fine not exceeding £100; and in the case of a continuing offence, a further fine not exceeding £10 for every day during which the offence is committed.[4]

Dismissal because of an equality claim

Where an employee is dismissed from her or his employment solely or mainly because she or he was involved in certain matters regarding the provisions of the 1977 Act, the employer is guilty of an offence, and liable on summary conviction to a fine not exceeding £100, or on conviction on indictment to a fine not exceeding £1,000.[5]

---

1   Section 10(2) of the 1974 Act.
2   Section 7(5) of the 1977 Act.
3   Section 8(3) of the 1977 Act.
4   Section 24(2) of the 1977 Act.
5   Section 25(1) of the 1977 Act.

Non-implementation of Labour Court award involving dismissal

The person to whom the direction is given is guilty of an offence and is liable on summary conviction to a fine not exceeding £100 and in the case of a continuing offence, to a further fine not exceeding £10 for every day during which the offence is continued.[1]

Offences relating to investigations

If a person fails or refuses to supply the EEA with information, refuses to attend as a witness before the EEA, refuses to take the oath or affirmation, or is in contempt of court before the EEA, she or he is guilty of an offence and liable on summary conviction to a fine not exceeding £100 or on conviction on indictment to a fine not exceeding £1,000. Also the court by which she or he is convicted may direct him/her to comply with what is so required by the EEA. If a person is requested to give certain information to the EEA and alters, suppresses, conceals or destroys a document specified in the notice from the EEA, or makes a false statement when supplying to the EEA information specified in the notice, he is guilty of an offence and liable on summary conviction to a fine not exceeding £100.[2]

6.1.6   CLASS ACTIONS

An equal pay claim is founded on the 'equal pay clause' in each individual contract of employment. Therefore each individual claimant must be specifically named as well as the comparator; and there is very little scope for class actions (for further discussion see §3.8.1 above).

An equal treatment claim is based on the 'equality clause' in each individual contract of employment. Section 20 suggests that the EEA may bring a claim for a group or a class of persons but it would be more correct under the Act to name the specific individuals as claimants; otherwise, technically, the reference may fail.

6.1.7   EXCLUSION OF JUDICIAL REDRESS

All claims must be initially referred to an Equality Officer or the Labour Court. Technically, there is no provision for judicial redress as the Labour Court is considered to be quasi-judicial. Arguably there is exclusion of judicial redress in that a determination of the Labour Court may only be appealed to the High Court on a point of law. Accordingly, the High Court does not hear the facts of the claim but only the legal points arising during the hearing of the claim.

---

1   Section 26(2) of the 1977 Act.
2   Section 41(1) and (2).

Generally, an application for judicial review would not consider the facts of the case but only the apparent breach of fair procedures at the earlier hearing. It has been argued by employers in a number of cases that the Labour Court does not have the power under the Constitution to award large amounts of compensation especially in equal pay claims. Their reasoning is that only the courts, with judges appointed under the Constitution, have such a right. This is a very technical point that has not yet been fully answered.[1]

6.1.8 TIME-LIMITS

Equal pay

There are no time-limits under the 1974 Act. Claimants must however be aware that they can only claim up to three years' back pay from the date of the reference of the dispute to the Equality Officer. Accordingly, if for example there had only been 'like work' for a specific period of time and if there had been a delay in the reference of the claim, a successful claimant might technically not receive any back pay.

Equal treatment

The issue of time-limits under the 1977 Act has been very problematic and the subject of much litigation. Section 19(5) provides that:

> save only where reasonable cause can be shown, ... a reference under this section shall be lodged not later than six months from the date of the first occurrence of the act alleged to constitute discrimination.

In *Aer Lingus Teo.* v. *The Labour Court*,[2] the Supreme Court considered that a claim brought outside the six-month period was outside the time-limit and could not succeed unless reasonable cause for the delay could be shown. The case involved alleged discrimination in relation to seniority against air hostesses who originally resigned due to the marriage bar and had since returned to work in the company. Some time later they brought a claim maintaining that they were discriminated against under the Act. Carroll J in the High Court considered the issue of alleged 'continuing discrimination' and whether this constituted new acts of discrimination which would have logically placed the claim within the six-month time-limit. She considered that if there were new acts of discrimination different from the original acts then this brought the claim within the time-limit.

---

1 See e.g. *Lissadell Towels Ltd* v. *56 Female Employees* DEP 2/1987; it should be noted that this determination was quashed by the High Court but not on this particular point.
2 [1990] ELR 113 and 125.

The next technical issue concerning time-limits is the actual date of reference of the claim and to what body. All claims under the 1977 Act are technically referred to the Labour Court, which then refers the claim to an Industrial Relations Officer for settlement or to an Equality Officer for investigation and recommendation. If an Industrial Relations Officer fails to effect a settlement, the matter can be referred to an Equality Officer. The Supreme Court in the *Aer Lingus* case considered that the Labour Court need not make an initial determination that a complaint is admissible before making the administrative decision to refer the matter to an Equality Officer for investigation. The Labour Court is free to have a preliminary hearing on the admissibility of the complaint if it so wishes, but it is not correct to say that it must hold such a hearing.

The effect of this ruling is that where the Labour Court does not decide to hold a preliminary ruling and the matter is referred to an Equality Officer, the latter must investigate the dispute and can also look at the issue of time-limits. Any recommendation that the Equality Officer makes on the issue of time-limits is strictly without prejudice to the Labour Court decision on the same issue. The Equality Officer can make a recommendation on both issues and both issues can be appealed to the Labour Court, which can then decide whether the claim is out of time.

6.2   COURTS AND TRIBUNALS

6.2.1   SPECIAL LABOUR COURT OR TRIBUNAL

6.2.1.1   Equality officer

In Ireland Equality Officers are individuals with a specialized knowledge of equality law, although they are not lawyers. Equality Officers (presently four in number) are organizationally part of the Labour Relations Commission. Invariably, they are recruited from within the public service, usually from the Department of Enterprise and Employment. They usually serve as Equality Officers for a number of years and may then be transferred to other parts of the public service (although they tend to remain within the Department of Enterprise and Employment).

Equal pay claims are referred directly to Equality Officers. Equal treatment claims are referred to the Labour Court which may either refer the matter to an Industrial Relations Officer of the Labour Relations Commission for conciliation purposes or, alternatively, may refer the matter directly to an Equality Officer. If the Industrial Relations Officer fails to effect a settlement, then the Labour Court or the Officer concerned may refer the case to an Equality Officer.

Under both Acts, hearings before Equality Officers are informal and are heard in private. Equality Officers investigate 'disputes', which may include carrying out work inspections and listening to various witnesses. Both parties usually provide written submissions. At the conclusion of the investigation, the Equality Officer issues a detailed written Recommendation.

The Equality Officer's recommendation is not legally binding; however, if for example an award is made in favour of a claimant but is not implemented, the claimant can refer the matter to the Labour Court for a determination within the six-week appeal period. If the employer does not pay during this period and if the employee does not apply for implementation, the employee is technically entitled to nothing. This can cause difficulties where an employee believes, or is even assured by the employer, that the recommendation is to be implemented, but this does not in fact occur.

6.2.1.2   Arbitration officer

The Labour Court is the body which acts as the industrial tribunal for equality cases. It sits in divisions with three members in each division and it hears and investigates appeals against Equality Officer recommendations. It may also implement an Equality Officer's recommendation, but it must investigate the claim again in such circumstances.[1]

The Labour Court issues written determinations which are binding on the parties unless appealed to the High Court on a point of law. The Labour Court hearing and determination may be judicially reviewed, and if quashed the matter is referred back to another division of the Court for determination.

The Labour Court hearings are normally held in private unless it is requested that they be public. Both parties provide written submissions and the Court may decide to visit the employer's premises. This often happens in equal pay cases, in order to investigate the work to be compared.

The Labour Court may, if it wishes, hold preliminary hearings about the admissibility of claims under the 1977 Act in relation to time-limits. More usually it does not, and the matter is referred straight to an Equality Officer.

6.2.1.3   Equal opportunities agency

The Employment Equality Agency (EEA) has power to refer cases to the Labour Court and act on behalf of a party in relation to a claim. Also the EEA may refer cases on its own behalf, with the EEA being the named claimant. The EEA can assist persons in bringing their claim to an Equality Officer or to the Labour Court. More generally the EEA gives informal advice to persons with potential grievances, and advises the Government on relevant matters. It has also made use of its power to issue codes of practice

---

1   See *Lissadell Towels Ltd* v. *56 Female Employees,* (1988) 7 JISLL 184 (HC).

by issuing its 1984 *Code of Practice for the Elimination of Sex and Marital Status Discrimination and the Promotion of Equality of Opportunity in Employment.*

The only enforcement powers that the EEA has arise in the context of investigations, which it may carry out under s. 39 of the 1977 Act. If as a result of an investigation the EEA takes the view that discriminatory practices are occurring, then under s. 44 of the Act it may issue a 'non-discrimination notice'. This will specify certain action to be taken by the employer(s) concerned, and the notice is legally binding, subject to an appeal to the Labour Court. The EEA also has other powers to obtain information, summon witnesses etc. in relation to such investigation.

For further details on the EEA, see §6.3 below.

6.2.1.4   Conciliation procedures

The Labour Court may refer an equal treatment claim (i.e. under the 1977 Act) to an Industrial Relations Officer to try to effect a settlement. This is most unusual; the vast majority of claims are referred to an Equality Officer. If a claim is referred to an Industrial Relations Officer, that Officer would use the normal industrial relations conciliation procedures to try to effect a settlement; but if a settlement cannot be effected, the Labour Court can refer the matter to an Equality Officer. Industrial Relations Officers are in the main concerned with industrial relations claims and work within the Labour Relations Commission.

6.2.2   SPECIALIZED TRAINING FOR JUDGES

There is no formal system of training for the judiciary in equality law. The judiciary rely on their formal legal training and their experience and knowledge of general law. For the last decade employment law has been a full course or subject in the universities and also in the professional law schools, but there is no specific requirement for judges to receive training in equality law and no in-service training or other facility for them to do so.

The Equality Officers and the members of the Labour Court are not required to be lawyers; they do not, therefore, have to have formal legal training. However, they may be formally trained in other disciplines and they often have considerable industrial relations experience, for example as trade union officials or as personnel managers or industrial relations negotiators with an employer body. They receive detailed 'in-service' training on new and existing equality and employment legislation.

6.2.3   SPECIALIZATION WITHIN THE SYSTEM

There are very few practising lawyers who specialize in employment law and even fewer with practical knowledge and experience of handling equality cases. There are also a small number of university academics with a good knowledge of equality law.

The vast majority of claimants are represented by their trade union officials, with the assistance of equality experts from their own union or Irish Congress of Trade Unions (ICTU). However, there are no lawyers employed by unions on a full-time basis specifically to handle equality issues. Employers are usually represented by an official from the Irish Business and Employers' Confederation (IBEC).

Trade unions regard equality matters as part of industrial relations and are resistant to the introduction of excessive 'legalism' in this area, believing that legal representation at Equality Officer or Labour Court level reduces the informality and accessibility which has characterized these institutions to date. The question of costs and resources is also relevant.

There have been a number of claims where the parties have been represented by lawyers, usually in individual equal treatment cases. Equal pay claims are more likely to be processed by trade union/employer body personnel assisted on occasions by specialized staff.

6.3   ENFORCEMENT AGENCY

6.3.1   TYPE

6.3.1.1   Labour inspectorate

There is no specific inspectorate in the Department of Enterprise and Employment or in the Department of Equality and Law Reform dealing with equality issues. However, there is an inspectorate in the Department dealing generally with certain terms and conditions of employment, e.g. holidays, certain rates of pay in some industries and services.

6.3.1.2   Equal opportunities agency

The 1977 Act made provision for the establishment of an Employment Equality Agency (EEA) which came into operation on 1 October 1977. This has the general function of promoting equality of opportunity between men and women in relation to employment and to oversee the operation of the equality legislation which existed at that time, namely the 1974 and 1977 Acts. It has no specific functions in relation to the subsequent equality legislation in respect of statutory social security and occupational benefit schemes, except to the extent that pensions and other occupational benefits have since 1977 been seen as falling within the scope of the 1974 Act.

The Board of the EEA consists of a chairperson and 10 members who represent trade unions, women's organizations and other interested parties. All are appointed by the Minister for Equality and Law Reform and are voluntary appointments. There is a full-time executive staff headed by a chief executive. Most of the staff are drawn from the public service, usually the Department of Enterprise and Employment. The EEA has an annual allocation of funds from the Department and must produce annual accounts. An annual report must also be presented to the Minister.

6.3.2   FUNCTIONS

6.3.2.1   Advice

Assistance to claimants

The EEA may provide assistance to a person who considers that there has been a breach of the 1974 or 1977 Acts but the wording of the 1977 Act limits the assistance that the EEA can offer; it only refers to 'assistance' in making a reference to the Labour Court or an Equality Officer.[1] There is no reference to financial assistance. Accordingly, the EEA can only provide assistance which, at its discretion, it sees fit within a non-financial context.

Assistance by the EEA is therefore limited, since no financial assistance is available to process an appeal on a point of law or judicial review proceedings to the High Court. The EEA can assist where it considers that discrimination is being generally practised and in matters where persons have allegedly been procuring a breach of the legislation, and in such cases the EEA would be the named plaintiff.

Invariably, EEA assistance takes the form of advice prior to the reference of a claim. If the claim is brought, assistance would also include the drafting of submissions and subsequent representation before the adjudicating bodies. For many years the EEA has had legally qualified staff who represent claimants before Equality Officers and the Labour Court.

However, the EEA must be satisfied that the proposed claim raises an important matter of principle and that the person would not otherwise be in a position to represent herself or himself adequately. Typically, such claimants are pursuing alleged discriminatory practices where their trade union may have been party to an agreement wherein the alleged discriminatory practice arose.

---

1   Section 48 of the 1977 Act.

Codes of practice

Section 37(2) of the 1977 Act provides that the EEA 'may draft and publish for the information of employers guidelines or codes of practice relating to discrimination in employment'. The EEA issued a code of practice in February 1984 in respect of the elimination of discrimination in employment. The code is not legally binding, but it is admissible in evidence before the adjudicating bodies and courts. In practice, use of the code in the hearing of discrimination cases is rare.

Review of the legislation

The EEA may carry out a review of legislation if it considers that existing legislation impedes the elimination of discrimination. However, the Minister for Equality and Law Reform must authorize it to do so. Over the years, the EEA has reviewed the 1974 and 1977 Acts and has made detailed recommendations for their amendment. It also submitted its views to the National Pensions Board on the appropriate manner of implementation of Directive 86/378/EEC, on equal treatment in occupational benefit schemes.

6.3.2.2 Research

The EEA may undertake and sponsor research and other activities relating to the dissemination of information. To date, it has commissioned research on women working in the electronics sector and has produced a video, mainly directed at schoolgirls, about women working in the electronics industry. A major report, *Women in the Labour Force*, was published in June 1989. The EEA has clearly been hampered by the lack of necessary financial resources. More recently (early 1992) the EEA published a booklet entitled *A Model Equal Opportunities Policy*, which gives a detailed overview of the implementation of such a policy. The same booklet includes a model grievance procedure to avoid sexual harassment in the workplace.

The EEA publishes a quarterly newsletter, *Equality News*. It has also advanced public awareness of equality issues through regular press releases and considerable coverage in the media.

6.3.2.3 Legal aid

There is no provision for financial legal aid. As stated at §6.3.2.1 above, the EEA provides direct legal assistance through its legally qualified staff.

6.3.3   REMEDIES

6.3.3.1   Notice

The EEA has power to conduct investigations[1] and these may be either requested by the Minister for Equality and Law Reform or carried out with the Minister's approval. Again the terms of reference of the investigation must be drawn up by the EEA or must have the Minister's approval if she or he has requested the investigation.

In summary, an investigation may only be carried out if the EEA or the Minister considers that there is or has been discrimination in the employment concerned; or if there has been discriminatory advertising; or if there has been an attempt to procure discrimination, or generally if there have been discriminatory practices. The EEA has statutory powers to obtain information and documents and to summon witnesses. If a person does not comply with such a request, that person is guilty of an offence and may be liable to a fine.[2]

When an investigation has been completed, the EEA prepares a report and makes recommendations. If the EEA is satisfied that there has been discrimination in employment, it may serve a non-discrimination notice on the employer or other person in question. The non-discrimination notice must detail the discriminatory practice. The Act provides for time-limits in which to respond to such notices and also in which to appeal to the Labour Court against the notice. If the notice has not been appealed, its contents will come into effect, e.g. the discriminatory practice must be discontinued. The Labour Court has power to hear the views of both sides on the appeal.

EEA investigations are very rare. They have only been carried out in two large undertakings to date.

6.3.3.2   Injunction

The EEA can request the High Court to grant an injunction against a discriminatory practice if the EEA considers that within five years of the operation of a non-discriminatory notice there is a likelihood of the discriminatory practice recurring.[3]

6.3.3.3   Compensation

Compensation may be awarded up to a maximum of 104 weeks' pay as the Court sees fit. There is no provision for compensation arising out of a

---

1   Section 39 of the 1977 Act.
2   Section 42 of the 1977 Act.
3   Section 47 of the 1977 Act.

non-discrimination notice unless there is a reference of the matter to the Labour Court.

6.4 COLLECTIVE AGREEMENTS

6.4.1 EQUAL PAY CLAUSE

Collective agreements may not contain provisions for pay differences based on, or related to, the sex of employees.[1] On the other hand, it is not obligatory for them to contain any positive commitment to equal pay or equal treatment. In practice, very few collective agreements contain equality clauses.

6.4.2 AUTOMATIC NULLITY

Section 5 of the 1974 Act provides that any provisions for differences in rates of remuneration in collective agreements or registered agreements, which are based on, or related to, the sex of the employees, will be null and void. However, the individual employee must still bring a claim under the Act in order to obtain redress; she or he must seek a recommendation or determination stating that she or he is entitled to equal pay and providing for back pay (if any). Thus the provision for automatic nullity, in the absence of any provision for automatic redress, has always been seen as unsatisfactory.

6.4.3 COLLECTIVE REDRESS

There is no provision for collective redress as claims are made on the individual contract of employment. In a claim under the 1974 Act, the legal advice to the Court concluded that 'each individual woman's claim for equal pay with a man' must be judged 'as a separate issue thus ruling out an approach which would judge the generality of the work done by a group of men in the same employment'. Furthermore, even if there are group claims, i.e. with claimants doing the same work, technically there have to be separate decisions for each individual claimant.

The 1977 Act appears to provide for wider remedies. For example, s. 22 provides that the Court can 'recommend to a person a certain course of action'. However, again each individual claim is founded on the individual contract of employment.

The EEA has powers to initiate proceedings and also to conduct investigations. Section 20 provides that the EEA can refer to the Labour Court alleged discrimination which is being practised against persons, discriminatory advertising, and attempts to procure discrimination. The EEA has not used its investigatory powers very frequently.

---

1   Section 5 of the 1974 Act.

To date most claims have arisen out of the individual contract of employment and hidden or structural discrimination has not been ventilated before the adjudicating bodies except in relation to a particular claim.

6.4.4   AGENCY MONITORING

The EEA continuously monitors rates of pay and equal treatment in all the industries and also in the general public service. It simply is not feasible to monitor each individual employment relationship.

6.4.5   CONTRACT COMPLIANCE

Contract compliance means that the awarding of public sector contracts should be dependent on the observance of the principles of non-discrimination. It is not a strategy which has been used in Ireland.

SOURCES OF
EQUALITY LAW

7. CONSTITUTION AND LEGISLATION

7.1 CONSTITUTIONAL PROVISIONS ON EQUALITY [1]

Art. 9–Nationality and citizenship

1.   1   On the coming into operation of this Constitution any person who was a citizen of Saorstát Éireann immediately before the coming into operation of this Constitution shall become and be a citizen of Ireland.
  2   The future acquisition and loss of Irish nationality and citizenship shall be determined in accordance with law.
  3   No person may be excluded from Irish nationality and citizenship by reason of the sex of such person.
2.   Fidelity to the nation and loyalty to the State are fundamental political duties of all citizens.

Art. 16–Dáil Éireann

1.   1   Every citizen without distinction of sex who has reached the age of twenty-one years, and who is not placed under disability or incapacity by this Constitution or by law, shall be eligible for membership of Dáil Éireann.
  2   Every citizen without distinction of sex who has reached the age of eighteen years who is not disqualified by law and complies with the provisions of the law relating to the election of members of Dáil Éireann, shall have the right to vote at an election for members of Dáil Éireann.
  3   No law may be enacted placing any citizen under disability or incapacity for membership of Dáil Éireann on the ground of sex or disqualifying any citizen from voting at an election for members of Dáil Éireann on that ground.
  4   No voter may exercise more than one vote at an election for Dáil Éireann, and the voting shall be by secret ballot.

Art. 40–Personal rights

1.   All citizens shall, as human persons, be held equal before the law.

---

[1]   The Irish Constitution of 1937 contains a number of references to equality between the sexes. It forbids any exclusions, by reason of sex, from Irish nationality and citizenship (art. 9.1.3), from eligibility for membership of Dáil Éireann (the national parliament), or from voting for members of Dáil Éireann (art. 16.1.1 and 16.1.2); and it prevents the enactment of any law excluding citizens from such membership, or such voting, on grounds of sex (art. 16.1.3). The most significant articles on equality are, however, arts 40 and 41 which deal, respectively, with 'Personal rights' and 'The family'. Article 45, on 'Directive principles of social policy', is also relevant.

This shall not be held to mean that the State shall not in its enactments have due regard to differences of capacity, physical and moral, and of social function.

Art. 41–The family

1.　1　The State recognizes the Family as the natural primary and fundamental unit group of Society, and as a moral institution possessing inalienable and imprescriptible rights, antecedent and superior to all positive law.

　　　2　The State, therefore, guarantees to protect the Family in its constitution and authority, as the necessary basis of social order and as indispensable to the welfare of the Nation and the State.

2.　1　In particular, the State recognizes that by her life within the home, woman gives to the State a support without which the common good cannot be achieved.

　　　2　The State shall, therefore, endeavour to ensure that mothers shall not be obliged by economic necessity to engage in labour to the neglect of their duties in the home.

3.　1　The State pledges itself to guard with special care the institution of Marriage, on which the Family is founded, and to protect it against attack.

　　　2　No law shall be enacted providing for the grant of a dissolution of marriage.

　　　3　No person whose marriage has been dissolved under the civil law of any other State but is a subsisting valid marriage under the law for the time being in force within the jurisdiction of the Government and Parliament established by this Constitution shall be capable of contracting a valid marriage within that jurisdiction during the lifetime of the other party to the marriage so dissolved.

Art. 45–Directive principles of social policy

　　　The principles of social policy set forth in this Article are intended for the general guidance of the Oireachtas. The application of those principles in the making of laws shall be the care of the Oireachtas exclusively, and shall not be cognisable by any Court under any of the provisions of this Constitution.

1.　The State shall strive to promote the welfare of the whole people by securing and protecting as effectively as it may a social order in which justice and charity shall inform all the institutions of the national life.

2.　The State shall, in particular, direct its policy towards securing:

　　(i)　That the citizens (all of whom, men and women equally, have the right to an adequate means of livelihood) may through their occupations find the means of making reasonable provision for their domestic needs.

　　(ii)　That the ownership and control of the material resources of the community may be distributed amongst private individuals and the various classes as best to subserve the common good.

(iii) That, especially, the operation of free competition shall not be allowed so to develop as to result in the concentration of the ownership or control of essential commodities in a few individuals to the common detriment.

(iv) That in what pertains to the control of credit the constant and predominant aim shall be the welfare of the people as a whole.

(v) That there may be established on the land in economic security as many families as in the circumstances shall be practicable.

3. 1 The State shall favour and, where necessary, supplement private initiative in industry and commerce.

2 The State shall endeavour to secure that private enterprise shall be so conducted as to ensure reasonable efficiency in the production and distribution of goods and as to protect the public against unjust exploitation.

4. 1 The State pledges itself to safeguard with especial care the economic interests of the weaker sections of the community, and, where necessary, to contribute to the support of the infirm, the widow, the orphan, and the aged.

2 The State shall endeavour to ensure that the strength and health of workers, men and women, and the tender age of children shall not be abused and that citizens shall not be forced by economic necessity to enter avocations unsuited to their sex, age or strength.

7.2   NATIONAL ACTS APPROVING INTERNATIONAL TREATIES IN MATTERS OF EQUALITY [1]

7.2.1   INTERNATIONAL LABOUR ORGANIZATION (ILO) CONVENTIONS

Ireland has ratified ILO Convention No 100 on Equal Remuneration, 1971. It has also ratified part of ILO Convention No 118 on Equality of Treatment (Social Security), 1962, ss (a) to (g) but not the remaining provisions.

Three earlier ILO Conventions on Night Work were also ratified by Ireland: Nos 4, 41 and 89 of 1919, 1934 and 1948 respectively. However, the first two of these were denounced as a result of the third; and No 89 was denounced in February 1983. Similarly, Convention No 45 on Underground Work (Women), 1935, was denounced by the Irish government in May 1988, to take effect from May 1989.

Other relevant Conventions, such as Nos 3 and 103 on Maternity Protection, No 111 on Discrimination (Employment and Occupation), and No 156 on Workers with Family Responsibilities, have not been ratified.

7.2.2   UNITED NATIONS (UN) CONVENTION ON THE ELIMINATION OF ALL FORMS OF DISCRIMINATION AGAINST WOMEN

In December 1985, Ireland acceded to the UN Convention on the Elimination of All Forms of Discrimination Against Women, entering a number of reservations. Two of these reservations were withdrawn in June 1986 following the enactment of the Irish Nationality and Citizenship Act 1986 and the Domicile and Recognition of Foreign Divorces Act 1986. The remaining reservations are as follows:

Article 13(b) and (c)

The question of supplementing the guarantee of equality contained in the Irish Constitution with special legislation governing access to financial credit and other services and recreational activities, where these are provided by private persons, organizations or enterprises is under consideration. For the time being Ireland reserves the right to regard its existing law and measures in this area as appropriate for the attainment in Ireland of the objectives of the Convention.

---

1   There are no national Acts which specifically approve international treaties in matters of equality. However, a number of ILO Conventions have been ratified (some of which were subsequently denounced); and in December 1985 Ireland acceded to the UN Convention on the Elimination of all Forms of Discrimination Against Women, with a number of reservations.

Article 15

With regard to paragraph 3 of this article, Ireland reserves the right not to supplement the existing provisions in Irish law which accord women a legal capacity identical to that of men, with further legislation governing the validity of any contract or other private instrument freely entered into by a women.

Article 16.1(d) and (f)

Ireland is of the view that the attainment in Ireland of the objectives of the Convention does not necessitate the extension to men of rights identical to those accorded by law to women in respect of the guardianship, adoption and custody of children born out of wedlock and reserves the right to implement the Convention subject to that understanding.

Article 11.1 and 13(a)

Ireland reserves the right to regard the Anti-Discrimination (Pay) Act 1974, and the Employment Equality Act 1977, and other measures taken in implementation of the European Economic Community standards concerning employment opportunities and pay as sufficient implementation of arts 11.1(b), (c) and (d).

Ireland reserves the right for the time being to maintain provisions of Irish legislation in the area of social security which are more favourable to women than men.

In August 1986, the then Minister of State for Women's Affairs circulated draft legislative proposals designed to allow the Irish Government to withdraw the above reservations on art. 13 of the Convention. The draft proposals provided for the extension of equal treatment to goods, services and facilities; and it was stated, in late 1986, that the Government's intention was to produce a Bill within three to six months and have it before the Parliament by Easter 1987. However, a change of government took place in February 1987, and the Equal Treatment Bill which had been prepared fell automatically as a result.

In the course of 1987 and 1988 it became apparent that the new administration had effectively shelved the legislation drafted by its predecessor.

The position is, therefore, that despite acceding to this UN Convention in 1985, the Irish Government's reservations on art. 13 (and others) still stand; and no national legislation has been enacted to implement the principles therein. The Government has however submitted a 'progress report' to the UN Secretariat detailing the measures which have been taken to give effect to the other provisions of the Convention (February 1987).

7.3   NATIONAL TEXTS CONTAINING GENERAL PROVISIONS ON EQUALITY

7.3.1   EMPLOYMENT

Until the equality legislation of 1974 and 1977, Irish employment law contained no specific provisions relating to sex discrimination. However, a number of Acts are considered to have contained discriminatory provisions. In some cases, these have been partly or wholly amended; in other cases, discussion continues as to the desirability or otherwise of amendments proposed. The most significant Acts and Regulations in this context are outlined below.

7.3.1.1   Industrial night-work

The Conditions of Employment Acts 1936 and 1944 prohibited the employment of women in industry between the hours of 10 pm and 8 am and stipulated a minimum interval of 11 hours between work periods. Although these provisions were in line with ILO Convention No 89, they attracted considerable criticism and were eventually denounced by the government with effect from February 1983. In March 1986, an order was issued under s. 14 of the Employment Equality Act 1977 amending ss 46 and 49 of the Conditions of Employment Act 1936 so as to remove the ban on women working at night and on Sundays. This regulation, the Employment Equality (Employment of Women) Order 1986, came into force on 4 May 1987.[1]

As a result of this change, employers are in most cases no longer required to obtain exclusion orders permitting the employment of women on shift work at night. However, as a result of negotiations with the Irish Congress of Trade Unions (which had expressed reservations about the removal of the ban on night-work for women in the absence of improved conditions for shift workers generally and pregnant shift workers in particular), the Department of Labour agreed in 1987 that when shift work licences were granted thereafter, in respect of night-work, and irrespective of the sex of the workers concerned, there would be attached to the licence (i) a requirement that the employer provide heating facilities for food, (ii) a recommendation that pregnant employees be given the option of transferring from night-work if this was considered medically advisable, and (iii) a recommendation that if public transport was not available to workers on night shift, consultations on alternative transport arrangements would take place. Other conditions sought by the ICTU were deemed to be matters for local negotiation (e.g. childcare arrangements and flexible working hours) and are not dealt with either as a requirement or a recommendation.

---

1   SI No 112 of 1987.

7.3.1.2 Weight-lifting

Regulation 2 of the Factories Act 1955 (Manual Labour) (Maximum Weights and Transport) Regulations 1972 lays down different maximum weights which can be lifted by men and women in industry (55 kilos for adult men, 16 kilos for adult women and men aged 16 to 18, 11 kilos for women aged 16 to 18, and 8 kilos for 14- to 16-year-olds of both sexes). Regulation 5(2) also limits the employment of pregnant women where medical opinion considers this harmful to herself or the child. These regulations are still in force. The Employment Equality Agency issued a report on the matter in 1981 recommending 'no change at this time' but seeking additional legislation to provide mechanical aids and weight-lifting devices; adequate training in, and supervision of, such aids and devices; frequent medical examinations for workers involved in weight-lifting; and exemption of pregnant workers from weight-lifting operations. No such legislation has yet been forthcoming.

7.3.1.3 Seats in shops

Section 56(1) of the Shops (Conditions of Employment) Act 1938 requires employers to provide seats for women but not for men. This is considered discriminatory against men but is still in force despite recommendations for deletion.

7.3.1.4 Mines and quarries

A number of sections of the Mines and Quarries Act 1965 have been identified as discriminatory. Sections 107(1) and (2) specify that no women shall be employed below ground at a mine and ss 110(1) to (6) set out conditions attaching to the employment of women at a mine.

In 1985, the Act was amended by the Employment Equality Act 1977 (Employment of Females in Mines) Order 1985.[1] Thus the employment of women in mines is now permitted for certain categories, such as non-manual management functions, health and welfare services, and necessary underground training as part of a study course.

In May 1988 Ireland registered its denunciation of ILO Convention No 45 of 1936. This took effect in May 1989, clearing the way for the amendment of the Mines and Quarries Act to permit the employment of all women below ground at a mine, although this has not yet happened.

7.3.1.5 Working with lead

Sections 68(1) and (2), 69, 70(1) and (2), and 90 of the Factories Act 1955 (as amended by the Safety in Industry Act 1980) have been identified

---

[1]   SI No 176 of 1985.

as discriminatory against women, along with associated regulations. The Employment Equality Agency has recommended amendment of these instruments while retaining the special mention of pregnant workers. It has also made detailed recommendations on the application in Ireland of Directive 82/605/EEC on the protection of workers from risks related to exposure at work to metallic lead and its ionic compounds.[1] However, regulations issued in September 1988 did not amend any of the above sections of the Safety in Industry Acts which were regarded as discriminatory.

7.3.2   TAXATION

Following the Supreme Court decision in *Murphy* v. *AG*,[2] which ruled that discrimination against married couples in the tax system contravened art. 41 of the Constitution (which commits the State to protecting the institution of marriage), the taxation system was changed to ensure that married couples would no longer receive less favourable tax treatment than unmarried persons living together. These changes were contained in ss 18 to 21 of the Finance Act 1980, which amended Chapter 1, Part IX of the Income Tax Act 1967 (ss 192 to 197 of that Act having been judged unconstitutional).[3]

7.3.3   JURY SERVICE

Under the Juries Act 1927 women were specifically excluded from serving as jurors (s. 5) unless they applied to be included and fulfilled the various other qualifications (which involved being a ratepayer aged between 21 and 65 years and having land with a rateable valuation in excess of a prescribed minimum). In *de Burca* v. *AG*,[4] it was established in evidence that only two women had served on juries within the previous ten years. The Supreme Court found that: (a) the exclusion of citizens who were not ratepayers; and (b) the conditional exclusion of women from the lists of jurors was inconsistent with the provisions of the Constitution. New legislation was subsequently enacted, with revised eligibility requirements: the Juries Act 1976 requires only that jurors be between the ages of 18 and 70 and enrolled on the electoral register for parliamentary elections.

---

1   Employment Equality Agency, *Report to Minister for Labour*, 1985.
2   [1982] IR 241 (SC); see below.
3   Sections 20 and 21 of the Finance Act 1980 were subsequently declared invalid by another constitutional challenge: see reference to *Muckley* v. *Ireland*, §8.1.3 below.
4   [1976] IR 38 (SC).

7.4 NATIONAL TEXTS IMPLEMENTING EC DIRECTIVES: EQUAL PAY

7.4.1 Anti-Discrimination (Pay) Act 1974[1]

1–Interpretation

(1) In this Act

'collective agreement' means an agreement relating to terms and conditions of employment made between parties who are or represent employers and parties who are or represent employees;

'the Court' means the Labour Court;

[[2]'dismissal' shall be taken to include the termination by an employee of her contract of employment with her employer (whether prior notice of the termination was or was not given to the employer) in circumstances in which, because of the conduct of the employer, the employee was or would have been entitled to terminate the contract without giving such notice, or it was or would have been reasonable for her to do so, and 'dismissed' shall be construed accordingly];

'employed' means employed under a contract of service or apprenticeship or a contract personally to execute any work or labour;

'the Minister' means the Minister for Labour;

'place' includes a city, town or locality;

'remuneration' includes any consideration, whether in cash or in kind, which an employee receives, directly or indirectly, in respect of his employment from his employer.

(2) In this Act a reference to a section is to a section of this Act unless it is indicated that reference to some other enactment is intended.

(3) In this Act a reference to a subsection is to the subsection of the section in which the reference occurs unless it is indicated that reference to some other section is intended.

2–Entitlement to equal pay

(1) Subject to this Act, it shall be a term of the contract under which a woman is employed in any place that she shall be entitled to the same rate of remuneration as a man who is employed in that place by the same employer (or by an associated employer if the employees, whether generally or of a particular class, of both employers have the same terms and conditions of employment), if both are employed on like work.

(2) For the purposes of this section two employers shall be taken to be associated if one is a body corporate of which the other (whether directly or

---

1   No 15 of 1974, implementing Directive 75/117/EEC. The Act came into force on 31 December 1975, and is printed here as amended by the Employment Equality Act 1977.

2   Inserted by s. 29 of the Employment Equality Act 1977.

indirectly) has control or if both are bodies corporate of which a third person (whether directly or indirectly) has control.

(3) Nothing in this Act shall prevent an employer from paying to his employees who are employed on like work in the same place different rates of remuneration on grounds other than sex.

3–Like work

Two persons shall be regarded as employed on like work —
(a) where both perform the same work under the same or similar conditions, or where each is in every respect interchangeable with the other in relation to the work, or
(b) where the work performed by one is of a similar nature to that performed by the other and any differences between the work performed or the conditions under which it is performed by each occur only infrequently or are of small importance in relation to the work as a whole, or
(c) where the work performed by one is equal in value to that performed by the other in terms of the demands it makes in relation to such matters as skill, physical or mental effort, responsibility and working conditions.

4–Equal pay entitlement implied

Where a woman is employed otherwise than under a contract, or is employed under a contract which does not include (whether expressly or by reference to a collective agreement or otherwise) a term satisfying section 2, the terms and conditions of her employment shall include an implied term giving effect to that section, and such an implied term shall, where it conflicts with an express term, override it.

5–Collective agreements, etc. basing remuneration on sex of employees

(1) Where after the commencement of this Act an agreement or order to which this section applies contains a provision in which differences in rates of remuneration are based on or related to the sex of employees, such a provision shall be null and void.
(2) This section applies to —
(a) a collective agreement made after the commencement of this Act,
(b) an employment regulation order within the meaning of Part IV of the Industrial Relations Act 1946, made after the commencement of this Act,
(c) a registered employment agreement within the meaning of Part III of the Industrial Relations Act 1946, registered in the Register of Employment Agreements after the commencement of this Act, and
(d) an order made by the Agricultural Wages Board under section 17 of the Agricultural Wages Act 1936, after the commencement of this Act.

6–[¹Equality officers]

(1) The Minister, after consultation with the Court and with the consent of the Minister for the Public Service, may appoint as [equality officers] of the Court, such and so many persons as he thinks fit and a person so appointed shall be known (and is in this Act referred to) as an [equality officer].

(2) An [equality officer] shall carry out the functions assigned to him by this Act and shall hold office on such terms and receive such remuneration as the Minister for the Public Service determines.

(3) An [equality officer] may provide for the regulation of proceedings before him in relation to an investigation by him under this Act.

(4) (a) An [equality officer] may, for the purpose of obtaining any information which he may require for enabling him to exercise his functions under this Act, do any one or more of the following things:
    (i) at all reasonable times enter premises,
    (ii) require an employer or his representative to produce to him any records, books or documents in the employer's power or control and which the officer has reasonable grounds for believing to contain information of the kind so required and to give him such information as he may reasonably require in regard to any entries in any such records, books or documents,
    (iii) inspect and copy or take extracts from any such records, books or documents,
    (iv) inspect any work in progress in the premises.

(b) Any person who obstructs or impedes an [equality officer] in the exercise of his powers under this subsection or does not comply with a requirement of an [equality officer] under this subsection shall be guilty of an offence under this section and shall be liable on summary conviction to a fine not exceeding £100 or on conviction on indictment to a fine not exceeding £1,000.

(5) An investigation by an [equality officer] shall be conducted in private.

7–Investigation by [equality officers]

(1) A dispute between an employer and an employee in relation to the existence or operation of a term (in this section referred to as an equal pay clause) included by virtue of section 2 in a contract of employment or implied by virtue of section 4 in terms and conditions of employment may be referred by a party to the dispute to an [equality officer] for investigation and

---

1   These officers were under the original terms of the Act referred to as Equal Pay Officers; this was changed to Equality Officer under s. 18 of the Employment Equality Act 1977.

recommendation and shall upon such reference be investigated in accordance with this Act and not under any other existing provision or arrangement.

(2) Where it appears to [¹the Agency] that an employer has failed to comply with an equal pay clause but that either no dispute has arisen in relation thereto or it is not reasonable to expect the employee concerned to refer a dispute in relation to such a clause to an [equality officer], the matter may be referred to an [equality officer] by the Minister and shall thereupon be dealt with as if it were a reference under subsection (1) of a dispute by an employee.

(3) Where a dispute is referred under this section to an [equality officer] he shall investigate the dispute and issue a recommendation thereon.

(4) A recommendation under this section shall be conveyed to the Court, to the parties to the dispute and, in the case of a dispute referred to in subsection (2), also to [²the Agency].

8–Investigation by Labour Court

(1) (a) A party to a dispute in relation to which an [equality officer] has made a recommendation may appeal to the Court against the recommendation or may appeal to the Court for a determination that the recommendation has not been implemented.

(b) The Court shall hear and decide an appeal under this subsection and shall convey its determination to the parties and, in the case of a dispute mentioned in section 7(2), also to [the Agency].

(c) (i) A hearing under this subsection shall be held in private, but the Court shall, if requested to do so by a party to the dispute, hold the hearing in public.

(ii) Where a hearing under this subsection is being held in public the Court may, if it is satisfied that any part of the hearing concerns a matter that should, in the interests of any party to the dispute, be treated as confidential, hold that part of the hearing in private.

(d) Sections 14 and 21 of the Industrial Relations Act 1946 shall apply to an appeal under this section.

(e) An appeal under this section shall be lodged in the Court not later than 42 days after the date of the [equality officer's] recommendation and the notice shall specify the grounds of the appeal.

(2) Any information obtained by an [equality officer] or by the Court in the course of an investigation or appeal under this Act as to any trade union or person or as to the business carried on by any person which is not

---

1   This function was originally given to the Minister for Labour, but was transferred to the Employment Equality Agency after its establishment by virtue of s. 36(1) of the Employment Equality Act 1977.

2   Amended by s. 36(1) of the Employment Equality Act 1977; the reference here is to the Employment Equality Agency.

available otherwise shall not be included in any recommendation or determination without the consent of the trade union or person concerned, nor shall any person concerned in proceedings before an [equality officer] or the Court disclose any such information without such consent.

(3) A party to a dispute determined by the Court under subsection (1) may appeal to the High Court on a point of law.

(4) (a) Where an employee complains to the Court that an employer has failed or neglected to implement a determination of the Court under this section, the following provisions shall have effect:

  (i) the Court shall consider the complaint and shall hear all persons appearing to the Court to be interested and desiring to be heard,

  (ii) if after such consideration the Court is satisfied that the complaint is well founded, the Court may by order direct the employer to do such things as will in the opinion of the Court result in the determination being implemented by the employer.

(b) If, where an order is made by the Court under paragraph (a), the direction contained in the order is not carried out within two months from the date of the making of the order (or, where there is an appeal under subsection (3), within two months of the date of the order of the High Court on the appeal) the person to whom the direction is given shall be guilty of an offence and shall be liable on summary conviction to a fine not exceeding £100 and, in the case of a continuing offence, a further fine not exceeding £10 for every day during which the offence is continued.

(c) (i) Where on a conviction for an offence under this section the court is satisfied that a person (in this paragraph referred to as the plaintiff) would be entitled to recover in a civil action arrears of remuneration, the court may, if it thinks fit and the plaintiff present or represented consents, impose on the convicted person, in addition to any other punishment, a fine not exceeding the amount which in the opinion of the court the plaintiff would be entitled to recover against the convicted person in respect of such arrears of remuneration.

  (ii) The amount of a fine imposed under subparagraph (i) shall be paid to the plaintiff.

  (iii) The payment by a convicted person of a fine imposed under subparagraph (i) shall be a good defence to any civil action brought by the plaintiff in respect of the arrears of remuneration referred to in that subparagraph.

  (iv) Without prejudice to any right of appeal by any other person, the plaintiff shall have a right of appeal limited to the amount of the fine, either (as the case may be) to the High Court or to the judge of the Circuit Court in whose circuit the district (or any part thereof) of the Justice of the District Court by whom the fine was imposed is situated, and the decision on such an appeal shall be final.

(5) In any proceedings brought by a person to recover arrears of remuneration to which he is entitled under this Act the person shall not be entitled to be awarded any payment by way of such arrears in respect of a time earlier than three years before the date on which the relevant dispute was referred under section 7 to an [equality officer].

9—Dismissal because of equal pay claim

(1) Where a woman claims from her employer the same rate of remuneration as a man employed by the same employer (or by an associated employer within the meaning of section 2) in the same place on like work and subsequent to the making of the claim the employer dismisses the woman from her employment solely or mainly because she made the claim, the employer shall be guilty of an offence and shall be liable on summary conviction to a fine not exceeding £100 or on conviction on indictment to a fine not exceeding £1,000.

(2) In a prosecution for an offence under this section the onus shall be on the employer to satisfy the court that the making of the claim was not the sole or principal reason for the dismissal.

(3) (a) [[1]On a conviction for an offence under this section, the court may, if it thinks fit and the dismissed woman is present or represented and consents —

   (i) order the re-instatement by the employer of the dismissed woman in the position which she held immediately before her dismissal on the terms and conditions on which she was employed immediately before her dismissal, together with a term that the re-instatement shall be deemed to have commenced on the day of the dismissal,

   (ii) order the re-engagement by the employer of the dismissed woman either in the position which she held immediately before her dismissal or in a different position which would be reasonably suitable for her on such terms and conditions as are reasonable having regard to all the circumstances, or

   (iii) impose on the convicted person, in addition to a fine imposed under subsection (1), a fine not exceeding the amount which in the opinion of the court the dismissed woman would have received from the employer concerned by way of remuneration if the dismissal had not occurred, but not in any case more than 104 weeks' remuneration.]

(b) The amount of a fine imposed under paragraph (a) shall be paid to the plaintiff.

(c) The payment by a convicted person of a fine imposed under paragraph (a) shall be a good defence to any civil action brought by

---

1   Inserted by s. 30 of the Employment Equality Act 1977.

the plaintiff in respect of the arrears of remuneration referred to in that paragraph.

(d) Without prejudice to any right of appeal by any other person, the plaintiff shall have a right of appeal limited to the amount of the fine, either (as the case may be) to the High Court or the judge of the Circuit Court in whose circuit the district (or any part thereof) of the Justice of the District Court by whom the fine was imposed is situated, and the decision on such an appeal shall be final.

10–Provisions applying to dismissal because of equal pay claim

(1) Where a woman, in respect of whose dismissal a prosecution for an offence under section 9 has not been brought, complains to the Court that she has been dismissed from her employment solely or mainly because she had claimed from her former employer the same rate of remuneration as a man employed by the same employer (or by an associated employer within the meaning of section 2) in the same place on like work, the following provisions shall apply:

(a) the Court shall investigate the complaint, and shall hear all persons appearing to the Court to be interested and desiring to be heard;

(b) an investigation under this subsection shall be held in private, but the Court shall, if requested to do so by a party to the dispute, hold the investigation in public;

(c) where an investigation under this subsection is being held in public the Court may, if it is satisfied that any part of the investigation concerns a matter that should, in the interests of any party to the dispute, be treated as confidential, hold that part of the investigation in private;

(d) [[1]if after such investigation the Court is satisfied that the complaint is well founded, the Court may —

  (i) order the re-instatement by the employer of the dismissed woman in the position which she held immediately before her dismissal on the terms and conditions on which she was employed immediately before her dismissal, together with a term that the re-instatement shall be deemed to have commenced on the day of the dismissal,

  (ii) order the re-engagement by the employer of the dismissed woman either in the position which she held immediately before her dismissal or in a different position which would be reasonably suitable for her on such terms and conditions as are reasonable having regard to all the circumstances, or

  (iii) by order direct the employer to pay to the dismissed woman such compensation as the Court considers reasonable in the circumstances, but not in any case more than 104 weeks' remuneration.]

---

1   Inserted by s. 31(1) of the Employment Equality Act 1977.

(2)   Subject to subsection (5), if where an order is made by the Court under subsection (1) the direction contained in the order is not carried out within two months of the date of the making of the order (or, where there is an appeal under subsection (5) against the order, within two months of the date of the order of the Circuit Court on the appeal), the person to whom the direction is given shall be guilty of an offence and shall be liable on summary conviction to a fine not exceeding £100 and, in the case of a continuing offence, to a further fine not exceeding £10 for every day during which the offence is continued.

(3)   (a)   [[1]On a conviction for an offence under this section, the court may, if it thinks fit and the dismissed person is present or represented and consents:

   (i)   order the re-instatement by the employer of the dismissed woman in the position which she held immediately before her dismissal on the terms and conditions on which she was employed immediately before her dismissal, together with a term that the re-instatement shall be deemed to have commenced on the day of the dismissal,

   (ii)   order the re-engagement by the employer of the dismissed woman either in the position which she held immediately before her dismissal or in a different position which would be reasonably suitable for her on such terms and conditions as are reasonable having regard to all the circumstances, or

   (iii)   impose on the convicted person, in addition to a fine imposed under subsection (2), a fine not exceeding the amount which in the opinion of the court the dismissed woman would have received from the employer concerned by way of remuneration if the dismissal had not occurred, but not in any case more than 104 weeks' remuneration.]

(b)   The amount of a fine imposed under paragraph (a) shall be paid to the plaintiff.

(c)   The payment by a convicted person of a fine imposed under paragraph (a) shall be a good defence to any civil action brought by the plaintiff in respect of the arrears of remuneration referred to in that paragraph.

(d)   Without prejudice to any right of appeal by any other person, the plaintiff shall have a right of appeal limited to the amount of the fine, either (as the case may be) to the High Court or to the judge of the Circuit Court in whose circuit the district (or any part thereof) of the Justice of the District Court by whom the fine was imposed is situated, and the decision on such an appeal shall be final.

---

1   Inserted by s. 31(1) of the Employment Equality Act 1977.

(4)   Save only where [¹a] reasonable cause can be shown, a complaint under this section shall be lodged not later than six months from the date of dismissal.

(5)   A person to whom a direction is given in an order under subsection (1) may, notwithstanding section 17 of the Industrial Relations Act 1946, appeal against the order to the judge of the Circuit Court in whose circuit the person carries on business.

11–Application of Act to men

Sections 2(1), 4, 9(1) and 10(1) shall be construed as applying equally, in a case converse to that referred to in those sections, to a man in relation to his remuneration relative to that of a woman.

12–Expenses

The expenses incurred in the administration of this Act shall, to such extent as may be sanctioned by the Minister for Finance, be paid out of moneys provided by the Oireachtas.

13–Commencement

This Act shall come into operation on the 31st day of December 1975.

14–Short title

This Act may be cited as the Anti-Discrimination (Pay) Act 1974.

---

1   Corrected by s. 31(1) of the Employment Equality Act 1977; the original text read: 'Save only where no reasonable cause can be shown ... '.

7.5   NATIONAL TEXTS IMPLEMENTING
EC DIRECTIVES: EQUAL TREATMENT

7.5.1   Employment Equality Act 1977[1]

1–Interpretation

(1) In this Act

'the Act of 1946' means the Industrial Relations Act 1946;

'the Act of 1974' means the Anti-Discrimination (Pay) Act 1974;

'act' includes a deliberate omission;

'advertisement' includes every form of advertisement, whether to the public or not and whether in a newspaper or other publication, on television or radio or by display of a notice or by any other means, and references to the publishing of advertisements shall be construed accordingly;

'the Agency' means the Employment Equality Agency established by section 34;

'close relative' means a wife, husband, parent, child, grandparent, grandchild, brother or sister;

'the Court' means the Labour Court;

'dismissal' shall be taken to include the termination by an employee of his contract of employment with his employer (whether prior notice of termination was or was not given to the employer) in circumstances in which, because of the conduct of the employer, the employee was or would have been entitled to terminate the contract without giving such notice, or it was or would have been reasonable for him to do so, and 'dismissed' shall be construed accordingly;

'employee' means a person who has entered into or works under (or, in the case of a contract which has been terminated, worked under) a contract of employment with an employer, whether the contract is (or was) for manual labour, clerical work or otherwise, is (or was) expressed or implied, oral or in writing, and whether it is (or was) a contract of service or apprenticeship or otherwise, and includes a civil servant of the State or of the Government and an officer or servant of a local authority within the meaning of the Local Government Act 1941, an officer or servant of a harbour authority, health board, vocational education committee or committee of agriculture, and cognate words or expressions shall be construed accordingly;

'employer', in relation to an employee, means the person by whom the employee is (or, in a case where the employment has ceased, was) employed under a contract of employment, and for the purposes of this

---

[1]   No 16 of 1977, implementing Directive 76/207/EEC; the Act came into force on 1 July 1977. The Act is printed here as amended by the European Communities (Employment Equality) Regulations 1982 (SI No 302 of 1982), and the European Communities (Employment Equality) Regulations 1985 (SI No 331 of 1985).

definition a civil servant of the State or of the Government shall be deemed to be employed by the State or the Government (as the case may be) and an officer or servant of a local authority within the meaning of the Local Government Act 1941, or of a harbour authority, health board, vocational educational committee or committee of agriculture shall be deemed to be employed by the local authority, harbour authority, health board, vocational educational committee or committee of agriculture (as the case may be);

'employment agency' means a person who, whether for profit or otherwise, provides services related to the finding of employment for prospective employees or the supplying of employees to employers;

'functions' includes powers and duties;

'investigation' means an investigation under section 39;

'the Minister' means the Minister for Labour;

'non-discrimination notice' means a notice under section 44;

'profession' includes any vocation or occupation;

'trade union' has the same meaning as it has in the Trade Union Acts 1871 to 1975;

(2) In this Act a reference to a section is to a section of this Act unless it is indicated that reference to some other enactment is intended.

(3) In this Act a reference to a subsection is to the subsection of the section in which the reference occurs unless it is indicated that reference to some other section is intended.

2–Discrimination for the purposes of this Act

For the purposes of this Act, discrimination shall be taken to occur in any of the following cases:

(a) where by reason of his sex a person is treated less favourably than a person of the other sex;

(b) where because of his marital status a person is treated less favourably than another person of the same sex;

(c) where because of his sex or marital status a person is obliged to comply with a requirement, relating to employment or membership of a body referred to in section 5, which is not an essential requirement for such employment or membership and in respect of which the proportion of persons of the other sex or (as the case may be) of a different marital status but of the same sex able to comply is substantially higher;

(d) where a person is penalized for having in good faith

   (i) made a reference under section 19 or under section 7 of the Act of 1974,

   (ii) opposed by lawful means an act which is unlawful under this Act or the Act of 1974,

   (iii) given evidence in any proceedings under this Act or the Act of 1974, or

   (iv) given notice of an intention to do anything referred to in subparagraphs (i) to (iii), and cognate words shall be construed accordingly.

3–Discrimination by employers prohibited

(1) A person who is an employer or who obtains under a contract with another person the services of employees of that other person shall not discriminate against an employee or a prospective employee or an employee of that other person in relation to access to employment, conditions of employment (other than remuneration or any condition relating to an occupational pension scheme), training or experience for or in relation to employment, promotion or re-grading in employment or classification of posts in employment.

(2) An employer shall not, in relation to his employees or to employment by him, have rules or instructions which would discriminate against an employee or class of employee, and shall not otherwise apply or operate a practice which results or would be likely to result in an act which is a contravention of any provision of this Act when taken in conjunction with section 2(c).

(3) Without prejudice to the generality of subsection (1), a person shall be taken to discriminate against an employee or prospective employee in relation to access to employment if —

(a)   in any arrangements he makes for the purpose of deciding to whom he should offer employment, or

(b)   by specifying, in respect of one person or class of persons entry requirements for employment which are not specified in respect of other persons or classes of persons where the circumstances in which both such persons or classes would be employed are not materially different, he contravenes subsection (1).

(4) Without prejudice to the generality of subsection (1), a person shall be taken to discriminate against an employee or prospective employee in relation to conditions of employment if he does not offer or afford to a person or class of persons the same terms of employment (other than remuneration or any term relating to an occupational pension scheme), the same working conditions and the same treatment in relation to overtime, shift work, short time, transfers, lay-offs, redundancies, dismissals (other than a dismissal referred to in section 25) and disciplinary measures as he offers or affords to another person or class of persons where the circumstances in which both such persons or classes are or would be employed are not materially different.

(5) Without prejudice to the generality of subsection (1), a person shall be taken to discriminate against an employee in relation to training or experience for or in relation to employment if he refuses to offer or afford to that employee the same opportunities or facilities for employment counselling, training (whether on or off the job) and work experience as he offers or affords to other employees where the circumstances in which that employee and those other employees are employed are not materially different.

(6)   Without prejudice to the generality of subsection (1), a person shall be taken to contravene that subsection if he discriminates against an employee in the way he offers or affords that employee access to opportunities for promotion in circumstances in which another eligible and qualified person is offered or afforded such access or if in those circumstances he refuses or deliberately omits to offer or afford that employee access to opportunities for promotion.

(7)   Without prejudice to the generality of subsection (1), a person shall be taken to discriminate against an employee or prospective employee, where he classifies posts by reference to sex and the classification is not a case referred to in section 17(2).

4–Equality clause

(1)   If the terms of a contract under which a person is employed do not include (whether directly or by reference to a collective agreement within the meaning of the Act of 1974 or otherwise) an equality clause, they shall be deemed to include one.

(2)   An equality clause is a provision which relates to terms of a contract (other than a term relating to remuneration or an occupational pension scheme) under which a person is employed and has the effect that where the person is employed in circumstances where the work done by that person is not materially different from that being done by a person of the other sex (in this section referred to as 'the other person') in the same employment

(a)   if (apart from the equality clause) any term of the contract is or becomes less favourable to the person than a term of a similar kind in the contract under which the other person is employed, that term of the person's contract shall be treated as so modified as not to be less favourable, and

(b)   if (apart from the equality clause) at any time the person's contract does not include a term corresponding to a term benefiting the other person included in the contract under which the other person is employed, the person's contract shall be treated as including such a term.

(3)   An equality clause shall not operate in relation to a variation between a person's contract of employment and the contract of employment of the other person if the employer proves that the variation is genuinely a consequence of a material difference (other than the difference of sex) between the two cases.

(4)   Where a person offers a person employment on certain terms, and if on his acceptance of the offer any of those terms would fall to be modified or any additional term would fall to be included by virtue of this section, the offer shall be taken to contravene sections 3 (1) and 3 (4).

5–Discrimination in relation to membership of certain bodies prohibited

A body which is an organization of workers, an organization of employers or a professional or trade organization or which controls entry to a profession or the carrying on of a profession shall not discriminate against a person in relation to membership of such body (or any benefits provided by it) or in relation to entry or the carrying on of the profession.

6–Discrimination in relation to vocational training prohibited

(1) Any person or educational or training body offering a course of vocational training shall not, in respect of any such course offered to persons over the age at which those persons are statutorily obliged to attend school, discriminate against a person (whether at the request of an employer, a trade union or a group of employers or trade unions or otherwise)

    (a) in the terms on which any such course or related facility is offered,

    (b) by refusing or omitting to afford access to any such course or facility, or

    (c) in the manner in which any such course or facility is provided.

(2) In this section 'vocational training' means any system of instruction which enables a person being instructed to acquire, maintain, bring up to date or perfect the knowledge or technical capacity required for the carrying on of an occupational activity and which may be considered as exclusively concerned with training for such activity.

7–Discrimination by employment agencies prohibited

(1) An employment agency shall not discriminate

    (a) in the terms on which it offers to provide any of its services,

    (b) by refusing or omitting to provide any of its services,

    (c) in the manner in which it provides any of its services.

(2) References in subsection (1) to a service of an employment agency include guidance on careers and any service related to employment.

(3) Subsection (1) does not apply where the service concerns only employment which an employer could lawfully refuse to offer to the person concerned.

(4) An employment agency shall not be under any liability under this section if it proves —

    (a) that it acted in reliance on a statement made to it by the employer concerned to the effect that, by reason of the operation of subsection (3), its actions would not be unlawful, and

    (b) that it was reasonable for it to rely on the statement.

(5) An employer who, with a view to obtaining the services of an employment agency, knowingly makes a statement such as is referred to in subsection (4)(a) and which in a material respect is false or misleading shall be guilty of an offence and shall be liable on summary conviction to a fine not exceeding £200.

8–Discriminatory advertising prohibited

(1) A person shall not publish or display, or cause to be published or displayed, an advertisement which relates to employment and indicates an

intention to discriminate, or might reasonably be understood as indicating such an intention.

(2) For the purpose of subsection (1), where in an advertisement a word or phrase is used defining or describing a post and the word or phrase is one which connotes a particular sex, or which, although not necessarily connoting a particular sex, is descriptive of or refers to a post or occupation of a kind previously held or carried on by members of one sex only, the advertisement shall be taken to indicate an intention to discriminate unless the advertisement contains a contrary indication.

(3) A person who makes a statement which he knows to be false with a view to securing publication or display in contravention of subsection (1) shall upon such publication or display being made be guilty of an offence and shall be liable on summary conviction to a fine not exceeding £200.

9–Procuring or attempting to procure discrimination prohibited

A person shall not procure or attempt to procure another person to do in relation to employment anything which constitutes discrimination.

10–Discrimination in collective agreements, etc.

(1) (a) Where an agreement or order to which this subsection applies contains a provision constituting discrimination, the provision shall be null and void.

(b) This subsection applies to
(i) a collective agreement,
(ii) an employment regulation order within the meaning of Part IV of the Act of 1946, and
(iii) a registered employment agreement within the meaning of Part III of the Act of 1946 registered in the Register of Employment Agreements.

(2) Where a contract of employment contains a term (whether expressed or implied) constituting discrimination, that term shall be null and void.

11–Provisions relating to midwives and public health nurses

(1) The Midwives Act 1944 (No 10 of 1944) is hereby amended by the substitution for the definition of 'midwife' in section 2 of the following:
'the word 'midwife' means a woman or man registered in the roll of midwives and, accordingly, every word importing the feminine gender shall be construed as if it also imported the masculine gender'.
[¹...]

---

1   Subsection (2) was deleted by the European Communities (Employment Equality) Regulations 1982 (SI No 302 of 1982).

12–Employments excluded from application of Act

(1) [[1]This Act does not apply to employment
(a) in the Defence Forces,
(b) which consists of the performance of services of a personal nature, such as the care of an elderly or incapacitated person in that person's home, where the sex of the employee constitutes a determining factor.]
(2) (a) Notwithstanding subsection (1), the Minister may by order declare that this Act shall apply to such class or classes of employment referred to in that subsection as may be specified in the order, and from the commencement of the order this Act shall apply to that class or those classes.
(b) Where the Minister proposes to make an order under this subsection, a draft of the proposed order shall be laid before each House of the Oireachtas and the order shall not be made until a resolution approving of the draft has been passed by each House.
(3) Sections 19, 20(b), 21 and 28 shall not apply to the selection, by the Local Appointments Commissioners or the Civil Service Commissioners, of a person for appointment to an office or position.

13–Saver for certain cases relating to non-performance of duties, etc.

Nothing in this Act shall require an employer
(a) to employ in a position a person who will not undertake the duties attached to that position or who will not accept the conditions under which those duties are performed, or
(b) to retain in his employment a person not undertaking the duties attached to the position held by that person.

14–Saver for, and repeal or amendment of, certain statutory provisions

(1) Notwithstanding any provision of this Act, nothing done by an employer in compliance with any requirement of or under an Act to which this section applies shall constitute discrimination in contravention of this Act.
(2) (a) The Minister may by order repeal or amend any Act to which this section applies or any provision of such an Act.
(b) Before making an order under this subsection the Minister shall consult such trade unions, employers' organizations and organizations of trade unions or of employers' organizations as he considers appropriate.
(c) Where the Minister proposes to make an order under this subsection, a draft of the proposed order shall be laid before each

---

[1]   Amended by the European Communities (Employment Equality) Regulations 1985 (SI No 331 of 1985).

House of the Oireachtas and the order shall not be made until a resolution approving of the draft has been passed by each House.

(3) This section applies to —

(a) the Conditions of Employment Act 1936,

(b) the Shops (Conditions of Employment) Act 1938,

(c) the Factories Act 1955,

(d) the Mines and Quarries Act 1965.

15–Saver for certain training courses, etc.

Nothing in this Act shall make it unlawful for any person to arrange for or provide training for persons of a particular sex in a type, form or category of work in which either no, or an insignificant number of, persons of that sex had been engaged in the period of twelve months ending at the commencement of the training, or to encourage persons of that sex to take advantage of opportunities for doing such work.

16–Saver for special treatment in connection with pregnancy, etc.

Nothing in this Act shall make it unlawful for an employer to arrange for or provide special treatment to women in connection with pregnancy or childbirth.

17–Exclusion of posts where sex is occupational qualification

(1) This Act does not apply to any act connected with or related to the employment of a person where the sex of the person is an occupational qualification for a post in relation to which the act occurs.

(2) For the purposes of this section, the sex of a person shall be taken to be an occupational qualification for a post in the following cases —

(a) where, on grounds of physiology (excluding physical strength or stamina) or on grounds of authenticity for the purpose of a form of entertainment, the nature of the post requires a member of a particular sex because otherwise the nature of the post would be materially different if carried out by a member of the other sex,

(b) where the duties of a post involve personal services and it is necessary to have persons of both sexes engaged in such duties,

[1...]

(e) where because of the nature of the employment it is necessary to provide sleeping and sanitary accommodation for employees on a communal basis and it would be unreasonable to expect the provision of separate such accommodation or impracticable for an employer so to provide,

---

1 Subsections (2)(c) and (d) were deleted by the European Communities (Employment Equality) Regulations 1982 (SI No 302 of 1982).

(f) where it is necessary that the post should be held by a member of a particular sex because it is likely to involve the performance of duties outside the State in a place where the laws or customs are such that the duties can only be performed by a member of that sex.

18–Equality officers

From the commencement of this section an equal pay officer shall be known (and is in this Act referred to) as an equality officer and, accordingly, all references in the Act of 1974 to an equal pay officer shall be construed as references to an equality officer.

19–Reference of disputes to Court

(1) Subject to sections 26, 27(1) and 27(2), a dispute as to whether or not a person has discriminated may be referred by any person concerned to the Court.

(2) Where a dispute is referred under this section to the Court, it shall endeavour to settle the dispute through an industrial relations officer of the Court or refer the dispute to an equality officer for investigation and recommendation, or make such a reference where the industrial relations officer fails to effect a settlement.

(3) Where a dispute is referred under this section to an equality officer he shall investigate the dispute and issue a recommendation thereon.

(4) A recommendation under this section shall be conveyed

(a) in the case of a dispute referred under this section, to the Court and the parties to the dispute, or

(b) in the case of a reference under section 20, to the Court, [[1]the Agency] and to such person or persons as appear to the equality officer to be concerned.

(5) Save only where a reasonable cause can be shown, a reference under this section shall be lodged not later than six months from the date of the first occurrence of the act alleged to constitute the discrimination.

(6) Subject to subsection (7) the powers conferred on an equality officer by section 6(4) of the Act of 1974 in relation to an employer may be exercised in relation to a person other than an employer.

(7) Nothing in this Act shall be construed as requiring any person to furnish any reference (or a copy thereof) from an employer or any report (or a copy thereof), whether of a confidential nature or otherwise, relating to the character or the suitability for employment of any other person, or to disclose the contents of such a reference or report.

---

1   The Employment Equality Agency; see s. 36 of the Act.

20–Reference to Court by [¹the Agency]

Where it appears to [the Agency] —

(a)   that discrimination is being generally practised against persons or that a practice referred to in section 3 (2) is being applied or operated,

(b)   that discrimination has occurred in relation to a particular person who has not made a reference under section 19 in relation to the discrimination and that it is not reasonable to expect such a reference by him,

(c)   that a person has procured or attempted to procure another person to do anything in relation to employment which constitutes discrimination, or

(d)   that a publication or display in contravention of section 8 has been made,

the matter may be referred to the Court by [the Agency] and shall be dealt with as if it were a reference under section 19 of a dispute.

21–Investigation of disputes by Court

(1)   A person or (in the case of a reference under section 20) [²the Agency] may appeal to the Court against a recommendation under section 19 or may appeal to the Court for a determination that the recommendation has not been implemented.

(2)   The Court shall hear and determine an appeal under this section and shall convey its determination —

(a)   in the case of a reference under section 19, to the parties, or

(b)   in the case of a reference under section 20, to [³the Agency] and such person or persons as appear to the Court to be concerned.

(3)   (a)   A hearing under this section shall be held in private, but the Court shall, if requested to do so by a party to the dispute or a person referred to in section 20, hold the hearing in public.

(b)   Where a hearing under this section is being held in public the Court may, if it is satisfied that any part of the hearing concerns a matter that should, in the interests of any party to the dispute, or of a person referred to in section 20, be treated as confidential, hold that part of the hearing in private.

(c)   Sections 14 and 21 of the Act of 1946 shall apply to an appeal under this section,

---

1   This function was originally given to the Minister for Labour, but was transferred to the Employment Equality Agency after its establishment by virtue of s. 36(1) of the Act.

2   This function was originally given to the Minister for Labour, but was transferred to the Employment Equality Agency after its establishment by virtue of s. 36(1) of the Act.

3   The Employment Equality Agency; see s. 36 of the Act.

(d) An appeal under this section shall be lodged in the Court not later than 42 days after the date of the relevant recommendation under section 19 and the notice shall specify the grounds of the appeal.

(4) A party to a dispute determined by the Court under subsection (2) or, in the case of such a determination in a matter referred under section 20, the Minister or a person concerned may appeal to the High Court on a point of law.

22–Decision of Court under section 21

A determination of the Court under section 21 shall do one or more of the following —
(a) hold that there was or (as the case may be) was not discrimination,
(b) recommend to a person or persons concerned a specified course of action,
(c) award compensation in accordance with this Act,
(d) in a case referred to the Court under section 20(c) or 20(d) hold that the person concerned has or (as the case may be) has not procured or attempted to procure another person to do in relation to employment anything which constitutes discrimination or that a publication or display in contravention of section 8 was or (as the case may be) was not made and, if the Court thinks fit, recommend a specified course of action to the person concerned.

23–Amount of compensation under section 22 or additional fine under section 25 or 26

(1) Compensation under section 22 shall be of such amount as the Court thinks reasonable having regard to all the circumstances of the case but shall not in any case exceed 104 weeks' remuneration at the rate the person concerned was receiving at the date of the discrimination or would have received but for the discrimination.

(2) The amount of an additional fine imposed under section 25 or 26 shall not in any case exceed 104 weeks' remuneration at the rate the person concerned was receiving at the date of the discrimination or would have received but for the discrimination.

24–Failure to implement determination of Court

(1) Where a person concerned or (in the case of a reference under section 20) [1the Agency] complains to the Court that a determination under section 22(b) to 22(d) has not been implemented, the following provisions shall have effect:
(i) the Court shall consider the complaint and shall hear all persons appearing to the Court to be interested and desiring to be heard;

---

1   The Employment Equality Agency; see s. 36 of the Act.

    (ii)   if after such consideration the Court is satisfied that the complaint is well founded, the Court may by order direct the person failing to implement the determination to do such things as will in the opinion of the Court result in the determination being implemented by that person.

(2) If, where an order is made by the Court under subsection (1) the direction contained in the order is not carried out within two months from the date of the making of the order (or, where there is an appeal under section 21(4), within two months of the date of the order of the High Court on the appeal), the person to whom the direction is addressed shall be guilty of an offence and shall be liable on summary conviction to a fine not exceeding £100 and, in the case of a continuing offence, a further fine not exceeding £10 for every day during which the offence is continued.

(3)   (a) On a conviction for an offence under this section the court may, in addition to imposing a fine, if it thinks fit and the person (in this subsection referred to as the plaintiff) in whose favour the determination was made either present or represented consents, award to the plaintiff a sum not exceeding such amount as in the opinion of the court the plaintiff would have received from the person against whom the determination was made by way of damages in respect of remuneration in relation to the matter the subject of the determination, but not in any case exceeding 104 weeks' remuneration.

    (b) Damages awarded under paragraph (a) shall be paid to the plaintiff.

    (c) The payment by a convicted person of a sum awarded under paragraph (a) shall be a good defence to any civil action brought by the plaintiff in respect of remuneration mentioned in that paragraph.

    (d) Without prejudice to any right of appeal by any other person the plaintiff shall have a right of appeal limited to the amount of damages, either (as the case may be) to the High Court or to the judge of the Circuit Court in whose circuit the district (or any part thereof) of the Justice of the District Court by whom the award was made is situated, and the decision on such an appeal shall be final.

25–Dismissal because of action under section 2

(1) Where an employee is dismissed from his employment solely or mainly because he did in good faith anything specified in section 2(d)(i) to 2(d)(iv), his employer shall be guilty of an offence and shall be liable on summary conviction to a fine not exceeding £100 or on conviction on indictment to a fine not exceeding £1,000.

(2) In a prosecution for an offence under this section the onus shall be on the employer to satisfy the court that the reason referred to in subsection (1) was not the sole or principal reason for the dismissal.

(3)   (a) On a conviction for an offence under this section, the court may, if it thinks fit and the employee concerned is present or represented and consents —

    (i) order the re-instatement by the employer of the employee in the position which he held immediately before his dismissal on the terms and conditions on which he was employed immediately before his dismissal, together with a term that the re-instatement shall be deemed to have commenced on the day of the dismissal,

    (ii) order the re-engagement by the employer of the employee either in the position which he held immediately before his dismissal or in a different position which would be reasonably suitable for him on such terms and conditions as are reasonable having regard to all the circumstances, or

    (iii) impose on the convicted person, in addition to a fine imposed under subsection (1), a fine not exceeding the amount which in the opinion of the court the employee would have received from the employer concerned by way of remuneration if the dismissal had not occurred.

(b) The amount of a fine imposed under paragraph (a) shall be paid to the employee concerned.

(c) Without prejudice to any right of appeal by any other person, the employee concerned shall have a right of appeal limited to the amount of the fine, either (as the case may be) to the High Court or to the judge of the Circuit Court in whose circuit the district (or any part thereof) of the Justice of the District Court by whom the fine was imposed is situated, and the decision on such an appeal shall be final.

(d) The payment by a convicted person of a fine imposed under paragraph (a) shall be a good defence to any civil action brought by the employee concerned in respect of the remuneration mentioned in that paragraph.

26–Provisions supplemental to section 25

(1) Where a person, in respect of whose dismissal a prosecution for an offence under section 25 has not been brought, complains to the court that he has been dismissed from his employment solely or mainly because he did in good faith a thing specified in section 2(d)(i) to 2(d)(iv), the following provisions shall apply:

(a) the Court shall investigate the complaint, and shall hear all persons appearing to the Court to be interested and desiring to be heard;

(b) an investigation under this subsection shall be held in private, but the Court shall, if requested to do so by either person concerned, hold the investigation in public;

(c) where an investigation under this subsection is being held in public the Court may, if it is satisfied that any part of the investigation concerns a matter that should, in the interests of any person concerned, be treated as confidential, hold that part of the investigation in private;

(d) if after such investigation the Court is satisfied that the complaint is well founded, the Court may —

(i) order the re-instatement by the employer concerned of the dismissed person in the position which he held immediately before his dismissal on the terms and conditions on which he was employed immediately before his dismissal, together with a term that the re-instatement shall be deemed to have commenced on the day of the dismissal,

(ii) order the re-engagement by the employer concerned of the dismissed person either in the position which he held immediately before his dismissal or in a different position which would be reasonably suitable for him on such terms and conditions as are reasonable having regard to all the circumstances, or

(iii) by order direct the employer concerned to pay to the dismissed person such compensation as the Court considers reasonable in the circumstances, but not in any case more than 104 weeks' remuneration;

(e) an employer or dismissed person in respect of whom an order under this subsection has been made may appeal to the High Court on a point of law.

(2) Subject to subsection (5), if an order made by the Court under subsection (1) is not carried out within two months of the date of the making of the order (or, where there is an appeal under subsection (5) against the order, within two months of the date of the order of the Circuit Court on the appeal or, where there is an appeal under subsection (1)(e), within two months of the date of the order of the High Court on the appeal), the person to whom the direction is given shall be guilty of an offence and shall be liable on summary conviction to a fine not exceeding £100 and, in the case of a continuing offence, to a further fine not exceeding £10 for every day during which the offence is continued.

(3) (a) On a conviction for an offence under this section, the court may, if it thinks fit and the dismissed person is present or represented and consents —

(i) order the re-instatement by the employer concerned of the dismissed person in the position which he held immediately before his dismissal on the terms and conditions on which he was employed immediately before his dismissal, together with a term that the re-instatement shall be deemed to have commenced on the day of the dismissal,

(ii) order the re-engagement by the employer of the dismissed person either in the position which he held immediately before his dismissal or in a different position which would be reasonably suitable for him on such terms and conditions as are reasonable having regard to all the circumstances, or

(iii) impose on the convicted person, in addition to a fine imposed under subsection (2), a fine not exceeding the amount which in the opinion of the court the dismissed person would have received from the employer concerned by way of remuneration if the dismissal had not occurred.

(b) The amount of a fine imposed under paragraph (a) shall be paid to the employee concerned.

(c) Without prejudice to any right of appeal by any other person, the employee concerned shall have a right of appeal limited to the amount of the fine, either (as the case may be) to the High Court or to the judge of the Circuit Court in whose circuit the district (or any part thereof) of the Justice of the District Court by whom the fine was imposed is situated, and the decision on such an appeal shall be final.

(d) The payment by a convicted person of a fine imposed under paragraph (a) shall be a good defence to any civil action brought by the employee concerned in respect of the remuneration mentioned in that paragraph.

(4) Save only where a reasonable cause can be shown, a complaint under this section shall be lodged not later than six months from the date of dismissal.

(5) A person to whom a direction is given in an order under subsection (1) may, notwithstanding section 17 of the Act of 1946, appeal against the order to the judge of the Circuit Court in whose circuit the person carries on business.

27–Reference to Court of disputes relating to dismissal under section 3(4)

(1) A dispute as to whether or not there has been a contravention of section 3(4) in relation to the dismissal of a person may be referred to the Court by that person.

(2) Where a dispute is referred under this section to the Court, section 26 shall apply to the dispute as if it were a complaint under that section.

(3) A person who accepts in respect of a particular dismissal redress awarded under section 9 or 10 of the Act of 1974 or under section 7 of the Unfair Dismissals Act 1977, shall not be entitled to accept redress awarded under this Act in respect of that dismissal, and a person who accepts in respect of a particular dismissal redress awarded under this Act shall not be entitled to accept redress awarded under section 9 or 10 of the Act of 1974 or under section 7 of the Unfair Dismissals Act 1977, in respect of that dismissal.

28–Right of employee, etc., to certain information

(1) Where a person (in this section referred to as the employee) proposes to refer under section 19 a dispute to the Court, he may ascertain from the other person concerned the reason for the act believed by the

employee to have constituted discrimination and that other person shall state the reason in writing to the employee.

(2) The Minister may by regulations prescribe forms to be used for the purposes of this section and specify time-limits for stating reasons under subsection (1).

[¹...]

32–Defence to certain prosecutions under Office Premises Act 1958

(1) It shall be a good defence in a prosecution for an offence consisting of a contravention of regulations under section 13 of the Office Premises Act 1958 for the defendant to show to the satisfaction of the court that it was not reasonable to expect compliance with the regulations having regard to all the circumstances of the case and, in particular, to the passing of this Act.

(2) This section shall cease to have effect five years after the making of the first order under section 55 or, where only one such order is made, five years after the making of that order.

33–Power of High Court to grant injunction

(1) In a case to which this section applies it shall be lawful for the High Court to grant an injunction on the motion of [²the Agency] to prevent discrimination, by a person specified in the order of the High Court, of a type so specified.

(2) This section applies to a case where [the Agency] satisfies the High Court that, following a determination of the Court in a matter referred to it under section 20 (other than section 20(b)), there is a likelihood of further discrimination, procuring or attempting to procure publication or display (as the case may be), by a person in relation to whom the determination was made, of the type the subject of that determination.

34–Establishment of Employment Equality Agency

(1) The Government may by order appoint a day to be the establishment day for the purposes of sections 34 to 52.

(2) On the establishment day there shall be established a body to be known as the Employment Equality Agency (in this Act referred to as 'the Agency') to perform the functions assigned to it by this Act.

(3) The Schedule to this Act shall apply to the Agency.

---

1   Section 29 of the Act amends s. 1 of the 1974 Act; s. 30 amends s. 9 of the 1974 Act; and s. 31 amends ss 10(1)(d), 10(3)(a) and 10(4) of the 1974 Act. The amended provisions of the 1974 Act are printed above in their amended form.

2   This function was originally given to the Minister for Labour, but was transferred to the Employment Equality Agency after its establishment by virtue of s. 36(1) of the Act.

35–General functions of the Agency

The Agency shall have, in addition to any functions assigned to it by any other provision of this Act, the following general functions —

    (a) to work towards the elimination of discrimination in relation to employment,

    (b) to promote equality of opportunity between men and women in relation to employment,

    (c) to keep under review the working of the Act of 1974 and this Act and, whenever it thinks it necessary, to make proposals to the Minister for amending either or both of those Acts.

36–Transfer to Agency of certain functions of Minister

(1) On the establishment day the functions conferred on the Minister by sections 20, 21(1) and 33 and by section 7(2) of the Act of 1974 shall, by virtue of this section, stand transferred to the Agency.

(2) On and from the establishment day the references to the Minister in sections 19(4) (b), 21(2)(b), 21(4) and 24(1), and in section 7(4) and 8(1)(b) of the Act of 1974, shall be construed as references to the Agency.

37–Research and informational activities

(1) The Agency may undertake or sponsor such research and undertake or sponsor such activities relating to the dissemination of information as it considers necessary and which appears expedient for the purposes of exercising any of its functions.

(2) Without prejudice to the generality of subsection (1), the Agency may draft and publish for the information of employers guidelines or codes of practices relating to discrimination in relation to employment.

(3) The Agency may make charges for any services provided by it under this section.

38–Review of legislation

(1) Where in the opinion of the Agency the working or effect of any Act to which section 14 applies, any provision of such an Act or any statutory instrument made under such an Act is likely to affect or impede the elimination of discrimination in relation to employment or the promotion of equality of opportunity between men and women in relation to employment, the Agency may if it thinks fit, and shall if required by the Minister, carry out a review of such an Act, provision or instrument or of its working or effect.

(2) For the purpose of assisting it in making a review under this section, the Agency shall consult such trade unions, employers' organizations and organizations of trade unions or of employers' organizations as it considers appropriate.

    (3) (a) Where the Agency makes a review under this section it may make to the Minister a report of the review, and shall do so where the review was required by the Minister.

(b) A report under this subsection may contain recommendations for amending any statute, statutory instrument or administrative provision so reviewed.

39–Agency's power to conduct investigations

(1) The Agency may, for any purpose connected with the performance of its functions, conduct an investigation and shall do so where required by the Minister.

(2) For the purpose of assisting it in the conduct of a particular investigation the Agency may, with the approval of the Minister, employ one or more than one person having qualifications which in the opinion of the Agency relate to that investigation.

(3) An investigation may be conducted by one or more than one member of the Agency delegated by the Agency for this purpose.

(4) An investigation shall not be conducted in relation to the selection by the Local Appointments Commissioners or the Civil Service Commissioners of a person for appointment to an office or position.

40–Terms of reference for investigations

The Agency shall not conduct an investigation until the following requirements have been complied with:
(a) terms of reference for the investigation shall be drawn up by the Agency or, if the investigation is one which the Minister has required the Agency to conduct, by the Minister after consultation with the Agency;
(b) notice of intention to conduct an investigation shall be given by the Agency by a notice published in at least one daily newspaper circulating in the State unless the terms of reference refer to a specified person in which case the notice shall be given in writing to that person.

41–Agency's power to obtain information and documents and to summon witnesses

(1) The Agency may for the purposes of an investigation do all or any of the following things —
(a) require any person, by notice delivered to him personally or by registered post, to supply to it such information as it specifies in the notice and requires for the purpose of the investigation,
(b) require any person, by notice delivered to him personally or by registered post, to produce to it or to send to it, any specified document in his power or control,
(c) summon witnesses, by notices delivered to them personally or by registered post, to attend before it,
(d) examine the witnesses attending before it.

(2) A notice under subsection (1) shall not be delivered unless the Agency has obtained the consent of the Minister to the delivery, or unless the terms of reference for the investigation specify that the Agency believes that a person named in the terms of reference —

(a) has discriminated or is discriminating,

(b) has failed or is failing to comply with an equality clause under section 4,

(c) has contravened section 8(1) or section 9,

(d) has engaged in or is engaging in a practice referred to in section 3 (2), or

(e) has failed or is failing to comply with an equal pay clause (within the meaning of section 7 of the Act of 1974).

(3) A witness before the Agency and a person sending a document to the Agency or supplying information to it shall be entitled to the same immunities and privileges as if he were a witness before the High Court.

(4) A notice under subsection (1) shall be signed by at least one member of the Agency.

(5) The Agency may make, to a person who attends before it as a witness, such payments in respect of subsistence and travelling expenses as may be determined by the Minister with the consent of the Minister for the Public Service.

42–Offence relating to investigations, etc.

(1) If a person —

(a) fails or refuses to supply to the Agency information required by it and specified in a notice under section 41(1) or to produce or send to the Agency any document in his power or control and required by the Agency in such a notice to be produced by him,

(b) on being duly summoned as a witness before the Agency fails or refuses to attend,

(c) being in attendance as a witness before the Agency refuses to take an oath or to make an affirmation when legally required by the Agency to do so or to answer any question to which the Agency may legally require an answer, or

(d) does anything which would, if the Agency were a court of justice having power to commit for contempt of court, be contempt of such court,

he shall be guilty of an offence and shall be liable, on summary conviction, to a fine not exceeding £100 or, on conviction on indictment, to a fine not exceeding £1,000, and where the offence is one referred to in paragraphs (a) to (c) of this subsection the court by which he is so convicted may direct him to comply with the paragraph in question.

(2) If a person to whom a notice under section 41(1) has been delivered alters, suppresses, conceals or destroys a document specified in the notice or makes a false statement when supplying to the Agency information specified in the notice, he shall be guilty of an offence and shall be liable on summary conviction to a fine not exceeding £100.

43–Recommendations and reports by Agency

(1) After it has conducted an investigation or in the course of an investigation the Agency may make to any person (including the Minister) recommendations arising out of the investigation for the purpose of promoting one or both of its general functions specified in sections 35(a) and 35(b).

(2) As soon as practicable after it has conducted an investigation the Agency shall prepare or cause to be prepared a report of the investigation, and such a report shall contain any findings of the Agency arising out of the investigation.

(3) Where the investigation was one required by the Minister a copy of the relevant report under this section shall be sent to the Minister as soon as practicable after its preparation.

(4) The Agency or (in the case of a report referred to in subsection (3)), the Minister shall, as soon as practicable after subsection (2) and (where appropriate) subsection (3) have been complied with cause a report under this section to be published or otherwise made available to the public and shall give notice to the public of such publication or availability.

(5) Any information obtained by the Agency by virtue of the powers conferred on it by section 41 as to any organization of workers or any person or as to the business carried on by any person, which is not available otherwise, shall not be included in a report under this section without the consent of the organization of workers or the person concerned (unless such non-inclusion would be inconsistent with the duties of the Agency and the object of the report), and any person concerned in any proceedings under this Act shall not disclose any such information without such consent.

44–Non-discrimination notice

(1) Where in the course of the conduct of an investigation or after an investigation has been conducted the Agency is satisfied that a person —
   (a) has discriminated or is discriminating,
   (b) has failed or is failing to comply with an equality clause under section 4,
   (c) has contravened section 8(1) or section 9,
   (d) has engaged in or is engaging in a practice referred to in section 3 (2), or
   (e) has failed or is failing to comply with an equal pay clause (within the meaning of section 7 of the Act of 1974),
it may serve a non-discrimination notice on that person.
   (2) (a) Where the Agency proposes to serve a non-discrimination notice it shall before serving it notify in writing the person on whom it is proposed to serve the notice of its proposal.
   (b) A notification under this subsection shall specify the act or omission constituting the discrimination, failure, contravention or practice and shall inform the person concerned that he may make

representations to the Agency regarding the proposal within a period specified in the notification.

(c)   A person who has received a notification under this subsection may make representations to the Agency regarding the proposed non-discrimination notice within 28 days of receipt of the notification.

(d)   Where representations are duly made under this subsection they shall be considered by the Agency before serving a non-discrimination notice.

(3)   A non-discrimination notice shall —

(a)   specify the act or omission constituting the discrimination, failure, contravention or practice,

(b)   require the person on whom it is served not to commit the discrimination or contravention or (where appropriate) to comply with the equal pay clause (within the meaning of section 7 of the Act of 1974) or the equality clause under section 4,

(c)   specify, in the case of a discrimination, what steps the Agency requires to be taken by the person on whom it is served in order not to commit the discrimination, and

(d)   require the person on whom it is served to inform the Agency, within a period specified in the notice, and any other persons so specified of what steps are taken in order to comply with the notice and to supply, within a period so specified, the Agency with any other information so specified.

(4)   A non-discrimination notice may be served by personal delivery or by registered post.

45–Appeal against non-discrimination notice

(1)   A person on whom a non-discrimination notice has been served may appeal to the Court within 42 days of the date of service against the notice or any requirement of the notice.

(2)   Where an appeal under subsection (1) is not made, a non-discrimination notice shall come into operation on the expiry of the 42-day period referred to in that subsection.

(3)   Where the Court has heard an appeal under subsection (1), it may either confirm the notice in whole or in part (with or without an amendment of the notice) or allow the appeal.

(4)   Where the Court confirms a non-discrimination notice, the notice (as so confirmed in whole or in part) shall come into operation on such date as the Court shall fix.

(5)   Where the Court allows an appeal under subsection (1), the non-discrimination notice appealed against shall cease to have effect.

46–Register of non-discrimination notices

The Agency shall keep a register, which shall be open to inspection by any person at all reasonable times, of every non-discrimination notice which has come into operation.

47–Power of Agency to seek injunctions

(1) In a case to which this section applies it shall be lawful for the High Court to grant an injunction, on the motion of the Agency, to prevent discrimination by a person specified in the order of the High Court of a type so specified.

(2) This section applies to a case where, in the period of five years beginning on the date on which a non-discrimination notice came into operation, the Agency satisfies the High Court that there is a likelihood of further discrimination or of a further contravention or failure referred to in section 44(1) by the person on whom the notice was served.

48–Assistance by Agency in certain references to Court or equality officer

(1) A person who considers that there is or has been discrimination in respect of him by another person, or that there is or has been a failure or neglect by such other person to comply with an equal pay clause (within the meaning of section 7 of the Act of 1974) or with an equality clause under section 4 or to implement a determination or order of the Court under section 21 or 26 or under section 8 or 10 of the Act of 1974, may apply to the Agency for assistance in making a reference to the Court or an equality officer.

(2) Where, having considered an application under subsection (1), the Agency is satisfied that the application raises an important matter of principle, or it appears to the Agency that it is not reasonable to expect the applicant adequately to present without assistance the case the subject of the proposed reference, the Agency may at its discretion provide assistance to the applicant in making the reference.

(3) Assistance under this section shall be in such form as the Agency at its discretion thinks fit.

49–Accounts and audits

(1) The Agency shall, in such form as may be approved by the Minister with the concurrence of the Minister for Finance, keep all proper and usual accounts of all moneys received or expended by it.

(2) Accounts kept in pursuance of this section shall be submitted annually by the Agency to the Comptroller and Auditor General for audit at such times as the Minister, with the concurrence of the Minister for Finance, directs and those accounts, when so audited, shall (together with the report of the Comptroller and Auditor General thereon), be presented to the Minister, who shall cause copies of the audited accounts and the report to be laid before each House of the Oireachtas.

50–Annual report, etc.

(1) The Agency shall in each year, at such date as the Minister may direct, make a report to the Minister of its activities during the preceding

twelve months ending on that date, and the Minister shall cause copies of the report to be laid before each House of the Oireachtas.

(2) The Agency shall supply to the Minister any information as he may from time to time require regarding its activities.

51–Grants to the Agency

(1) In each financial year there may be paid to the Agency out of moneys provided by the Oireachtas a grant of such amount as the Minister, with the concurrence of the Minister for Finance, may sanction towards the expenses of the Agency in the performance of its functions.

(2) The Agency may invest money in such manner as the Minister may approve.

52–Power of the Agency to borrow

The Agency may, with the consent of the Minister, given with the concurrence of the Minister for Finance, borrow temporarily by arrangement with bankers such sums as it may require for the purpose of providing for current expenditure.

53–Regulations

(1) The Minister may make regulations for the purpose of giving effect to this Act.

(2) (a) The Minister may by regulations provide that a particular provision (or particular provisions) of this Act specified in the regulations shall not apply to an appointment to which this subsection applies.

(b) This subsection applies to an appointment to an office or position specified in the regulations and made or to be made before the expiry of the period of six months from the commencement of this section consequent on a selection by the Local Appointment Commissioners or the Civil Service Commissioners.

54–Expenses

The expenses incurred in the administration of this Act shall, to such extent as may be sanctioned by the Minister for Finance, be paid out of moneys provided by the Oireachtas.

55–Commencement

This Act (other than sections 34 to 52) shall come into operation on such day or days as may be appointed by order or orders of the Minister, either generally or with reference to a particular purpose or provision, and different days may be fixed for different purposes and different provisions of this Act.

56—Short title and construction

(1) This Act may be cited as the Employment Equality Act, 1977.

(2) The Act of 1974 and this Act shall be construed together as one Act.

SCHEDULE

EMPLOYMENT EQUALITY AGENCY

1. The Agency shall be a body corporate with perpetual succession and power to sue and be sued in its corporate name and to acquire, hold and dispose of land.

2. The Agency shall consist of a chairman (in this Schedule referred to as 'the chairman') and ten ordinary members.

3. The chairman may at any time resign his office by letter addressed to the Minister and his resignation shall take effect as on and from the date of the receipt of the letter by the Minister.

4. The Minister may at any time remove the chairman from office.

5. Where the chairman or an ordinary member of the Agency becomes a member of either House of the Oireachtas, he shall, upon his becoming entitled under the Standing Orders of the House to sit therein, cease to be the chairman or such ordinary member.

6. A person who is for the time being entitled under the Standing Orders of either House of the Oireachtas to sit therein shall be disqualified from being either the chairman or an ordinary member of the Agency.

7. The chairman shall be appointed by the Minister either in a whole-time or a part-time capacity and shall hold office for not more than five years on such terms and conditions as the Minister determines with the consent of the Minister for the Public Service.

8. The chairman shall be paid, out of moneys provided by the Oireachtas, such remuneration and allowances and expenses incurred by him as the Minister, with the consent of the Minister for the Public Service, may determine.

9. Of the ordinary members of the Agency —

(a) two shall be workers' members;

(b) two others shall be employers' members, and

(c) the remaining six, three of whom shall be representative of women's organizations, shall be nominated by the Minister.

10. Each ordinary member of the Agency shall be a part-time member and, subject to this Schedule, shall hold office for five years on such terms and conditions as the Minister determines with the consent of the Minister for the Public Service.

11. The chairman and an ordinary member of the Agency whose term of office expires by effluxion of time shall be eligible for re-appointment.

12. The Minister may at any time remove an ordinary member of the Agency from office.

13. An ordinary member of the Agency may resign his office as such member by letter addressed to the Minister and the resignation shall take effect as on and from the date of the receipt of the letter by the Minister.

14. A member of the Agency shall be disqualified from holding and shall cease to hold office if he is adjudged bankrupt or makes a composition or arrangement with creditors or is sentenced by a court of competent jurisdiction to suffer imprisonment or penal servitude or ceases to be ordinarily resident in the State.

15. Each ordinary member of the Agency shall be paid, out of moneys provided by the Oireachtas, such expenses as the Minister, with the consent of the Minister for the Public Service, may sanction.

16. The Minister shall appoint one of the ordinary members of the Agency to be vice-chairman of the Agency with the function of acting as chairman in the absence of the chairman.

17. Where a casual vacancy occurs among the workers' members, the employers' members or the women's organizations members of the Agency, the Minister shall forthwith invite the organization which previously nominated that member to nominate a person for appointment to fill the vacancy and the Minister shall appoint the person nominated to fill the vacancy.

18. (1) The Minister, with the consent of the Minister for the Public Service, may appoint such officers and servants as he thinks necessary to assist the Agency in the performance of its functions.

(2) The officers and servants so appointed shall hold office on such terms, and receive such remuneration, as the Minister for the Public Service determines.

19. (1) The Agency shall hold such and so many meetings as may be necessary for the performance of its functions and may make arrangements for the regulation of its proceedings and business.

(2) Such arrangements may, with the approval of the Minister provide for the discharge, under the general direction of the Agency, of any of its functions by a committee of the Agency.

20. The Minister may fix or sanction the date, time and place of the first meeting of the Agency.

21. The quorum for a meeting of the Agency shall be five members.

22. At a meeting of the Agency

(a) the chairman shall, if present, be the chairman of the meeting,

(b) in the absence of the chairman or, if the office of chairman of the Agency is vacant, the vice-chairman of the Agency shall act as chairman,

(c) if, and so long as, the chairman is not present, or if the office of chairman of the Agency is vacant and the vice-chairman is not present or the office of vice-chairman is vacant, the members of the Agency present shall choose one of their number to be chairman of the meeting.

23. The chairman and each ordinary member of the Agency attending a meeting of the Agency shall have one vote.

24. Every question at a meeting of the Agency shall be determined by a majority of the votes cast on the question and, in the case of an equal division of votes, the chairman of the meeting shall have a second or casting vote.

25. The Agency may act notwithstanding one or more than one vacancy among its members.

26. Subject to this Schedule, the Agency shall regulate its procedure and business.

27. (1) The Agency shall, as soon as may be after its establishment, provide itself with a seal.

(2) The seal of the Agency shall be authenticated by the signature of the chairman or some other member of the Agency authorized by it to act in that behalf and by the signature of an officer of the Agency authorized by it to act in that behalf.

(3) Judicial notice shall be taken of the seal of the Agency and any document sealed with the seal shall be received in evidence.

7.6   NATIONAL TEXTS IMPLEMENTING EC DIRECTIVES: SOCIAL SECURITY

7.6.1   Social Welfare (No 2) Act 1985[1]

1–Interpretation

In this Act 'the Principal Act' means the Social Welfare (Consolidation) Act 1981.

2–Increase of social insurance benefits

The Principal Act is hereby amended by the substitution for Parts I to V of the Second Schedule (inserted by the Social Welfare Act 1985) of the Parts set out in the Second Schedule to this Act.

3–Amendment of section 2 of Principal Act (interpretation generally)

Section 2 of the Principal Act is hereby amended by the substitution in subsection (1) for the definition of 'adult dependant' of the following definition:

'adult dependant, subject to section 199, means in relation to any person
- (a) a spouse who is wholly or mainly maintained by that person but does not include
  - (i) a spouse in employment (other than employment specified in paragraphs 4, 5 or 10 of Part II of the First Schedule), or
  - (ii) a spouse who is self-employed, or
  - (iii) a spouse who is entitled to, or is in receipt of, any pension, benefit, assistance or allowance (other than supplementary welfare allowance) under Parts II or III of this Act, or disabled person's maintenance allowance under section 69 of the Health Act 1970;
- (b) a person over the age of 16 years being wholly or mainly maintained by that person and having the care of one or more than one qualified child who normally resides with that person where that person is

---

1   Directive 79/7 was implemented by this Act which became law in July 1985, although none of its provisions was activated until 1986. With the exception of s. 6 which was activated in May 1986 by the Social Welfare Act 1986, the 1985 Act was brought into force in November 1986 by the Social Welfare (No 2) Act 1985 (Commencement) Order 1986. As a consequence a number of regulations were issued at the same time, namely: SI No 367 of 1986 (definition of 'child dependants'); SI No 368 of 1986 (payments of adult dependants' allowances); SI No 369 of 1986 (definitions of 'adult dependants', specifies calculations of earnings of employed and self-employed persons); SI No 422 of 1986 (transitional payments necessitated by 'equal treatment' changes).
The Act is printed here as amended by the Social Welfare (No 2) Act 1989.

(i) a single person, or

(ii) a widow, or

(iii) a widower, or

(iv) a married person who is not living with and is neither wholly or mainly maintaining, nor being wholly or mainly maintained by, such married person's spouse, or

(c) such person as the Minister, with the consent of the Minister for Finance, may by regulations specify to be an adult dependant for the purposes of this Act.'

4—Amount of increases payable in respect of qualified child normally resident with beneficiary in certain cases

(1) Subject to subsection (2), any increase of benefit or pension, as the case may be, payable pursuant to sections 21, 32, 44, 55, 81, 86 or 91 of the Principal Act in respect of a qualified child who normally resides with a beneficiary or pensioner and with the spouse of a beneficiary or pensioner shall be payable at the rate of one-half of the appropriate amount in any case where the spouse of the beneficiary or pensioner is not an adult dependant, and the said sections 21, 32, 44, 55, 81, 86 and 91 shall be construed and have effect accordingly.

(2) The provisions of subsection (1) shall not apply in any case where a spouse of a beneficiary or pensioner is living apart from the beneficiary or pensioner, as the case may be, and is not making a financial contribution to the maintenance of the qualified child.

5—Increase of maternity allowance

The Principal Act is hereby amended by the insertion after section 26 of the following section:

'26A—Increase of maternity allowance

(1) Subject to subsection (2), the weekly rate of maternity benefit shall be increased by the appropriate amount set out in column (4), (4a), (5) or (5a) of Part I of the Second Schedule in respect of each qualified child who normally resides with the beneficiary.

(2) The increase payable pursuant to subsection (1) in respect of a qualified child who normally resides with the beneficiary and with the spouse of the beneficiary shall be payable at the rate of one-half of the appropriate amount in any case where the spouse of the beneficiary is not an adult dependant.

(3) The provisions of subsection (2) shall not apply in any case where the spouse of the beneficiary is living apart from the beneficiary and is not making a financial contribution to the maintenance of the qualified child.'

6–Amendment of section 34 of Principal Act (duration of payment)

Section 34 of the Principal Act is hereby amended by
(a) the substitution for subsection (1) of the following subsection:
'(1) A person who, in respect of any period of interruption of employment, has been entitled to unemployment benefit for 156 days shall not thereafter, subject to subsection (3), be entitled to that benefit for any day of unemployment (whether in the same or a subsequent period of interruption of employment) unless before that day he has requalified for benefit or unless, in the case of a person over 65 years of age, he has qualifying contributions in respect of not less than 156 contribution weeks in the period between his entry into insurance and the day for which unemployment benefit is claimed';
(b) the substitution for subsection (3) of the following subsection:
'(3) Subsection (1) shall, in respect of a person who is over the age of 18 years, have effect as if "390 days" were substituted for "156 days";' and
(c) the substitution for subsection (6) of the following subsection:
'(6) Where in a period of interruption of employment a woman who was formerly entitled to 312 days' unemployment benefit has exhausted her right to 312 days' unemployment benefit within the period of 78 days ending on the date on which this subsection comes into operation, she shall be entitled to such benefit in respect of each day, up to a maximum of 78 days, of unemployment after that date, up to the 393rd day of unemployment in that period of interruption of employment'.

7–Amendment of section 43 of Principal Act (disablement benefit)

Section 43 of the Principal Act is hereby amended by
(a) the substitution for paragraph (b) of subsection (7) of the following paragraph:
'(b) The scale prescribed for the purposes of paragraph (a) shall be the same for all persons, except that a lower amount may be fixed for cases where, at the beginning of the period taken into account by the assessment, the beneficiary is under the age of 18 years and may be made to depend on the date on which the beneficiary will attain that age:
Provided that:
   (i)   such lower amount shall not in any case be less than two-thirds of the amount to which the beneficiary would otherwise be entitled, and
   (ii) the higher rate shall be payable if the beneficiary would, if he were in receipt of injury benefit rather than disablement gratuity, be entitled to an increase of that benefit for a qualified child or children or for an adult dependant or would

be so entitled but for the fact that his spouse is in employment (other than employment specified in paragraphs 4, 5 or 10 of Part II of the First Schedule), is engaged in self-employment or is entitled to, or in receipt of, any benefit, assistance or allowance (other than supplementary welfare allowance) under Parts II or III of this Act or disabled person's maintenance allowance under section 69 of the Health Act, 1970';

(b) the substitution for subsection (8) of the following subsection:

'(8) Where the extent of the disablement is assessed for the period taken into account as amounting to 20 per cent or more, disablement benefit shall be a pension (in this Chapter referred to as a disablement pension) for that period at the weekly rate set out in column (2) of Part III of the Second Schedule appropriate to the degree of disablement:

Provided that:

(a) where that period is limited by reference to a definite date, the pension shall cease on the death of the beneficiary before that date, and

(b) where the beneficiary is under the age of 18 years, the weekly rate for any degree of disablement shall be the rate set out in column (3) of Part III of the Second Schedule appropriate to the degree of disablement unless the beneficiary would, if in receipt of injury benefit rather than disablement pension, be entitled to an increase of that benefit for a qualified child or qualified children or for an adult dependant or would be so entitled but for the fact that his spouse is in employment (other than employment specified in paragraphs 4, 5 or 10 of Part II of the First Schedule), engaged in self-employment or is entitled to, or in receipt of, any benefit, assistance or allowance (other than supplementary welfare allowance) under Parts II or III of this Act, or disabled person's maintenance allowance under section 69 of the Health Act, 1970'; and

(c) the substitution for subsection (9) (b) (i) of the following paragraph:

'(i) the scale shall be the same for all persons, except that a lower amount may be fixed thereby for cases where the beneficiary is under the age of 18 years, unless the beneficiary would, if in receipt of injury benefit rather than disablement pension, be entitled to an increase of that benefit for a qualified child or qualified children or for an adult dependant or would be so entitled but for the fact that his spouse is in employment (other than employment specified in paragraphs 4, 5 or 10 of Part II of the First Schedule), is engaged in self-employment or is entitled to, or in receipt of, any benefit, assistance or allowance (other than supplementary welfare allowance) under Parts II or III of this Act or disabled person's maintenance allowance under section 69 of the Health Act, 1970'.

8–Amendment of section 87 of Principal Act (title to benefit)

Section 87 of the Principal Act is hereby amended by the insertion in subsection (1) after 'husband' of the words 'provided that he is incapable of self-support by reason of some mental or physical infirmity', and the said subsection, as so amended, is set out in the Table to this section.

TABLE

'(1) Subject to this Act, on the death of a woman to whom an old age (contributory) pension or retirement pension was payable at an increased weekly rate by virtue of section 81(1) or 86(1) in respect of a period ending on such death, her husband, providing that he is incapable of self-support by reason of some mental or physical infirmity, shall be entitled to benefit the weekly rate of which is equal to the rate of widow's (contributory) pension, including increases, in respect of qualified children where appropriate, which would be payable to him under the provisions of this Part if he were a widow.'

9–Amendment of section 136 of Principal Act (qualification certificates)

Section 136 of the Principal Act is hereby amended by the substitution for paragraph (c) of subsection (3) of the following paragraph:
'(c) that his means, calculated in accordance with this Chapter, do not exceed an amount per annum equal to 52 times
  (i) twice the amount of unemployment assistance set out in column (2) at reference 1A(1)(i) in Part I of the Fourth Schedule, and
  (ii) in case he has a qualified child or qualified children, so much of the unemployment assistance set out at reference 1A(1)(i) in Part I of the Fourth Schedule applicable to the person as would be payable in respect of that child or those children, as the case may be; and'.

10–Amendment of section 139 of Principal Act (rates of assistance)

Section 139 of the Principal Act is hereby amended by the insertion after 'section 140' of 'and to section 12 of the Social Welfare (No 2) Act 1985', and the said section, as so amended, is set out in the Table of this section.

TABLE

'139   Subject to section 140 and to section 12 of the Social Welfare (No 2) Act 1985, the rate (in this Chapter referred to as the scheduled rate) of unemployment assistance shall be the weekly rate set out in column (2) of Part I of the Fourth Schedule, increased by

(a) the amount set out in column (3) of that Part for any period during which the applicant or recipient has an adult dependant, subject to the restriction that the applicant or recipient shall not be entitled to an increase of assistance under this paragraph in respect of more than one person, and

(b) the appropriate amount set out in column (4), (4a), (5) or (5a) of that Part in respect of each qualified child who normally resides with the applicant or recipient.'

11–Amount of unemployment assistance in respect of qualified children in certain cases

(1) Subject to subsection (2), any increase of unemployment assistance payable pursuant to section 139 of the Principal Act in respect of a qualified child who normally resides with the applicant or recipient and with the spouse of the applicant or recipient shall be payable at the rate of one-half of the appropriate amount in any case where the spouse of the applicant or recipient is not an adult dependant, and the said section 319 shall be construed and have effect accordingly.

(2) The provision of subsection (1) shall not apply in any case where a spouse of an applicant or recipient is living apart from the applicant or recipient and is not making a financial contribution to the maintenance of the qualified child.

12–Unemployment assistance — married couples

(1) [[1]In the case of a couple both of whom are entitled to be paid unemployment assistance, the total amount payable to them pursuant to Chapter 2 of Part III of the Principal Act shall not exceed the amount which would be payable if only one of them was entitled to be paid unemployment assistance and the other was an adult dependant, and each of them shall be entitled to be paid one-half of the amount which would be payable to him if the other were his adult dependant.]

(2) Where the spouse of an applicant for unemployment assistance is not an adult dependant, the unemployment assistance payable to the applicant shall be at a rate equal to the scheduled rate reduced by 5p for every 10p or part of 10p of his means and whenever the rate of unemployment assistance payable as a result of such calculation is not an even multiple of 5p, the amount payable shall be rounded up to the nearest 5p.

(3) Subsection (2) of this section shall not apply in any case where the spouse is living apart from the applicant.

---

[1] The original provisions were found to be unconstitutional in *Hyland* v. *Minister for Social Welfare*, see §§8.1.4 and 8.4.5 below. The text printed here was inserted by s. 1 of the Social Welfare (No 2) Act 1989.

[¹(4) Where one of a couple is entitled to disability benefit, unemployment benefit, injury benefit, disablement pension, old age (contributory) pension, old age pension, retirement pension or invalidity pension and the other is entitled to unemployment assistance, the total of the amount payable to them by way of such benefit or pension, as the case may be, and such unemployment assistance (in this subsection referred to as 'the relevant amount') shall not exceed the total amount of benefit or pension, as the case may be, or the total amount of unemployment assistance, whichever is the greater (in this subsection referred to as 'the greater amount'), that would be payable if only one of the couple were in receipt of benefit, pension or unemployment assistance, as the case may be, and the benefit, pension or unemployment assistance included an increase in respect of the other as his adult dependant; and, if the relevant amount would but for this subsection exceed the greater amount, the amount of unemployment assistance payable to the spouse who is entitled to such unemployment assistance shall be reduced by the amount of the excess.

(5) In this section 'couple' means a married couple who are living together or a man and woman who are not married to each other but are cohabiting as man and wife.

(6) In subsection (4) of this section 'spouse' means each person of a couple in relation to the other.]

13–Calculation of means

The Principal Act is hereby amended by the substitution for section 146 thereof of the following section:

'146–Calculation of means

(1) In the calculation of the means of a person for the purposes of this Chapter, the following things and no other things shall be deemed to constitute the means of a person:

    (a)   the yearly value ascertained in the prescribed manner of all property belonging to him or to his spouse (not being property personally used or enjoyed by him or by his spouse or a farm of land leased either by him or by his spouse under a lease which has been certified by the Irish Land Commission to be *bona fide* and in accordance with sound land use practice) which is invested or otherwise put to profitable use or is capable of being, but is not invested or put to profitable use;

    (b)   all income which he or his spouse may reasonably expect to receive during the succeeding year in cash, whether as contributions to the expenses of the household or otherwise, but excluding

        (i)   any income or money coming within any other paragraph of this subsection,

---

1   Inserted by s. 1 of the Social Welfare (No 2) Act 1989.

(ii)   all moneys earned by him or by his spouse in respect of current personal employment under a contract of service,

(iii)   any moneys received by way of unemployment assistance under this Chapter,

(iv)   any moneys received by way of supplementary welfare allowance,

(v)   any moneys received by way of disability benefit, unemployment benefit, maternity benefit, children's allowance or family income supplement,

(vi)   any income arising from a bonus under a scheme administered by the Minister for the Gaeltacht for the making of special grants to parents or guardians resident in the Gaeltacht or Breac-Ghaeltacht (as defined in such scheme) of children attending primary schools,

(vii)   an amount of an allowance, dependant's allowance (not being a dependant's allowance to which paragraph (viii) relates), disability pension or wound pension under the Army Pensions Act, 1923 to 1980, or a combination of such allowances and such pensions so far as such amount does not exceed £80 per year,

(viii) a dependant's allowance under the Army Pensions Act 1923 to 1980 arising out of service in the period from the 23rd day of April 1916, to the 30th day of September 1923,

(ix)   any moneys received by way of training allowance from an organization while undergoing a course of rehabilitation training provided by the organization (being an organization approved of by the Minister for Health for the purposes of the provision of such training),

(x)   any moneys, except so far as they exceed £104 per year, received by such person or by the spouse of such person in respect of work of the kind referred to in paragraph 7 of Part I of the First Schedule, under a scheme that is, in the opinion of the Minister, charitable in character and purpose,

(xi)   where he or his spouse is engaged on a seasonal basis in the occupation of fishing, one-half of so much of the income derived there from as does not exceed £120 per year and one-third of so much of such income as exceeds £120 per year but does not exceed £300 per year,

(xii)   any moneys received under a statutory scheme administered by the Minister for Labour in respect of redundancy or by way of financial assistance to unemployed persons changing residence;

(c)   the yearly value ascertained in the prescribed manner of any advantage accruing to him or to his spouse from:

(i)   the use of property (other than a domestic dwelling or farm building owned and occupied, furniture and personal effects) which is personally used or enjoyed by him or by his spouse, and

(ii)   the leasing by him or by his spouse of a farm of land under a lease which has been certified by the Irish Land Commission to be *bona fide* and in accordance with sound land use practice;

(d)   all income and the yearly value ascertained in the prescribed manner of all property of which he or his spouse have directly or indirectly deprived themselves in order to qualify for the receipt of unemployment assistance;

(e)   the yearly value of any benefit or privilege enjoyed by him or by his spouse, including the estimated value to the household in the succeeding year deriving from all income earned by his spouse in respect of current personal employment under a contract of service.

(2)   For the Purposes of subsections (1)(b) and (1)(e), the income of a person shall, in the absence of other means of ascertaining it, be taken to be the income actually received during the year immediately preceding the date of calculation.

(3)   For the purposes of this section, 'spouse', in relation to a person, means a spouse who is living with, and not apart from, that person'.

14–Amendment of section 161 of Principal Act (rates of pension and increases for child dependants)

Section 161 of the Principal Act is hereby amended by the insertion after subsection (1) (inserted by the Social Welfare Act 1982) of the following subsection:

'(1A)   The increase payable pursuant to subsection (1) in respect of a qualified child who normally resides with the pensioner and the spouse of the pensioner shall be payable at the rate of one-half of the appropriate amount in any case where the spouse of the pensioner is entitled to any benefit, assistance, allowance (other than supplementary welfare allowance) or any other pension under this Act or to disabled person's maintenance allowance under section 69 of the Health Act 1970'.

15–Amendment of section 162 of Principal Act (increases for incapacitated and married pensioners)

Section 162 of the Principal Act is hereby amended by the substitution for paragraph (d) of subsection (1) of the following paragraph:

'(d) by the amount calculated in accordance with Part III of the Fourth Schedule where the pensioner is living with, or is wholly or mainly maintaining, his spouse and the spouse is not in receipt of any benefit, pension, assistance or allowance under Part II or this Part'.

16–Amendment of section 199 of Principal Act (interpretation Part III Chapter 6)

Section 199 of the Principal Act is hereby amended by the insertion after the definition of 'the Act of 1939' of the following definition:

'adult dependant means

(a) the spouse of the recipient who is being wholly or mainly maintained by him, or

(b) a person over the age of 16 years being wholly or mainly maintained by the recipient and having the care of one or more than one qualified child who normally resides with the recipient where the recipient is

    (i) a single person, or

    (ii) a widow, or

    (iii) a widower, or

    (iv) a married person who is not living with and is neither wholly nor mainly maintaining, nor being wholly or mainly maintained by, such married person's spouse'.

17–Amendment of section 210 of Principal Act (calculation of means)

Section 210 of the Principal Act is hereby amended by the substitution in paragraph (a) of subsection (2) for 'income as head of the household' of 'household income', and the said paragraph, as so amended, is set out in the Table to this section.

TABLE

'(a) all income in cash, including the net cash value of any non-cash earnings derived from personal exertions and the actual or estimated amount of any household income, whether as contributions to the expenses of the household or otherwise, but excluding:

    (i) any sums received by way of children's allowance under Part IV,

    (ii) any sums received by way of allowance for domiciliary care of handicapped children under section 61 of the Health Act 1970, and

    (iii) any sums arising from the investment or profitable use of property (not being property personally used or enjoyed by such person or a farm of land leased by him under a lease which has been certified by the Irish Land Commission to be *bona fide* and in accordance with sound land use practice).'

18–Amendment of Rule 1 of Third Schedule to Principal Act (rules as to calculation of means)

Rule 1 (4) of the Third Schedule to the Principal Act is hereby amended by:

(a) the substitution for subparagraphs (g)(i) and (g)(ii) of the following:
'£312, plus £208 if his spouse is living with or is wholly or mainly maintained by him or, being a single person, widow or widower, is maintaining wholly or mainly a person over the age of 16 years having the care of one or more than one qualified child who normally resides or reside with him, plus £140 for each qualified child normally residing with him of whom account has not already been taken in accordance with this paragraph in calculating the means of another person'; and

(b) the insertion in subparagraph (i) (inserted by the Social Welfare Act 1982) after 'each such child' of 'of whom account has not already been taken in accordance with this paragraph in calculating the means of another person', and the said subparagraph, as so amended, is set out in the Table to this paragraph.

TABLE

'(i) in the case of a person who is not a blind person, and who has a qualified child or qualified children who normally resides or reside with him, all earnings derived by him from his personal exertions except and in so far as the annual amount of such earnings is calculated to exceed £104 (or for the purposes of widow's (non-contributory) pension, £312) for each such child of whom account has not already been taken in accordance with this paragraph in calculating the means of another person.'

19–Payment of increases in respect of qualified children

The Minister may provide by regulations for the payment of increases in respect of qualified children at the full rate to either parent of the children concerned notwithstanding that each parent is entitled to an increase in benefit, pension or assistance, as the case may be, in respect of qualified children.

20–Regulations securing continuity of Act with provisions repealed, amended, etc.

The Minister may, subject to the consent of the Minister for Finance, make regulations for the purpose of securing the continuity of this Act with any provision repealed or amended by this Act or otherwise for the preservation of rights conferred under or by virtue of any of those provisions.

21–Calculation of benefit, pension or allowance

In calculating the amount of any benefit, allowance or pension which, pursuant to section 4, section 26A of the Principal Act (inserted by this Act), section 11 or section 161 (1A) of the Principal Act (inserted by this Act), is payable at one-half of the appropriate amount, fractions of one penny shall be rounded up to the nearest penny.

22–Removal of difficulties

(1) If in any respect any difficulty arises in the administration or operation of this Act, the Minister may, subject to the approval of the Minister for Finance, by order do anything further which appears to be necessary or expedient for bringing this Act into operation, and any such order may modify the provisions of this Act so far as may be necessary or expedient for carrying the order into effect.

(2) Every order made by the Minister under this section shall be laid before each House of the Oireachtas as soon as may be after it is made, and if a resolution is passed by either House of the Oireachtas within the next twenty-one days on which that House has sat after the order is laid before it annulling the order, the order shall be annulled accordingly, but without prejudice to the validity of anything previously done under the order.

(3) No order may be made under this section after the expiration of one year after the commencement of this section.

23–Repeals

Each provision of the Principal Act mentioned at a particular reference number in column (1) of the First Schedule to this Act is hereby repealed to the extent specified in column (2) of that Schedule.

24–Commencement

This Act shall come into operation on such day or days as may be fixed therefor by order or orders of the Minister and different days may be so fixed for different purposes and different provisions of this Act.

25–Short title, construction and collective citation

(1) This Act may be cited as the Social Welfare (No 2) Act 1985.
(2) The Social Welfare Acts 1981 to 1985 and this Act shall be construed as one.
(3) The collective citation 'the Social Welfare Acts 1981 to 1985' shall include this Act.

7.6.2   Social Welfare (No 2) Act 1989

...

2–Certain claims

(1) A person who, on or after the 9th day of May 1989, claims or has claimed, in respect of a period before the passing of this Act, unemployment assistance of an amount to which he would not be entitled if section 12 were applicable shall be entitled to be paid such assistance only in accordance with section 12.

(2) (a) A person who has not, before the 9th day of May 1989, specifically claimed, in respect of a period before the passing of this Act, any additional amount for unemployment assistance being an amount to which he would not be entitled if section 12 were applicable shall not be entitled to be paid the additional amount.

(b) In paragraph (a) of this subsection 'claimed' means claimed in writing from the Minister or claimed in proceedings instituted against the Minister in any court.

(3) In this section 'section 12' means subsections (1), (4), (5) and (6) of section 12 (as amended by this Act) of the Social Welfare (No 2) Act 1985.

3–Non-recoverability

An amount properly paid to any person before the passing of this Act by way of unemployment assistance which as a result of this Act would be recoverable by the Minister shall not be so recoverable.

4–Short title, construction and collective citation

(1) This Act may be cited as the Social Welfare (No 2) Act 1989.

(2) The Social Welfare Acts 1981 to 1989 and this Act shall be construed as one.

(3) The collective citation 'the Social Welfare Acts 1981 to 1989' shall include this Act.

8. CASES

8.1 DECISIONS ON EQUALITY IN GENERAL

The Irish Constitution contains a number of references to equality between the sexes. The most significant of these are in arts 40, 41 and 45 which deal, respectively, with 'Personal rights', 'The family' and 'Directive principles of social policy'.[1] These articles have been cited in a number of constitutional cases which have been brought, over the years, in the areas of employment, jury service, taxation, social welfare, family and property law and adoption. Examples of each of these areas are given below.

8.1.1 EMPLOYMENT

Murtagh Properties Ltd v. Cleary [2]

In *Murtagh Properties Ltd* v. *Cleary* Kenny J decided that an action designed to deprive women of employment, purely on grounds of sex, was unconstitutional. In March 1971, granting an injunction against such action, Kenny J referred to art. 45.2 of the Constitution and expressed the view that:

> Its purpose was to emphasize that, insofar as the right to an adequate means of livelihood was involved, men and women were to be regarded as equal. It follows that a policy or general rule under which anyone seeks to prevent an employer from employing men or women on the ground of sex only is prohibited by the Constitution ... . What is or is not an adequate means of livelihood is a matter for decision by the Oireachtas, but a demand ... that women should not be employed at all in any activity solely because they are women ... is a breach of this right.

In November 1972 Kenny J granted the plaintiffs a perpetual injunction in the general terms of his March 1971 order.

8.1.2 JURY SERVICE

De Burca v. AG [3]

In *de Burca* v. *AG* the Supreme Court held that those sections of the Juries Act 1927 which excluded women from jury service unless they (a) specifically applied to be included and (b) fulfilled various other qualifying conditions (such as owning property with a rateable valuation in excess of a prescribed minimum) were unconstitutional. Indeed, both the conditional

---

1   See §7.1 above.
2   [1972] IR 330 (SC).
3   [1976] IR 38 (SC).

exclusion of women, and the exclusion of citizens who were not ratepayers (i.e. property owners) were found to be inconsistent with the provisions of the Constitution. A new Juries Act 1976 was subsequently introduced, with non-discriminatory eligibility requirements for jurors.

Interestingly, in this judgment, Henchy J and Griffin J first located specific rights guaranteed by the Constitution (the right to a jury trial and the right to work); and then considered whether the exclusion of women was consistent with those rights. The equality issue was a secondary one. However, Walsh J focused mainly on the equality question and stated that the Juries Act 1927 was:

> ... undisguisedly discriminatory on the ground of sex only. It would not be competent for the Oireachtas to legislate on the basis that women, by reason only of their sex, are physically or morally incapable of serving and acting as jurors. The statutory provision does not seek to make any distinction between the different functions that women may fulfil and it does not seek to justify the discrimination on the basis of any social function. It simply lumps together half of the members of the adult population, most of whom have only one thing in common, namely their sex. In my view, it is not open to the State to discriminate in its enactments between the persons who are subject to its laws solely upon the ground of the sex of those persons. If a reference is to be made to the sex of a person, then the purpose of the law that makes such a discrimination should be to deal with some physical or moral capacity or social function that is related exclusively or very largely to that sex only.

8.1.3   TAXATION

Murphy v. *AG* [1]

In the Supreme Court decision in *Murphy* v. *A G* Kenny J ruled that discrimination against married couples in the taxation system contravened art. 41 of the Constitution (which commits the State to protecting the institution of marriage).

Significantly, however, in this judgment Kenny J also expressed the view that such discrimination could be justified under art. 40 because of the 'social function of married couples living together'. This confirms the possibility that the proviso in art. 40 (that the State in its enactments may 'have due regard to differences of capacity, physical and moral, and of social function'), when read in conjunction with the 'recognition' which art. 41 extends to women's 'life within the home', does permit unequal treatment between men and women in certain respects. Specifically, it appears to permit inequalities in relation to the position of (a) women working outside the home (especially married women) and (b) men working within the home.

Following the *Murphy* case, which judged ss 192 to 197 of the Income Tax Act 1967 to be unconstitutional, the offending sections were amended

---

[1]   [1982] IR 241 (SC).

by ss 18 to 21 of the Finance Act 1980. The main effect of these amendments was to increase the tax-free allowances of married couples to twice the amounts applying to single persons and to ensure that the tax bands applying to married couples were double those of single people.

Muckley v. Ireland [1]

Section 21 of the Finance Act 1980 was subsequently challenged in the High Court and found to violate both arts 40.3 and 41 of the Constitution.

Section 21 of the 1980 Act was, in effect, an attempt by the State to recover unpaid taxes from married couples for periods prior to 1980, albeit on a different basis from that judged unconstitutional in *Murphy* v. *AG*.

In *Muckley* v. *Ireland* Barrington J said that s. 21 of the 1980 Act was unconstitutional and that the State could not recover taxes assessed under it. The ruling was accepted by the defendants and ss 20 and 21 of the Finance Act 1980 were both deemed invalid thereafter.

8.1.4   SOCIAL WELFARE

In two more recent cases which came before the High Court, discrimination against married couples in the social welfare system was also deemed to be contrary to art. 41 of the Constitution (as in the *Murphy* case at §8.1.3 above). In both cases, the question of whether the relevant sections contravened Directive 79/7/EEC was side-stepped and the issue was decided solely by reference to the Constitution.

Hyland v. Minister for Social Welfare [2]

In *Hyland* v. *Minister for Social Welfare and AG (1988)*, Barrington J referred to the *Murphy* case and said that he, too, was satisfied that the relevant section of the social welfare code 'violated the State's pledge in art. 41.3 to guard with special care the institution of marriage and protect it against attack'. The Supreme Court upheld this view in May 1989.

Healy v. Eastern Health Board [3]

Shortly after the judgment in *Hyland*, Keane J in *Healy* v. *Eastern Health Board* referred both to the *Murphy* and the *Hyland* cases and held an analogous provision of the Health Act 1970 (providing for a payment known as the disabled person's maintenance allowance) to be similarly unconstitutional. He then added that:

---

[1]   1984, unreported (HC).
[2]   [1989] ILRM 196 (HC); [1990] ILRM 213 (SC).
[3]   1988, unreported (HC).

In these circumstances, it is unnecessary and indeed undesirable for me to express any opinion on the ... submission advanced ... that the determination is in contravention of the EEC Directive ... .

At the time of the Supreme Court judgment in *Hyland*, the *Healy* case was under appeal, but this was subsequently withdrawn.

Dennehy v. *Minister for Social Welfare* [1]

In an earlier claim to the High Court, for equal treatment in social security law with women who provide the sole or main support and care for their children, a man in similar circumstances sought payment of a benefit provided exclusively to women deemed to be 'deserted' by their husband.

However, in *Dennehy* v. *Minister for Social Welfare*, Barron J ruled that the claimant was not entitled to the deserted wife's benefit (payable only to married women raising children on their own, or married women 'deserted' after the age of 40). In his view, the State was entitled under art. 41.2 'to protect financially deserted wives who are mothers and who have dependent children residing with them, or to recognize that mothers who have had to care for children will have lost out in the labour market and so are likely to need similar protection when similarly deserted'. By implication, however, there was no obligation to protect fathers in similar circumstances.[2]

MacMathuna v. *Ireland* [3]

In an action against the State, Mr and Mrs MacMathuna, a married couple with several children, claimed that both the Social Welfare and Finance Acts discriminated against marriage and the family as defined in arts 41 and 42 of the Constitution. This was because the State had abolished tax-free allowances for children and allowed only £3.47 per week for each child of married parents (by way of child benefit); whereas the children of unmarried parents were entitled to £16 per week through welfare allowances. In a reserved judgment Carroll J dismissed the action, stating that in her view the extra support directed to single parents was child-centred and could not be designated as an attack on the institution of marriage. Nor did she accept the plaintiffs' argument that the State had made it more advantageous to be an unmarried mother than to be married with children and had therefore failed in its duty to protect the institution of marriage: the burden of parental responsibility was unquestionably greater for a single parent than for a married couple living together. At the time of writing it was not clear

---

1   26 July 1984, unreported (HC).

2   The *Dennehy* case did not reach the Supreme Court, as intended by Mr Dennehy, because of his premature death. However, a similar case was initiated in August 1989 by a Mr Anthony Lowth, and this was expected to be heard in 1993.

3   27 January 1989, unreported (HC).

whether the MacMathunas intended appealing this judgment to the Supreme Court.

8.1.5   FAMILY AND PROPERTY

BL v. ML (1988) [1]

Article 41 of the Constitution also featured prominently in a High Court action concerning the property rights of a woman working within the home. In a written judgment (October 1988) on a family law case held in camera, Barr J decided that the special recognition in the Constitution (art. 41) for the role of a wife who works in the home gives her the right to own up to half of the family property. This was the first time the High Court had been asked to consider a wife's entitlement to a beneficial interest in matrimonial property in the context of art. 41. Irish courts had already recognized that the financial contribution (e.g. through mortgage repayments or contributions to the family budget) of a wife working outside the home entitled her to a proportional share in the ownership of a family home. However, as Barr J noted in his judgment:

> ... women without independent means who adopt the role of full-time mother in accordance with the philosophy of art. 41 receive no credit under existing law for their labours in the home, however devoted they may have been and for however long ... .
> It seems to me that if effect is to be given to the spirit and objective of art. 41 as to the status of the mother and her crucial role within the family unit, then in assessing her contribution to the acquisition by the husband of the family home and/or furnishings at or about the time of or subsequent to the marriage, regard must be had to the value of her work in the home.
> It should be measured by the court in the light of its nature, quality and duration. I take the view that in making that assessment the course which the court should adopt is to measure the wife's beneficial interest in such family property arising out of her work in the home in percentage terms of ownership as between husband and wife and, bearing in mind that because marriage is an equal partnership, the wife's entitlement so derived ought not to exceed 50 per cent of ownership unless there are exceptional circumstances which justify assessing her beneficial interest in the family home as being greater than that of the husband.

This ruling was appealed to the Supreme Court by the claimant's husband, on the basis that the remedy granted by Barr J was unknown to the law. On 5 December 1991 the Supreme Court overturned the judgment of Barr J, holding that to grant such a remedy amounted to a failure to award 'any known principle of common law', but was rather 'to identify a brand new right'. According to Finlay CJ it was the task of Parliament, not of the courts, to decide whether new ownership rights of this kind should be granted to wives and mothers. The Supreme Court decision gave rise to considerable

---

1   October 1988, unreported (HC); 5 December 1991, unreported (SC).

public concern about the status and property rights of women working in the
home.[1]

8.1.6   ADOPTION

O'G v. AG [2]

The most clear-cut case of legislative provisions being struck down on
the grounds of unconstitutional sex discrimination was O'G v. AG. A
provision in the Adoption Acts which required widowers to satisfy more
onerous conditions than widows when adopting children was described by
McMahon J as being 'founded on the idea of difference in capacity between
men and women which has no foundation in fact'; consequently, it was an
'unwarranted denial of human equality'.

---

1   See also EN v. RN and MC, 5 December 1991, unreported (SC), in which the
    Supreme Court reached a similar decision in principle. In this case, however, the
    court did grant the woman an increased share in the beneficial ownership of the
    home, but based on considerations which were unrelated to her role as wife and
    mother.
2   1985, unreported (HC).

8.2   DECISIONS ON EQUAL PAY

8.2.1   INTRODUCTION

Between 1 January 1976 and 31 December 1991 a total of 423 recommendations by Equality Officers and 170 determinations by the Labour Court were issued under the Anti-Discrimination (Pay) Act 1974 (the 1974 Act). Of these, seven were appealed to the High Court, two to the Supreme Court, and one to the ECJ.[1]

The key cases are arranged below under broad headings corresponding to relevant sections in the 1974 Act, with, in some instances, sub-headings arranged alphabetically. Within each heading or sub-heading, cases are shown in chronological order.

For ease of reference, all cases are cited with the employer name first and then the claimant reference.

8.2.2   SCOPE AND ENTITLEMENT

8.2.2.1   Contemporaneous employees

Champion Fire Defence Ltd v. *Byrne* [2]

The Equality Officer considered that there was nothing in the 1974 Act 'to suggest that a woman cannot be entitled to the same rate of pay as a man who had previously performed the same job as her and that an entitlement under the Act can arise only in respect of a period during which a man and a woman are employed contemporaneously.'

8.2.2.2   Deceased employee

University College Galway v. *EEA* [3]

The husband of a deceased female employee was entitled to the same benefits as those enjoyed by the survivors of married male employees.[4]

8.2.2.3   Definition of employee

Department of the Public Service v. *Robinson* [5]

A member of the national Parliament, the Oireachtas, was held to be 'employed' for the purposes of the Act.[6]

---

1   See §8.2.7.5 below.
2   EP 8/1985; see also §8.2.5 below.
3   EP 18/1984; DEP 2/1985.
4   See §8.2.8.7 below. See also *Department of Education* v. *EEA*, EP 19/1984; DEP 3/1987.
5   EP 36/1978; DEP 7/1979.
6   See §8.2.8.7 below. See also *P. C. Moore & Co.* v. *Flanagan*, EP 13/1978; DEP 12/1978: a partner in a firm of solicitors was held not to be an employee.

8.2.2.4   Former employee

Revenue Commissioners v. *O'Sullivan* [1]

Mr O'Sullivan was not an employee when he originated his claim. There is no definition of employee in the 1974 Act but the definition of employee in the Employment Equality Act 1977 was applied. That definition encompasses former employees.[2]

8.2.2.5   Waiver of equal pay entitlement

Insurance Corporation of Ireland v. *8 Female Staff* [3]

The Labour Court stated that a collective agreement purporting to implement equal pay could not be allowed to deprive individual employees of the right to avail themselves of the procedures set out in the Act.

PMPA Insurance Co. v. *15 Insurance Officials* [4]

The applicants were 15 female insurance officials who, prior to 1978, had been on a separate female grade and had thus been denied equal pay. In 1978 a collective agreement was concluded between the company and the employees' trade union under which a new unisex salary scale was implemented as from January 1978. The applicants then sought equal pay for the period between 31 December 1975 (the date on which the 1974 Act came into force) and 31 December 1977. The company refused this, stating that the benefits (including some benefits in addition to the new salary scale) conferred by the 1978 collective agreement had been offered, and accepted, expressly on the understanding that they were 'in full and final settlement of all claims'. The company considered that this was a binding agreement. This case involved arrears of equal pay only; current entitlement was not at issue.

The Labour Court accepted the principle that the collective agreement was enforceable. However, the Court found that:

> an agreement not to pursue an equal pay claim through the procedures laid down by the Oireachtas, even if the agreement forms part of an individual's contract of employment, should be regarded as void to that extent on the grounds that it is contrary to public policy.

On appeal to the High Court, Carroll J took the different view that a claim for arrears of equal pay could be waived if the agreement were

---

1   EP 10/1983; DEP 7/1983.
2   See §8.2.8.5 below. See also *Bank of Ireland* v. *Kavanagh* (1987) 6 JISLL 192 (HC).
3   EP 8/1977; DEP 6/1977.
4   EP 20/1980; DEP 1980, [1983] IR 330, *sub nom. PMPA Insurance Co.* v. *Keenan* (HC).

On appeal to the High Court, Carroll J took the different view that a claim for arrears of equal pay could be waived if the agreement were 'supported by consideration'. However, she upheld the Labour Court's decision on the grounds that no waiver of the right to claim arrears was necessarily implied in the agreement under consideration.

On further appeal to the Supreme Court (July 1983), Henchy J stated that any compromise of the women's claim for less than their entitlement under the 1974 Act would be unlawful and that a person can only waive or be deprived of their entitlement to equal pay in the most exceptional of circumstances.

Data Products (Dublin) Memories Ltd v. *Simpson* [1]

An employee had accepted a redundancy payment 'as final settlement' of remuneration claims on the company but the Labour Court said that '... even if there was an express term in that agreement waiving the right to equal remuneration it would be over-ridden by s. 4 of this Act'.

8.2.3   SAME PLACE

PMPA Insurance Co. Ltd (Waterford) v. *3 Women Insurance Officials* [2]

The claimants worked in the company's Waterford office and argued that their work was equal in value to that of a male insurance official in the company's Kilkenny office. The company said that they were not performing 'like work' and that Waterford and Kilkenny (some 30 miles apart) were not in the 'same place'. However, the Equality Officer was satisfied that the claimants were performing 'like work' with the Kilkenny official; and that since staff salaries were centrally determined by the company on a nation-wide basis, without regional or geographical variations, the Kilkenny comparison was a valid one.

Midland Health Board v. *Stokes* [3]

The Board submitted that Portlaoise and Tullamore General Hospitals were in different counties and not the 'same place'. The Equality Officer held that the two towns (18 miles apart) were within the same locality and thus in the 'same place'.[4]

---

1   EP 20/1978; DEP 1/1979.
2   EP 29/1981.
3   EP 26/1982.
4   See also *Plunder and Pollak* v. *ATGWU*. Employees were in plants eight miles apart, but the claim was considered under other headings. See §8.2.8.2 below.

Department of Posts and Telegraphs v. 6 Employees [1]

Dublin and Cork were not considered to be the 'same place'.

North-Western Health Board v. Brady [2]

The claim was that Sligo and Portlaoise should be seen as the 'same place' because the pay rates in both were determined at national level. The Equality Officer said this implied that 'same place' included the entire State, which would render the Act's definition of 'place' pointless. The claim was rejected and the Labour Court upheld the recommendation.

Leaf Ltd v. 49 Female Employees [3]

The claimants sought equal pay with 10 men, of whom five were working with them in the company's Co Kildare factory and five were in the Roscommon factory. The Equality Officer said these towns were 75 miles apart and could not be viewed as being in the same 'locality'. The question of whether restricting entitlements under the 1974 Act to people employed in the 'same place' was in conflict with EC law, was also considered; and the Equality Officer concluded that a decision from the ECJ would be required to clarify this point.

Schiesser International (Ireland) Ltd v. ATGWU [4]

Clonmel and Carrick-on-Suir (less than 12 miles apart) were found to be in the same 'locality'.

8.2.4   ASSOCIATED EMPLOYER

Clonskeagh Hospital v. 2 Telephonists [5]

The claimant worked in a different hospital from the male comparator but could claim equal pay as both hospitals were run by the same health board.

8.2.5   SAME WORK

Department of Posts and Telegraphs v. Kennefick [6]

The claimant, a post office clerk, sought equal pay with male clerks. The Department refused, arguing that the male employees had in their

---

1   EP 9/1983.
2   EP 12/1985; DEP 9/1985.
3   EP 10/1988; DEP 4/1989.
4   EP 11-15/1988; DEP 1/1989.
5   EP 40/1979.
6   EP 9/1979; DEP 2/1980.

contract of employment an 'attendance liability and range of duties' which did not apply to the claimant. However, the Equality Officer and the Labour Court found that in practice she performed substantially the same work as the male clerks so that she was entitled to receive equal pay. Also, the actual work performed, rather than the liability to perform particular work, was what was relevant.

Champion Fire Defence v. Byrne [1]

The work of the claimant was compared with that of a former male employee. The Equality Officer said that the Act did not preclude such a comparison [2] but rejected the claim on the grounds that the work being compared was not, in fact, the same.[3]

8.2.6   SIMILAR WORK

Mater Misericordiae Hospital v. ITGWU [4]

The claimant and the male comparator worked as a team in the stores area. The hospital said that the man did heavier physical work, on a regular basis, which the claimant could not do. However, it was considered that they were doing 'like work' within the meaning of s. 3(b) of the 1974 Act because 'the work ... was divided up between them for their own mutual convenience'. The man tried to take on 'some of the heavier or more awkward lifting ... [but] ... this was not significant in volume'.

Toyota Motor Distributors (Ireland) Ltd v. Kavanagh [5]

Both workers were employed in the company's spare parts office under the supervision of an assistant parts manager. The male worker was classified by the company as a 'partsman' and was paid the same rate of pay as other 'partsmen' in the office and in the adjoining spare parts stores. The female worker was classified as a 'stock control clerk' and was the only employee of the company in that category. Her rate of pay was lower than that of the male worker and the other partsmen. On 25 January 1985 the company interchanged the two workers. The female worker subsequently claimed equal pay with the male worker but her claim was rejected by the company. On 11 March 1985 the company reverted the workers to their

---

1   EP 8/1985.
2   See §8.2.2.1 above.
3   See also *CIE* v. *Rail Operatives*, EP 1/1976 (employees not interchangeable); *St Luke's Hospital* v. *ITGWU*, EP 1/1978 (like work conceded); and *St Loman's Hospital* v. *25 Employees*, EP 35/1979 (like work conceded).
4   EP 50/1978.
5   EP 17/1985; DEP 1/1986.

original positions and a dispute arose as to whether or not this was done to frustrate the female worker's claim.

The claim was referred to an Equality Officer, who held as follows:

10. Having regard to these job descriptions, and having inspected the work described at first hand, it seems to me that both workers perform what are essentially two clerical jobs. Therefore, and despite the different impression possibly created by their respective job titles, I consider that their work may reasonably be regarded as being similar in nature for the purpose of s. 3(b) of the Act.

11. The next question, therefore, is whether or not the differences between the two jobs are of small importance in relation to the work as a whole. Having examined the jobs, I am satisfied that there are some differences between them in terms of the factors mentioned by the company. The real question, however, is whether or not these differences, to whatever extent they exist, are sufficiently important to justify the payment of a higher rate of pay to Mr Melbourne.

12. In this regard, it seems to me that whether or not a difference between the two jobs warrants a difference in pay is generally dependent on the grading structure in the particular employment concerned. For example in a company with a large number of job grades, a relatively small difference between two jobs could be sufficient to warrant a difference in pay. In another company, however, one with only a small number of grades each consisting of broadly similar jobs, the same difference might well be considered unimportant and warrant no difference in pay.

13. In order to decide the question in this case, I have, therefore, examined the work performed by other persons who are in the same grade and in receipt of the same rate of pay as Mr Melbourne, i.e. all other 'partsmen'. This examination clearly showed that the work performed by most of these other men, particularly those in the stores area, does not require any special experience, knowledge or judgment, or any type of responsibility which could reasonably be equated with the responsibilities emphasized by the company in arguing the importance of Mr Melbourne's job ... . The examination also showed that Ms Kavanagh is performing work which is at least as demanding as that performed by these other partsmen in the stores area. As Mr Melbourne is therefore being paid the same rate of pay as other partsmen in spite of the additional demands of his job as outlined by the company, and as Ms Kavanagh is performing work which is at least as demanding as that of those same other men, I can see no justifiable reason why those additional demands of Mr Melbourne's work should be regarded as sufficiently important to warrant the payment to him of a higher rate of pay than to Ms Kavanagh. I therefore consider Mr Melbourne and Ms Kavanagh to be employed on like work within the meaning of s. 3(b) of the Act.

This recommendation was upheld on appeal to the Labour Court.

Dowdall O'Mahony & Co. Ltd v. *ITGWU* [1]

All three parts of s. 3 were used in this case, but the decisions under s. 3(b) are most significant; and the approach used in this and the *Toyota* case[2] has been followed by claimants in subsequent s. 3(b) cases. In deciding

---

[1]   EP 2/1987; DEP 6/1987.
[2]   See the previous case.

whether or not to uphold the Equality Officer's finding of 'like work', the Labour Court considered (i) whether the work performed by each claimant was similar in nature to that performed by each comparator; (ii) whether there were differences between their work; (iii) whether such differences occurred infrequently; and (iv) whether they were of small importance in relation to the work as a whole. Its findings were, essentially, that the work performed was of a similar nature; that there were differences; that the differences occurred on an ongoing basis and thus frequently; but that the differences were not of such importance as to justify different rates of pay. In reading the last of these conclusions, the Court pointed out that the Act did not stipulate the basis for deciding what is or is not 'of small importance'. This was therefore a matter for judgment. In this case, it was difficult to establish what criteria had been used to classify the jobs (which had formerly been described simply as 'male' and 'female') and the company admitted that classification had been a matter of judgment and experience. After examining the jobs in question, the Court decided that the major difference was that of physical effort. However, if the sex of the workers had not been a factor, this difference would not have been important enough to justify different grades and different rates of pay. It therefore upheld the recommendation in favour of equal pay.

Charles Bell (Ireland) Ltd v. 3 Female Employees [1]

Again, there were differences in the work performed by the claimants and comparators, but these were considered to be 'of small importance in relation to the work as a whole'.

University College Cork v. 2 Female Laboratory Aides [2]

The Equality Officer found that pay differences were not justified in terms of extra responsibility (as the work of the claimants was as responsible as that of the comparators), or of flexibility (since none of the comparators was called upon to be flexible and it was 'work actually performed' that counted). In reality, therefore, the differences cited did not really exist and equal pay was recommended.[3] The Labour Court subsequently upheld this

---

1   EP 7/1987.
2   EP 4/1988; DEP 1/89.
3   See also *Aer Rianta* v. *ITGWU*, EP 23/1978; DEP 8/1979: 'differences were of small importance ...'; *Bord Iascaigh Mhara* v. *WUI*, EP 46/1978: claim by shorthand typist failed as comparator (a general assistant) had more responsibility; *St Mary's Hospital* v. *24 Employees*, EP 28/1979: differences were 'infrequent and of small importance'; *St Clare's Home* v. *9 Employees*, EP 29/1979: extra responsibility did not justify difference in pay; *National Medical Rehabilitation Centre* v. *19 Employees*, EP 49/1980: nurses were denied equal pay with medical attendants because latter's job had far greater physical element and this was crucial in a centre for disabled and injured people; the difference in work performed was 'frequent and of large importance'.

view: it determined that the claimants were performing 'like work' with their comparators and should be paid the same hourly rate of pay as them.

8.2.7   WORK OF EQUAL VALUE

8.2.7.1   Actual performance

Youghal Carpets v. ITGWU [1]

The Equality Officer found that although the claimants, who were female operatives, were doing different work from the male operatives, roughly 'the same amount of physical effort had to be expended by all', so they were entitled to equal pay.

Department of Posts and Telegraphs v.
Post Office Workers' Union [2]

A strict application of the principle of 'actual performance' led the Equality Officer to conclude that '... the time at which the work is performed should be disregarded in considering whether ... (the claimants and the comparators) ... are employed on like work'.

8.2.7.2   Balancing

Youghal Carpet (Yarns) Ltd v. Canteen Attendants [3]

The Equality Officer considered that the work of a number of canteen attendants was equal in value in terms of s. 3(c) with a male night attendant who performed mostly cleaning duties and to a lesser extent canteen duties. The demands of the claimants' work under the headings of skill and responsibility was greater than the male's as they were involved in checking in goods on arrival as well as checking, counting and recording cash receipts. The physical effort expended by the male was higher, mainly because of lifting and transporting heavy items. His working conditions, although the same in many respects, were more demanding as he was required to clean a number of toilets on a regular basis. On balance, the demands on the claimants and the male comparator were regarded as equal in value.

City of Dublin VEC v. 124 Cleaners [4]

It was agreed that the claimants all performed 'like work'. The male comparators were general operatives (i.e. performing general duties in

---

[1]   EP 25/1981.
[2]   EP 4/1979.
[3]   EP 21/1982.
[4]   EP 13/1986; DEP 1/1987.

schools, such as cleaning classrooms, or gardening). The VEC argued that the males could be transferred between schools/colleges. It was held that this did not justify different payment. Accordingly, the claimants were entitled to the same basic hourly rate with assimilation into the general operative scale on the basis of corresponding points. [1]

8.2.7.3   Job evaluation

Lissadell Towels Ltd v. *56 Female Employees* [2]

56 female employees claimed equal basic remuneration with certain male employees and the payment of production bonus at the same minimum level of performance. The claim was on the basis that the females were doing work of equal value. The company argued that the work performed by the women was not as demanding as the men's and therefore was not 'like work' as per s. 3(c) of the Act.

In assessing the case, the Equality Officer considered the meaning of s. 3(c) and stated that in his view 'work of equal value' was work which warranted the same rate of remuneration; and 'like work' was work which warranted the same rate of remuneration because of the demands it made on those performing it. Thus 'work of equal value' was intended to mean more work which was equally demanding; indeed, it was common practice for employers to pay the same rate for jobs that had been evaluated as being appropriate to the same grade, even where they were not necessarily equally demanding.

Having investigated the jobs of the claimants and comparators, the Equality Officer concluded that the differences in pay were, in reality, based on sex, rather than on the different demands made by the individual jobs. These differences did not warrant unequal pay; therefore the women were entitled to the same rate of basic pay and production bonus as the men.

The company argued that this recommendation had been made entirely on a point of law and that the Equality Officer had made no comparison of the work under the headings of skill, responsibility, physical and mental

---

1   See also *Borg Warner (Ireland) Ltd* v. *16 Female Employees*, EP 11/1982 (claim failed); *Borg Warner (Ireland) Ltd* v. *128 Female Employees*, EP 10/1982; DEP 10/1982 (claim succeeded); *Arthur Guinness Son & Co. Ltd* v. *2 Female Waiters*, EP 18/1982; DEP 8/1983 (claim failed); *North Western Health Board* v. *A Seamstress*, EP 24/1982 (claim failed); *Eastern Health Board* v. *O'Brien*, EP 1/1984 (claim succeeded); *Burlington Hotel* v. *43 Employees*, EP 3/1984; *Howmedica International Inc.* v. *4 Pleur Evac Operators*, EP 2/1986 (claim succeeded); *Ryan Plastics* v. *3 Female Employees*, EP 16/1986 (claim failed).

2   EP 10/1986; DEP 2/1987; (1988) 7 JISLL 184 (HC); DEP 3/1989. See also *Polymark (Ireland) Ltd* v. *ITGWU*, EP 14/1984; DEP 7/1985; *State (Polymark (Ireland) Ltd)* v. *Labour Court* [1987] ILRM 357. See §8.2.10.3 below.

effort, and working conditions, as required under the Act. It therefore appealed the recommendation on points of both law and fact.

The Labour Court overturned the Equality Officer's recommendation and rejected its interpretation of s. 3(c), stating that:

> The question of whether the work of a claimant is equal in value to the work of a comparator should be decided by the Equality Officer in terms of the demands which the work makes — not on the particular individuals performing it, or by reference to the pay of the persons performing it — but objectively assessed.
>
> Factors such as skill, physical or mental effort, responsibility and working conditions are examples of the kind of demands which may be taken into account in the evaluation process.
>
> As a general rule the factors which are in use in the particular employment either explicitly, as in a formal job evaluation scheme, or implicitly in a job grading classification system of pay, should be adopted by the Equality Officer, except of course where there is an element of sex bias in the factors themselves. This is often the case.
>
> The Court does not consider that the Equality Officer's opinion at para. 14 of his recommendation is correct. To accept, as he does, that, 'equal in value' means 'work that warrants the same rate of remuneration' introduces circularity into the argument. The Court therefore upholds this basis of the appeal.

As well as rejecting the Equality Officer's interpretation of 'equal value', the Labour Court also held that the recommendation had been based on an incorrect interpretation of 'equal rate of remuneration'. It allowed the appeal solely on these questions of interpretation; and did not deal in detail with the facts of the case.

The claimants then applied to the High Court for a judicial review of the Labour Court's determination, on the grounds that the Labour Court's failure to make a finding on the validity of the claim itself left them in limbo. The High Court directed that the matter be remitted to the Labour Court for an investigation of the validity of the claim [1].

Kayfoam Woolfson v. *7 Female Employees* [2]

The Equality Officer said that the value of the work in terms of the demands specified in s. 3(c) was 'the value which is or would be reflected in the rates of remuneration in the absence of discrimination on the basis of sex'. She considered that, in terms of assessing whether two jobs were equal in value, the point to be addressed was whether there were differences in demands between the two jobs which would have convinced the employer to allocate the jobs to different grades had both jobs been performed by males.

The Labour Court upheld this recommendation.[3]

---

[1] See §§ 3.5.2 above and 8.2.10.3 below.

[2] EP 4/1987; DEP 6/1988.

[3] See also *Dowdall O'Mahoney & Co.* v. *ITGWU*, EP 2/1987, DEP 6/1987. As in the *Lissadell* and *Kayfoam Woolfson* cases above, the Court stressed that in order to apply s. 3(c) an assessment of work performed is required. See §8.2.6 above.

8.2.7.4 Overall responsibility

Blood Transfusion Board v. *O'Sullivan* [1]

The Equality Officer stated that 'responsibility is more important than physical effort'.[2]

8.2.7.5 Work of higher value

An Bord Telecom Éireann v. *Murphy* [3]

Both the Equality Officer and the Labour Court had rejected the equal pay claim on the basis that the claimants were doing work which was of higher value than the comparators. Keane J considered that this issue should be referred to the ECJ as:
- the construction of s. 3(c) would result in equal pay for unequal work, an outcome which could not have been intended by the legislature;
- an intention to partly remedy the situation could not be read into the Act;
- where the Act itself had not addressed itself to a particular issue, it was not for the Court to accept a meaning to the Act;
- a possible outcome of s. 3(c) was that the claimants may lawfully be paid lower wages than a male employee whose work was of lesser value. It was a question of EC law and Irish law whether such a position was reconcilable with art. 119 of the EEC Treaty.

The ECJ held:

> Article 119 of the EEC Treaty must be interpreted as covering the case where a worker who relies on that provision to obtain equal pay within the meaning thereof is engaged in work of higher value than that of the person with whom a comparison is to be made. Art. 119 requires the application of the principle of equal pay for men and women solely in the case of equal work or in the case of work of equal value, and not in the case of work of unequal value. Nevertheless, if that principle forbids workers of one sex engaged in work of equal value to that of workers of the opposite sex to be paid a lower wage than the latter on grounds of sex, *a fortiori* it prohibits such a difference in pay where the lower paid category of workers is engaged in work of higher value.

> To adopt a contrary interpretation would be tantamount to rendering the principle of equal pay ineffective and nugatory, since an employer would be able to

---

1   EP 23/1981.

2   See also *Irish Containers* v. *ATGWU*, EP 1/1979; DEP 14/1979; *PMPA* v. *4 Employees*, EP 33/1980; *Linson* v. *27 Stomahesive Operatives*, EP 32/1981; *Addis* v. *19 Employees*, EP 20/1981.

3   *An Bord Telecom Éireann* v. *Murphy* EP 28/1983; DEP 6/1984; *Murphy* v. *Bord Telecom Éireann* [1986] ILRM 483 (HC); Case 157/86, [1988] ECR 673 (ECJ), [1989] ILRM 53 (ECJ and HC); DEP 7/1988.

circumvent the principle by assigning additional or more onerous duties to workers of a particular sex, who could then be paid a lower wage.

The High Court in April 1988 ordered that the case be remitted to the Labour Court with a direction that the applicants' claim be determined on the basis that 'like work' existed. The Labour Court granted equal pay to the claimants.[1]

8.2.8   REMUNERATION

8.2.8.1   Accommodation

Midland Health Board v. *Stokes* [2]

The Equality Officer held that staff accommodation provided by the employer below the cost of similar private accommodation constituted remuneration. This recommendation was overruled by the Labour Court on the basis that the accommodation was only 'incidentally available'.

8.2.8.2   Bonus payments

Plunder and Pollak v. *ATGWU* [3]

The company maintained that the men's additional earnings consisted solely of 'rest allowances' which could not be described as 'remuneration'. The Labour Court held that the latter term covered 'equal basic rates and equal basic earnings for equal levels of output'.

Lissadell Towels Ltd v. *56 Female Employees* [4]

In this case[5] the Equality Officer considered the question of what is meant by 'rate of remuneration'. The case involved a claim for equal basic pay, and payment to the claimants of a production bonus at the same minimum level of performance as their male comparators. The bonus was being paid to the women at 85 per cent of standard performance, whereas the men's bonus started at 70 per cent. On the other hand, the women's bonus reached a maximum at 117 per cent of standard performance, whereas the men's did not until 120 per cent. The Equality Officer recommended payment of the women's bonus at the same minimum level of performance as the men (i.e. 70 per cent); and said he saw no reason why they should have to accept some other disimprovement (such as a raising of their maximum to

---

1   See also *Department of Agriculture* v. *ITGWU* EP 28/1978; DEP 6/1979; *Arthur Guinness Son & Co. (Dublin) Ltd* v. *FWUI (EP 17/1983, DEP 11/1983)*; *Department of Posts and Telegraphs* v. *29 Female Post Office Factory Workers (EP 28/1983)*.

2   EP 26/1982; DEP 2/1983.

3   EP 30/1978; DEP 3/1979.

4   EP 10/1986; DEP 2/1987; but note (1988) 7 JISLL 184 (HC); DEP 3/1989.

5   See §8.2.7.3 above and §8.2.10.3 below.

120 per cent) as a *quid pro quo*. The company appealed the recommendation on this and other grounds; and the Labour Court upheld the appeal, stating that total remuneration was what counted.

Galway Crystal v. ATGWU [1]

The claimants sought the retention of bonus payments granted before the implementation of equal pay. The company wanted to stop the payments, but the Equality Officer concluded that this was not permissible since they related to productivity; and said '... it would amount to something less than the full implementation of equal pay ... if ... [they] ... were to be abolished'.

Group 4 Securitas (Ireland) Ltd v. 26 Female Store Detectives [2]

The company's store detectives were an all-female grade while its guards were predominantly male. Both groups were on different pay scales. The female employees requested the same unsocial hours allowance, Sunday work allowance and uniform allowance as were paid to the male guards.

The company conceded that the claimants and the comparators were employed on 'like work'. Therefore the only question for consideration was whether there were 'grounds other than sex' for the non-payment to the claimants of the allowances.

The company argued that the non-payment of the unsocial hours allowance had nothing to do with sex, as it was based on the liability of the guards to work over a 24-hour period. The Equality Officer accepted the company's argument in respect of this allowance. However, the Equality Officer considered that there were no 'grounds other than sex' to explain the more favourable Sunday work allowance or uniform allowance paid to the men, and that these were 'remuneration' within the terms of the 1974 Act.

8.2.8.3   Commission

Clery (1941) Ltd v. 25 Female Employees [3]

Commission paid to sales assistants was accepted as being an element of their remuneration.

8.2.8.4   Definition of 'same rate'

Lissadell Towels Ltd v. 56 Female Employees [4]

Basic pay and bonus pay were calculated on a different basis between the sexes. The Labour Court rejected the Equality Officer's finding that

---

1   EP 22/1978.
2   EP 3/1991.
3   EP 26/1983; DEP 2/1984.
4   EP 10/1986; DEP 2/1987; (1988) 7 JISLL 184 (HC); DEP 3/1989. See also § 3.5.2.

individual aspects of remuneration could be compared without having regard to total remuneration.

Metropole Hotel v. 7 Waitresses [1]

The hotel maintained that the female claimants received a lower basic rate of pay than the male waiter comparator as the former were in receipt of living accommodation. However, there was no evidence to prove that this was the reason as to why the females were on a lower rate. They were both doing 'like work' and the Equality Officer concluded that they should receive 'the same rate' of remuneration. Even if the option to live-in constituted remuneration, payment of a lower basic rate, plus an option to live-in, did not constitute payment of the same rate; they must, therefore, be paid the higher rate. The Labour Court upheld this recommendation.

Krups Engineering v. 16 Armature Winders [2]

The Labour Court stated that investigations must be concerned with total remuneration in the first instance and that the significance of different elements in its make-up must then be decided on the facts of each case.

8.2.8.5   Marriage gratuities

Revenue Commissioners v. O'Sullivan [3]

The Commissioners argued that as the claimant was entitled to deferred pension benefits his remuneration was not less than that of a female who received a marriage gratuity but had no entitlement to deferred benefits. The Equality Officer considered, however, that a preserved superannuation benefit could not be regarded as the 'same rate of remuneration' as a marriage gratuity. She also considered that female officers who had a choice between a marriage gratuity or preserved benefits were being treated more favourably than males who were only entitled to preserved benefits. On appeal the Labour Court upheld the recommendation but stated as follows:

> The Court however is not satisfied that in all cases of the same nature, the remedy lies in the payment to the claimant of a marriage gratuity on the same basis as that paid to the worker with whom the claimant compares his case. The present case hinges on the claimant not having been given an option as between gratuity and deferred superannuation and the remedy recommended is valid because he obviously holds that the gratuity claimed in his particular case comes up to the value of the alternative. This element may not be present in other cases and, therefore, this cannot be taken as a precedent for all such cases.

---

1   EP 19/1986; DEP 4/1987.
2   EP 8/1986; DEP 1/1988.
3   EP 10/1983; DEP 7/1983.

Bank of Ireland v. *Kavanagh* [1]

Prior to 1974 all female officials in the bank were required to resign on marriage. At the time of resignation and on production of their marriage certificate all female officials were paid a marriage gratuity. In March 1974 an agreement was entered into between the Banks' Staff Relations Committee and the Irish Bank Officials Association which *inter alia* abolished the marriage bar but retained the gratuity for all pre-1974 staff. Mr Kavanagh was employed in the bank from 1969 until his resignation in 1984. He had married in 1980 and shortly before he left the bank's employment he applied for the gratuity. The dispute was referred to an Equality Officer who recommended payment of the gratuity, thus confirming its status as part of remuneration. The recommendation was upheld by the Labour Court. The bank appealed to the High Court and was successful in arguing that the payment had been made on 'grounds other than sex'.[2] Costello J held:

> A female employee who qualifies for the gratuity and thus gets paid a higher remuneration than her male colleague doing like work gets higher pay not because she is a woman, but because she is a woman who has fulfilled certain conditions, namely that she has (a) married and (b) entered the bank's employment before 1974. Her higher pay is not based on her sex but on grounds other than her sex, a point convincingly demonstrated by the fact that all of her female colleagues who marry and are doing like work will be treated differently from her and on the same footing as men if they entered the bank's service after 1 January 1974.

This decision was appealed to the Supreme Court but settled prior to the hearing. An out-of-court settlement of £14,013 was agreed, with the bank stating that although this represented the amount of the gratuity claimed, it was not in fact the gratuity but 'purely and simply' a payment offered by the bank to avoid legal costs. The Supreme Court was advised on 17 January 1989 that the appeal could be struck out by consent of the parties (*Irish Times*, 19 January 1989).[3]

8.2.8.6 Payment-in-kind

CIE v. *ITGWU* [4]

The female claimant, a cook, was doing 'like work' with the male comparator but received a lower basic rate of remuneration as she was in receipt of free living accommodation etc. The Equality Officer held and the Labour Court confirmed that for the present the differential should remain but if the female stopped taking advantage of free accommodation, she should be paid the same rate as the male cooks.

---

1   EP 11/1985; DEP 10/1985.
2   See §8.2.9.10 below.
3   The High Court judgment was also followed in *National Irish Bank* v. *Deeney*, EP 4/1991.
4   EP 13/1977; DEP 1/1978.

8.2.8.7   Pensions

Linson v. ASTMS [1]

The inclusion of pension schemes within the scope of 'remuneration' was first established in this case, where there were both different entry and retirement ages in the scheme. The Equality Officer stated that 'pension benefits or allowances based on the wage or salary received by an employee are within the scope of the Act'. The Labour Court determined that there should be equal pension benefits for men and women.

Department of Public Service v. Robinson [2]

Equality of survivors' benefits were considered in this case. Senator Mary Robinson maintained that the non-provision of a widower's pension was discriminatory. It was held that the provision of such benefits was part of employees' remuneration 'and the fact that they are paid after the death of the employee does not put them outside the scope of the Act'. Thus the claim succeeded (and most public servants subsequently became eligible for spouses' pensions).

University College Dublin v. IFUT [3]

The Labour Court considered that the provision of a contributory widows' and children's plan for men only was discriminatory.

University College Galway v. Employment Equality Agency [4]

The claimant was the spouse of a deceased employee. The Equality Officer held that a claim relating to the actual amount of benefit was outside the scope of the Act as the payment was being claimed by a person other than the employee of the employer.

The EEA appealed this recommendation to the Labour Court, which overruled it. The Court considered that the Equality Officer should not have concentrated on who the claimant was but whether an implied term operated or existed in the employee's contract of employment that her husband would be paid the same survivor's benefit as would the wife of a deceased male employee. The Court ruled that her husband was entitled to the same benefits as those enjoyed by the survivors of male employees.[5]

---

1   EP 1/1977; DEP 2/1977.
2   EP 36/1978; DEP 7/1979. In 1990 the claimant in this case, Mrs Mary Robinson, was elected President of Ireland.
3   EP 7/1979; DEP 17/1979.
4   EP 18/1984; DEP 2/1985.
5   See also Department of Education v. EEA, EP 19/1984; DEP 3/1987.

8.2.8.8   Permanent health insurance: income continuance plan

Shield Insurance Co. Ltd v. *2 Female Employees* [1]

An Equality Officer held that membership of a permanent health insurance plan, provided and paid for by the company, constituted remuneration. Accordingly, the claimants were entitled to be eligible under the terms of the plan for benefit in respect of disablement related to pregnancy or childbirth.

McCarren & Co. Ltd v. *Jackson*[2]

The Equality Officer held that membership of an income continuance scheme constituted remuneration; and that equality in such remuneration included eligibility for benefit in respect of pregnancy-related illness or disability.

8.2.8.9   Redundancy

Grant, Barnett & Co. Ltd v. *Kiernan* [3]

The Equality Officer concluded that a redundancy lump sum payment, in excess of the statutory amount, formed part of remuneration.

8.2.8.10 Sick leave

North-Western Health Board v. *Brady* [4]

The claimant, who was pregnant, was denied paid sick leave and was advised by the Board to take unpaid additional maternity leave. The Equality Officer considered that such treatment was indirectly discriminatory on grounds of sex since the policy was 'naturally and exclusively' to the detriment of Board's female employees. However, the Equality Officer did not recommend equal pay as the claimant and the male comparator were not employed in the 'same place'. On appeal, the Labour Court upheld the recommendation.

8.2.8.11 Staff uniforms

Educational Building Society v. *Male Employees* [5]

The claimants maintained that they were entitled to a uniform on the same basis as female employees, or compensation in lieu of uniform. The

---

1   EP 8/1984.
2   EP 5/1987.
3   EP 6/1983.
4   EP 12/1985; DEP 9/1985.
5   EP 9/1987.

Educational Building Society provided its female employees with a uniform
free of charge. The contract of employment provided that 'dress as
considered appropriate by management must be worn at all times; uniforms
where provided must be worn'. The Equality Officer decided that the
provision of uniforms in this case did not fall within the definition of
remuneration under the Act since it was a condition of employment that the
uniform must be worn. Thus the uniform was not 'consideration' in respect of
the women's employment: it was not given in return for something given or
promised by the employee under the contract of employment.

British Home Stores (Dublin) Ltd v. 127 Catering Assistants [1]

The claimants maintained that as the two male comparators had their
uniforms laundered free of charge, they were entitled to such free laundering
also. All catering assistants were doing like work and were on the same rates
of pay. However the union maintained that the females were, in reality, on a
lower rate of pay as they had to launder their own uniforms. The union
claimed approximate amounts of money for soap powder, their time, etc.

The Equality Officer considered that the employer was not providing the
laundering of the uniforms in return for something given or promised by the
male employees under the contract of employment. Both males and females
were employed subject to the condition that they wore uniforms which were
clean at all times. Accordingly, the provision of laundered uniforms to the
males did not constitute any part of their consideration and thus the females'
claim claim did not fall within the scope of the Act. The recommendation
was upheld by the Labour Court.

8.2.9   GROUNDS OTHER THAN SEX

8.2.9.1   Actuarial factors

Shield Insurance Co. Ltd v. 2 Female Employees [2]

The Company maintained that differences in remuneration (in an
income continuance scheme) were due to the application of actuarial factors
which differed between the sexes. Also, the different treatment of women
(the exclusion of pregnancy-related illnesses) was at the insistence of another
company (the insurance company with whom the income continuance
scheme had been arranged) and not through any intention of Shield Insurance
itself to discriminate. The Equality Officer rejected both arguments and said
that the company was obliged under the Act to provide equal benefits
regardless of any differences in costs.[3]

---

[1]   EP 1/1988; DEP 5/1988.
[2]   EP 8/1984.
[3]   See §8.2.8.8 above.

8.2.9.2 Age/service

Inter-Beauty (Ireland) Ltd v. *Bobbett* [1]

The company maintained that the claimant was paid a different rate of pay because the male operator had longer service. However, his longer service was not allied to annual increments. Accordingly, the claimant was entitled to equal pay.

Irish Plastic Packaging v. *ITGWU* [2]

The Equality Officer accepted that 'an age-related wage structure, in itself, does not constitute discrimination ... as it is a differentiation in pay based on age rather than sex'.

8.2.9.3 Attendance

Navan Carpets (Yarns) Ltd v. *92 Female Employees* [3]

The Equality Officer could not accept that the higher basic rate being paid to the males derived from their liability to do night-work and was not sex-based.

8.2.9.4 Capacity for extra duties

Nitrigin Éireann Teo v. *ITGWU* [4]

The actual range of duties performed by the male comparator was also performed by the female claimants. Accordingly, there was an entitlement to equal pay.

Dunne's Stores (Parkway) Limerick Ltd v. *28 Female Employees* [5]

The male comparators had a flexibility for doing extra duties over and above their main work. Accordingly the claimants were not entitled to equal pay.

8.2.9.5 Compassion

Nitrigin Éireann Teo. v. *ITGWU* [6]

The company contended that the male general labourer was paid a higher rate than the female cleaners on grounds other than sex, i.e. on

---

1   EP 41/1981.
2   EP 25/1978.
3   EP 46/1979. See also *Department of Posts and Telegraphs* v. *POWU*, EP 4/1979. However, in *Department of Posts and Telegraphs* v. *POMSA*, EP 7/1977, it was accepted that a more onerous attendance liability constituted valid 'grounds other than sex' for payment of a higher rate.
4   EP 49/1979; DEP 16/1980.
5   EP 6/1987.
6   EP 2/1977; DEP 4/1977.

compassionate grounds, as he could not carry out the full range of physical duties due to his condition. The Labour Court accepted the company's argument.[1]

8.2.9.6   Former position/personal rate

Irish Dunlop Ltd v. *Cronin* [2]

The Equality Officer accepted the company's argument that the male comparator received a higher rate of pay than the claimant 'on grounds other than sex'. The male comparator had previously held a supervisory position in another department and had retained his personal rate of pay 'because of his former position'.[3]

8.2.9.7   Grading structures

Howmedica International Inc. v. *4 Pleur-Evac Operators* [4]

The claimants and the male comparator worked in different departments but the Equality Officer rejected the argument that their pay differences were for reasons other than sex and said that the women were entitled to equal pay. However, in several other cases, it was accepted that the payment of different rates to differently-graded employees was not sex related.[5]

8.2.9.8   Industrial action/industrial relations

Brooks Thomas Ltd v. *ASTMS* [6]

As a result of job evaluation, the rates of pay of all employees were set in a non-discriminatory manner. However, the company subsequently hired men to do work graded as F and G and the union insisted that these men be paid at grade D and E rates (the original male ones). The company agreed to do so and the women in grades F and G then claimed equal pay with the new male entrants. The Equality Officer considered that by paying the new men grade D and E rates, 'the company had re-established rates of pay for grades F and G which differentiated on the basis of sex'. However, the Labour Court

---

1   Similar decisions were also given in *Central Bank of Ireland* v. *1 Female Cleaner*, EP 48/1980; and *CIE* v. *2 Females*, EP 46/1981.

2   EP 39/1978; DEP 4/1979.

3   Similar arguments were accepted in *Boart Hardmetals Europe Ltd* v. *3 Women Canteen Assistants*, EP 64/1980; and *Cadbury (Ireland) Ltd* v. *8 Female Employees*, EP 5/1985.

4   EP 2/1986.

5   See *Bord na Móna* v. *Keightly*, EP 16/1985; *Measurex Ireland Ltd* v. *2 Female Calibration Laboratory Technicians*, EP 9/1985; *Meath Hospital* v. *Male Night Porters*, EP 12/1986; DEP 9/1986.

6   EP 6/1977; DEP 7/1977.

disagreed, saying that the money 'was paid by the company on grounds other than sex, i.e. threat of industrial action'. It also pointed out that s. 9 of the Employment Equality Act 1977 prohibited procuring, or attempting to procure, discrimination; thus the circumstances which gave rise to this determination should nowhere be repeated.[1]

8.2.9.9   Juvenile rates

Youghal Carpet (Yarns) Ltd v. ITGWU [2]

The issue before the Labour Court was that a male juvenile received the general adult rate when transferred on to an adult operation on a temporary basis. A female juvenile, however, received the general juvenile rate regardless of the fact that she was engaged full-time on adult work. The Labour Court upheld the Equality Officer's recommendation that the females were entitled to equal pay.

8.2.9.10   Marital status

Bank of Ireland v. Kavanagh [3]

The High Court found that payment of marriage gratuities to certain women was made on grounds other than sex (i.e. marital status and entry to the employment prior to a certain date) and was, therefore, permissible.[4]

8.2.9.11   Maternity/indirect discrimination

North-Western Health Board v. Brady [5]

Refusal to grant paid sick leave (because the claimant could have made use of unpaid maternity leave at the time) was held to be indirectly discriminatory and hence not permissible [6].

8.2.9.12   Part-time employees

Dunne's Stores (Navan) Ltd v. 2 Female Employees [7]

The Equality Officer had to consider the question of whether two female part-time employees were entitled to equal pay with a male full-time employee. The company maintained that the case was merely an attempt by

---

1   See *Grant Barnett and Co. Ltd* v. *Kiernan*, EP 6/1983 and EE 6/1983. The Labour Court held that there may be differences in pay arising from the industrial relations process, and that such differences may be justifiable as long as they are not inherently discriminatory. Thus the difference was allowed on 'grounds other than sex'.
2   EP 9/1986; DEP 8/1986.
3   EP 11/1985; DEP 10/1985; (1987) 6 JISLL 192 (HC).
4   See §8.2.8.5 above.
5   EP 12/1985; DEP 9/1985.
6   See §8.2.8.10 above.
7   EP 15/1982.

the union (IUDWC) to obtain a recommendation from the Equality Officer that part-time staff should be paid at the same rate as full-time staff. The company paid its full-time employees, whether male or female, the same rate; and part-time employees likewise. However the Equality Officer found that the males on full-time work did not perform the same work as the females, nor did the part-time males perform the same work as the females.

It was held that the female claimants were performing work equal in value with the named male. The Equality Officer further ruled that the payment of different rates on the grounds of full-time or part-time status were not valid grounds *per se* in terms of s. 2(3) of the Act, i.e. the defence of 'grounds other sex'; nor was she satisfied that the employer had any economically justifiable reasons for maintaining the differential. The women were therefore to be paid the same hourly rate and to be assimilated onto the full-time salary scale on the basis of cumulative hours worked, although it would obviously take them longer to reach various service points on the scale.

St. Patrick's College, Maynooth v. ITGWU [1]

The Labour Court held that female workers of a particular category, working reduced hours, were entitled to the same incremental progression as a male worker in the same category working full-time hours.

8.2.9.13 Qualifications

Department of Agriculture and County Committees of Agriculture v. Instructors in Farm Home Management and in Poultry Keeping [2]

The Labour Court upheld the appeal of the Department of Agriculture, which had claimed that the male comparators required higher educational qualifications (i.e. a degree as opposed to a diploma) and that this difference justified their higher rate of pay.[3]

---

[1]   EP 4/1984; DEP 10/1984.

[2]   EP 23/1978; DEP 10/1979.

[3]   See also *ACOT* v. *Irish Agricultural Advisers' Organization*, EP 13/1984; DEP 8/1985; 1989, unreported (HC): different employment records as well as different educational qualifications, were also at issue here. The Labour Court concluded that the pay differences were, in reality, based on sex rather than the other factors. ACOT appealed to the High Court on a point of law on four grounds. In a reserved judgment on 13 April 1989 Carroll J rejected two of these grounds, including the contention that the Labour Court had been wrong in determining that discrimination had not been on grounds other than sex.

8.2.9.14 'Red circle'

Hanson Ltd v. McLoughlin [1]

The male comparator had a higher rate of pay as a result of an over-evaluation of his job prior to the introduction of a job evaluation scheme. The Equality Officer held that this constituted 'grounds other than sex': it was a genuine case of 'red circling' and had been explained to the claimant when she first sought and accepted the job.

Micromotors Groschopp Ireland Ltd v. ITGWU [2]

Following an equal pay claim and a subsequent job evaluation exercise, 16 men and 1 woman were found to have been 'over-rated', but were allowed to retain their old rates on a personal basis. Four other women later claimed equal pay with a number of the 'red circled' men, arguing that the 'red-circling' had only perpetuated earlier sex discrimination. The company maintained that the 'red circling' was non-discriminatory; and the Equality Officer accepted this in relation to three of the claimants. The fourth claimant, however, had been employed at the time of the job evaluation and was doing like work with one of the comparators, but had not been similarly 'red circled'. The Equality Officer was satisfied that had she been a man, her rate of pay prior to the job evaluation would have been the same as the comparator's; she would therefore have been 'red circled' in the same way as him. Consequently, her claim succeeded. The Labour Court upheld this recommendation.

Eastern Health Board v. Coffey [3]

The claimants were 62 female domestic staff who considered they were doing 'like work' with named male attendants. 'Like work' was conceded and the employers relied on 'grounds other than sex'. It was argued that the males had been 'red circled', holding their rate on a personal basis. The Labour Court accepted that 'red circling' is a recognized practice in industrial relations. However, if 'red circling' is a defence, the Court must consider the reasons for 'red circling' and must be satisfied that the parties had acknowledged its existence. On the facts of the case, there had been a change in the male duties some years previously. Nineteen of the comparators stated in writing that they were not aware of any agreement, and the Court thus considered that the defence had failed and that there was an entitlement to equal pay.

---

1   EP 45/1979.
2   EP 18/1986; DEP 5/1987.
3   EP 8/1990; DEP 5/1991.

8.2.9.15 Salary and service

Bord Telecom Éireann v. *Ní Oireachtaigh* [1]

The claimant argued sex discrimination in relation to pension and lump sum entitlements (and other payments), which were much lower than those of the comparators. However, the Equality Officer concluded that this was mainly because her salary and service were lower and these were so for reasons other than sex. No discrimination had occurred in the calculation of her salary or service and a man in the same situation would have received the same pension and lump sum.

8.2.10   PRACTICE AND PROCEDURE

8.2.10.1 Appeals to the Labour Court

Dunne's Stores (Northside) Ltd v. *5 Female Employees* [2]

The Equality Officer had recommended that there was no entitlement to equal pay. The claimants appealed the recommendation to the Labour Court. The Labour Court considered that the union's appeal was not valid as it did not challenge any matter of fact or law as contained in the recommendation; it merely sought to challenge the effects of the recommendation.

Eastern Health Board v. *Coffey* [3]

For the facts see §8.2.9.14 above. Both the Health Board and trade union appealed to the Labour Court under s. 8 of the 1974 Act; the Health Board appealed against the recommendation, and the trade union sought a determination that the recommendation had not been implemented. The notice of appeals from the Health Board did not state its grounds of appeal as is required under the Act. The Court found that the appeal did not comply with s. 8(1) of the 1974 Act.

8.2.10.2 Application of EC law

Bord Telecom Éireann v. *Murphy* [4]

For the facts see §8.2.7.5 above. The High Court held that the Labour Court, in discharging its statutory functions, was as much bound to apply EC law as was the High Court. Furthermore, where national law and EC law conflicted, it had to give precedence to EC law.

---

[1]   EP 9/1988.
[2]   EP 6/1988; DEP 4/1988.
[3]   EP 8/1990; DEP 5/1991. See §8.2.9.14 above.
[4]   See §8.2.7.5 above.

8.2.10.3 Procedures of the Court

Change in comparator

Polymark (Ireland) Ltd v. ITGWU [1]

This case highlighted the point that a claimant cannot change comparator during the course of hearing the claim (*inter alia*). It was held that such a change in comparator was in effect a new claim.

Investigation

Lissadell Towels Ltd v. 56 Female Employees [2]

The claimants referred the Labour Court determination to the High Court for judicial review requesting the High Court to order the Labour Court to investigate the validity of their claim. The Labour Court had overturned an Equality Officer's interpretation of 'equal value' and 'same rate of remuneration', but this had left the claimants with no means of having their case examined on its merits. Further they maintained that the Labour Court had an obligation to investigate the facts of the original case and not just base its decision on the Equality Officer's findings.

Egan J granted the claimants' application for judicial review. He held that the whole claim be referred back to the Labour Court for a full hearing and investigation. The Labour Court appealed the High Court judgment to the Supreme Court but that appeal was subsequently withdrawn..

Natural Justice

State (Polymark (Ireland) Ltd) v. Labour Court [3]

The High Court said that where the members of the Labour Court took legal advice from their Registrar, they:

> should first inform the parties of their intention to ask the Registrar for legal advice; then, having obtained the advice they should, at a resumed hearing, inform the parties of the nature of the advice they had obtained and give the parties an opportunity of making submissions in regard to it, and finally, having heard the submissions, the members of the Court should, on their own, without further reference to the Registrar, arrive at their own conclusions on the issue.

---

1   EP 14/1984; DEP 7/1985, [1987] ILRM 357. See also *Lissadell Towels Ltd v. 56 Female Employees*, §8.2.8.4 above and immediately below.
2   See preceding footnote.
3   [1987] ILRM 357 (HC): review of *Polymark (Ireland) Ltd v. ITGWU*, see footnote 1 above.

State (Cole and Others) v. Labour Court [1]

The High Court quashed the original Labour Court determination on the basis that the Labour Court hearing did not conform to natural justice as an expert's confidential report, obtained by the Court, was not raised with both parties so that their submissions on it could be heard. Also, the union's failure to object, initially, to the procedure used, did not preclude it from appealing later to the High Court, since it was not clear, at the time, what the nature of the report would be and how it would be used.

8.2.10.4 Time-limits

Dunnes Stores (Parkway) Limerick Ltd v. 28 Female Employees [2]

The company contended that the equal pay claim was out of time. Section 56(2) of the Employment Equality Act 1977 provided that the 1974 and 1977 Acts should be construed as one Act. Accordingly, the time-limit of six months contained in s. 19(5) of the 1977 Act applied also to equal pay claims. The Equality Officer rejected this argument as the time-limit only referred to claims under ss 19 and 20 of the 1977 Act.

---

1   (1984) 3 JISLL 124 (HC).
2   EP 6/1987.

8.3 DECISIONS ON EMPLOYMENT EQUALITY

8.3.1 INTRODUCTION

Between 1 July 1977 and 31 December 1991 a total of 232 recommendations by Equality Officers and 62 determinations by the Labour Court were issued under the Employment Equality Act 1977 (the 1977 Act). Of these, four were appealed to the High Court, three to the Supreme Court.

The key cases are arranged below under broad headings corresponding to relevant sections in the 1977 Act. Within these, there may be sub-headings arranged in alphabetical order and cases are shown in chronological order.

For ease of reference, all cases are cited with the employer name first and then the claimant reference.

8.3.2 ACCESS TO EMPLOYMENT

8.3.2.1 Access to employment (part-time)

HB Ice Cream v. *Ryan* [1]

The claimant maintained that he was refused access to a job of part-time factory operative on the basis of his sex. He said that he was told at interview that the jobs were for females only. There was conflict of evidence in this case. The Equality Officer found in favour of the company.

Packard Electric Ireland Ltd v. *EEA* [2]

The employees alleged that certain employees on the part-time twilight shift were barred from entry to full-time employment. The practice arose from a clause in the union/management agreement (to which the co-respondent unions were party) which provided that employees who had been laid-off or made redundant from the twilight shift could not apply for full-time work with the company until a period of 26 weeks had elapsed from the date of redundancy. If such employees made application for full-time work after 26 weeks, they would automatically be removed from the twilight shift recall list. The twilight shift comprised mainly married women.

The Equality Officer considered that the clause was not an essential requirement. It discriminated indirectly against the married women in comparison with the fewer single women who did not have to comply with the 26-weeks-break requirement. The Equality Officer recommended that this practice be discontinued immediately and that the next 30 appointments

---

[1] EE 4/1981.
[2] EE 14/1985.

to full-time positions be made from the twilight shift, subject to sufficient applications being received from the twilight shift workers and the company's normal requirements on suitability for full-time employment being met. The company was ordered to make these appointments within three months from the date of the recommendation.

8.3.2.2 Access to employment (temporary)

Mid-Western Health Board v. *Brassil* [1]

The claimant, who had acted as a temporary relief nurse on a number of occasions in a hospital, was informed by the matron that six weeks' continuous employment would be available to her. However, the work in respect of two of those weeks was re-allocated subsequently to another nurse. The matron informed the claimant that the decision to re-allocate work to the other nurse was because the other nurse 'was a single girl'.

In view of the undisputed evidence that preference was given to the other nurse because she was single, the Equality Officer was satisfied that the claimant was treated less favourably than the other nurse because of her marital status and that this constituted discrimination within the meaning of s. 2(b) of the Act. The Equality Officer recommended that she be paid for the weeks she would have worked but for the discrimination. She was awarded £300.

Central Statistics Office v. *O'Shea* [2]

This case concerned the alleged discrimination against the claimant on the basis of her sex or marital status, in a competition for field supervisor in the 1986 Census of Population. The key issue in this case was that the Office was giving preference to persons registered as unemployed or otherwise in economic need. As a consequence, the claimant was refused employment; but the Office also maintained that she would not have got the job on merit, either.

At the time, under social welfare regulations, a wife who was living with or being wholly or mainly maintained by her husband was deemed to be an 'adult dependant' and was not eligible to draw unemployment assistance or benefit, whereas a husband was considered an 'adult dependant' only if he was incapable of self-support and being wholly or mainly maintained by his wife. The claimant said that as she was a married woman, it was more difficult for her to comply with the requirement to be unemployed. Details of persons registered as unemployed were provided which showed fewer married women in receipt of unemployment assistance/benefit.

---

[1]   EE 3/1986.
[2]   EE 7/1987.

The Equality Officer considered that a substantially higher proportion of men than women and a substantially higher proportion of unmarried women than married women could comply with the requirement to be unemployed or in economic need. These figures showed that a much larger proportion of married females could not comply with such requirement. One way or another, the claimant would not have been appointed; but she was awarded £500 for distress.

8.3.2.3 Advertisements (discriminatory)

Galway Social Service Council v. EEA [1]

The EEA referred the matter of the Council's advertisement for male staff for its proposed hostel for destitute men. The Equality Officer recommended that the advertisement was discriminatory and that the Council could not rely on the 'occupational qualification' exemption, as there was no requirement for the Council to provide staff with sleeping accommodation and the sanitary facilities could be used by persons of both sexes.

Sunday Independent v. EEA [2]

An advertisement placed by a catering company appeared for a 'head waiter/manager' in the *Sunday Independent*. The EEA referred the matter to the Labour Court which in turn referred the case to an Equality Officer. The Equality Officer considered that the job title implied a reference to a particular sex and that the prospective employer and the newspaper were thus in breach of s. 8 of the 1977 Act.[3]

Cork Examiner Publications v. EEA [4]

The case concerned an advertisement for a 'female supervisor in a health and fitness clinic'. The Equality Officer ruled that the advertisement was discriminatory and the newspaper had to run a notice for four consecutive weeks drawing the attention of employers to the fact that ss 17(2)(c) and 17(2)(d) of the 1977 Act had been repealed.

8.3.2.4 Discriminatory statements (at interview)

University College Dublin v. Chaney [5]

Mrs Chaney alleged that University College Dublin refused her access to permanent employment as a copying office operator because she was a married woman with children. The claimant maintained that she was

---

1   EE 13/1983.
2   EE 17/1991.
3   For further details see §4.7.3 above.
4   EE 13/1991.
5   EE 15/1983.

discriminated against at the interview as she was asked how many children she had and how she would have them minded if she got the job. The College did not say that they asked the same questions of male interviewees. The Equality Officer considered it quite reasonable for an employer to require prospective employees to be in a position to take up employment. However, he also considered that, if in the case of a prospective male employee an employer is willing to assume, without making specific enquiries, that any children that he might have would not affect his ability to take up employment and to give reliable service, the employer should also do so in the case of women.

The Equality Officer considered that the questioning of women at interviews in the way the claimant was questioned constituted unfair treatment and was likely to prove discouraging and to lead to suspicions of discrimination. The claimant was awarded £30 on the basis of direct discrimination. The reason why the award was so low was because discriminatory questions may only result in the claimant losing a right to be considered for the job.

Coombe Lying-in Hospital v. Tuite [1]

The claimant furnished a list of questions allegedly asked of her at interview; she had repeated the questions asked both to her sister and to a nursing colleague, on the day of the interviews, as she had been upset by them. The Hospital denied asking the questions and said they would not have been asked in that manner. The full interview board was not prepared to attend a joint hearing with the Equality Officer. The Equality Officer considered that questions concerning how the claimant's husband felt about her studying, whether she had any children, and if she would be able to study and be a housewife at the same time, amounted to placing an onus on the claimant to show that her marital status would not interfere with her ability to undertake the commitment to the post.

The Equality Officer found that the claimant was treated less favourably than unmarried female candidates who had no such onus placed on them. As she was successful in finding a similar post in another hospital, it was not necessary for the Equality Officer to make a decision on whether or not the claimant would have been successful in obtaining the post but for the discrimination. She was awarded £200.

Medical Council v. Barrington [2]

This case highlighted the issue of application forms and alleged discrimination at interview. The claimant applied for the position of assistant

---

[1]   EE 17/1985.
[2]   EE 9/1988.

administrative officer. She maintained that when the interviewer confirmed certain details on her application form (such details included her marital status) she was asked if she was thinking of getting married. She said she replied 'No', that the interviewer then allegedly stated 'so you're not thinking of getting married' and then remarked that 1988 was a leap year and that she could ask someone. The claimant also stated that the interviewer informed her that a woman whom he had previously hired, married shortly after taking the post and subsequently left.

The claimant said she found these remarks to be objectionable, distasteful and embarrassing, but that she tried to continue with a normal interview. The Medical Council denied that such questions were asked or statements made; the Council considered the claimant did not have the experience for the job.

The Equality Officer accepted that there was no basis for the allegation that her non-appointment was as a result of discrimination. Accordingly, £400 was awarded for distress only.[1]

8.3.2.5 Discriminatory statements (not at interview)

Alfred Beit Foundation v. *Gahan* [2]

The Foundation had invited applications for the post of administrator. When the claimant applied he was advised that a married man was required for the post. The Foundation argued that a married couple was essential for the position. The Equality Officer held that the marital status of a person was not an occupational qualification and therefore, the claimant was discriminated against. He was awarded only £175 as there was no guarantee that he would have been selected for the position even if he had been considered.

8.3.3 BURDEN OF PROOF

North Western Health Board v. *Martyn* [3]

Discrimination must be proved by the person alleging it. To this end, very detailed statistical evidence may be required.

---

1   See also *Model School, Limerick* v. *Culloo*, EE 8/1987, §8.3.10 below.
2   EE 18/1983.
3   EE 14/1981; DEE 1/1982; [1985] ILRM 226 (HC); [1988] ILRM 519 (SC). See also *Revenue Commissioners* v. *Irish Tax Officials' Union*, EE 6/1986, DEE 2/1987, at §8.3.13 below.

8.3.4   COMPENSATION

Cork Corporation v. 4 Pool Attendants [1]

The Labour Court had found that the rostering arrangements for male and female swimming pool attendants were discriminatory to the four female claimants and had awarded them compensation in a sum equal to 2.64 hours pay per week between 1977 and 16 December 1983. The Corporation argued that compensation should be limited to the six-month time-limit or else the three years' retrospection as provided in s. 8(5) of the 1974 Act.

Murphy J held that the power to assess compensation was provided for in the 1977 Act under s. 23 which provides that compensation will be of such an amount as the Labour Court thinks reasonable having regard to all the circumstances of the case but will not exceed 104 weeks' remuneration.

8.3.5   CONDITIONS OF EMPLOYMENT

8.3.5.1   Accommodation

Southern Health Board v. Kennedy [2]

The Equality Officer stated that he was 'satisfied that the provision in this case of accommodation which is subject to a charge less than its commercial value forms part of a person's remuneration and that consequently Mr Kennedy's complaint does not come within the scope of the 1977 Act'.[3]

8.3.5.2   Allocation of duties

St Brigid's Boys NS Foxrock, Co. Dublin v. McGuinness [4]

The claimant maintained that she had suffered discrimination in the allocation of teaching classes over a period of years. On learning that she was to continue teaching a junior class during the school year 1979/1980, instead of a more senior class which she had long sought, she referred her claim.

The claimant said that being allocated junior classes affected her chances of gaining a wide range of experience and that male teachers had a greater access to higher classes; and that their willingness to take boys for games may have been a factor. The Equality Officer found that there had

---

1   EE 17/1984; DEE 1/1985; 2 May 1987, unreported (HC).
2   EE 26/1984.
3   See §8.2.8.1 above.
4   EE 3/1979.

been discrimination and recommended a change of allocation in the 1980/1981 school year or earlier if a vacancy occurred.

8.3.5.3   Demotion

Roma Food Products Ltd v. Mulhern [1]

The claimant maintained that the company had appointed a man as packing department supervisor when she in fact held that position. The effect was that she was demoted and suffered a reduction in status; and discrimination had thereby occurred. A conflict of evidence arose in the manner of the claimant's appointment. The company showed evidence that she had been appointed as a charge hand. However, she produced the original letter of appointment which stated 'I am pleased to confirm your appointment as packing department supervisor'.

The Equality Officer held that the company was perfectly within its rights to create the new position of packing supervisor and appoint whomsoever it so wished. The Labour Court upheld the company position. The claim failed.

8.3.5.4   Disciplinary measures

Rank Xerox (Ireland) Ltd v. Molloy [2]

The claimant maintained that the disciplinary measures imposed on her by the company were more strict than those applied to male employees, in particular, in relation to the use of the telephone for personal calls. The Equality Officer noted that the claimant made a number of lengthy personal calls. It was held that there was no discrimination.

8.3.5.5   Dress

Norwich Union Insurance v. 131 Female Clerical Staff [3]

The Equality Officer found that a ban on the wearing of jeans or trousers by women was discriminatory.

---

[1]   EE 4/1982; DEE 7/1982.
[2]   EE 3/1983.
[3]   EE 19/1981.

8.3.5.6   Experience/training

School of Physiotherapy, University College Dublin v. Corrigan [1]

The claimant was denied access to the School because it would only accept females. Both the Equality Officer and the Labour Court held this to be discriminatory. The Court increased his compensation and determined that the College accept the claimant for the course commencing in the academic year 1980-81.

8.3.5.7   Leave for adoptive fathers

Aer Rianta v. 37 Male Employees
Aer Rianta v. Labour Court [2]

The claimants argued that the company's adoptive leave scheme, which applied only to women, discriminated against them contrary to s. 2(a), taken in conjunction with s. 3, of the 1977 Act. One of the company's responses was that the claim was 'out of time' (as the scheme had applied since 1984) and the issue of procedures and 'time-limits' became the subject of judicial review by the High Court. On a matter of the adoptive leave scheme itself, the company's main argument was that it did not discriminate unlawfully on the basis of sex as it was saved by the operation of s. 16 of the 1977 Act which should be interpreted widely and in accordance with art. 2(3) of Directive 76/207/EEC.[3] The company referred to an earlier case[4] in which an Equality Officer had accepted the provisions of s. 16 as applying to adoption. However, in this case the Equality Officer took the view that since neither pregnancy nor childbirth were involved in adoption, s. 16 did not apply. In his view, s. 16 did not go beyond the limits of the exceptions permitted by the Directive but provided a lesser derogation which was within those limits. Therefore, where adoptive leave was provided, it should be made available to both men and women on equal terms.

The Labour Court overturned the Equality Officer's recommendation and held that since the 1977 Act was introduced to give effect to Directive 76/207/EEC, s. 16 of the Act should be interpreted in accordance with the ECJ judgment in *Commission* v. *Italian Republic* [5] that different provisions for adoptive leave for adoptive mothers and fathers did not amount to discrimination. The ECJ had held that the distinction was justified 'by the legitimate concern to assimilate as far as possible the conditions of entry of the child into the adoptive family to those of the arrival of a new-born child'.

---

1   EE 13/1979; DEE 6/1980.
2   EE 11/1987; 16 March 1989, unreported (HC).
3   The terms of the derogation permitted by s. 16, which refers to 'pregnancy and childbirth', are narrower than those in the Directive, which refer to 'pregnancy and maternity'.
4   *ESB* v. *ESBOA*, EE 3/1980.
5   Case 163/82, [1983] ECR 3273 (ECJ).

The Labour Court therefore held that Aer Rianta was not in breach of s. 16 of the 1977 Act.

8.3.5.8 Loan scheme

Central Bank of Ireland v. ASTMS [1]

The Bank operated a staff house loan scheme and the ASTMS complained that its terms were discriminatory. The Equality Officer agreed and recommended that the terms be amended to give the same benefits to both male and female staff. The Labour Court upheld this recommendation.

8.3.5.9 Working hours

Cork Corporation v. 4 Pool Attendants [2]

Rostering arrangements for male and female swimming-pool attendants were found to be discriminatory as they denied the women equal access to overtime. The question of appropriate compensation was then the subject of a Labour Court determination and a High Court ruling.

Kildare Vocational Education Committee v. 3 Female Cleaners [3]

The claimants were part-time cleaners at a vocational school. For a number of years they worked ten hours a week over five days. In May 1988 they were advised by the school principal that their hours were to be reduced to 7.5 hours a week with a consequent reduction in pay.

All the part-time cleaners were female, and the Committee had not considered reducing the hours of the male caretakers or of the female full-time cleaner. The Equality Officer was satisfied that the reduction in hours was because of their part-time status and not their sex; there was therefore no direct discrimination. The Equality Officer considered however that there was indirect discrimination on the basis of sex as all the males could comply with the requirement to work full-time, and approximately 72 per cent of the part-time jobs were held by women. The claimants were awarded £400 for loss of earnings and distress.

8.3.5.10 Redundancies/lay-offs

Food Products (Donegal) Ltd v. Kelly [4]

The Equality Officer considered that the employer's argument about the need to lift heavy weights was not a valid reason for not re-employing the female claimants because 'there were sufficient males available to perform

---

1   EE 4/1980; DEE 7/1980.
2   EE 17/1984; DEE 1/1985. See §8.3.4 above and §8.3.5.12 below.
3   EE 9/1989.
4   EE 5/1982; DEE 8/1982.

any necessary heavy physical work that occurred'. This finding was upheld by the Labour Court.

Michael O'Neill & Sons Ltd v. 2 Female Employees [1]

Two female part-time employees claimed that they were unfairly selected for redundancy. It was accepted that there was a redundancy situation. The company/union agreement provided that in the event of a lay-off or redundancy arising, service with the employer would be a deciding factor; subject, however, to the need of the employer to retain the skills and ability necessary for the viable operation of the business. In the event of lay-off or redundancy arising, consultation with the union should take place. The union maintained that the selection of two part-time married females was discriminatory. If 'last-in, first-out' had applied, these persons would not have been selected.

The claimants argued that as a greater number of women than men worked on a part-time basis and a greater number of married women than single women also worked on a part-time basis, the proportion of married women who could not comply with the requirement of working full-time was greater than the proportion of single women. Thus, the selection for redundancy of the two claimants constituted indirect discrimination. In order to avoid selection for redundancy, the women claimants had to be working full-time.

The Labour Court considered that this was indirect discrimination and that the sole basis for the company decision was that the claimants were part-time. Accordingly, as a greater proportion of males than single women could comply with the requirement of working full-time, there was indirect discrimination. The Court awarded each claimant £250 compensation and noted that the company would be prepared to re-employ the claimants when there was an improvement in trading conditions.

8.3.5.11 Remuneration

North Western Health Board v. Brady [2]

The claimant argued that the employer's refusal to pay salary in respect of sick leave, where an entitlement to unpaid maternity leave existed, was discriminatory under the 1977 Act. The policy was held to be indirectly discriminatory under the 1974 Act as the issue of remuneration was involved. However, she received no award as she was not working in the 'same place' as her male comparator.

---

[1] DEE 1/1988.
[2] EE 9/1985; DEE 9/1985. See §8.2.8.10 above.

8.3.5.12 Shift rosters

Cork Corporation v. *4 Pool Attendants* [1]

Rostering arrangements for men and women were found to be discriminatory by an Equality Officer. The question of appropriate compensation subsequently went to the Labour Court and the High Court.

8.3.5.13 Sick leave

North Western Health Board v. *Brady* [2]

Refusal to grant paid sick leave, on the grounds that the claimant was entitled to make use of unpaid maternity leave, was held to be discriminatory (under the 1974 rather than the 1977 Act).

8.3.5.14 Transfers

National Institute for Higher Education, Limerick v. *Bolton* [3]

The claimant was refused a transfer because the Institute did not consider it appropriate that a secretary should work in the same area as her husband if the area concerned was considered a sensitive one. She contended that this constituted both direct and indirect discrimination on grounds of marital status. The Equality Officer was satisfied that the Institute was operating a policy which was intended to apply to relatives and which was not confined to married women. There was no direct discrimination.

The Equality Officer also concluded that it could not be held that a substantially higher proportion of single rather than married women would be able to comply with the requirement not to be a spouse or relation of the other employee; and he found, therefore, that the Institute had not indirectly discriminated against the claimant.

8.3.5.15 Working conditions

University College Dublin v. *Zeuli* [4]

The claimant was employed as an assistant librarian. Prior to the birth of her child she was absent due to a pregnancy-related illness; she then went on maternity leave. She had difficulty weaning her child, so when she came back to work she requested flexibility in her working time, namely evening

---

[1]   EE 17/1984; DEE 1/1985. See §8.3.4 above.
[2]   EE 9/1985; DEE 9/1985. See §8.2.8.10 above.
[3]   EE 7/1984; EE 12/1989.
[4]   EE 4/1987.

duties and the amalgamation of breaks during the day. The College authorities refused; she resigned her employment. The Equality Officer considered that the refusal was directly discriminatory and that her absence would have caused minimal disruption. She was awarded £1,500 compensation.

8.3.6   DISMISSALS

8.3.6.1   Dismissal

Irish TV Rentals v. *Brady* [1]

The claimant was employed as a sales receptionist at one of the company showrooms for about four months before being made redundant. Some weeks later she was re-employed as a temporary sales receptionist to cover for one of the two remaining workers who was absent on sick leave. On the return of that worker the claimant's temporary employment was terminated. On the day following the effective date of termination of her employment, a male worker commenced employment in the showroom. The claimant had not been made aware that a vacancy existed in the company and considered that access to the position had been denied her because of her sex.

In deciding how the company's preference for a male worker affected the claimant, the Equality Officer noted that the company had approached the National Manpower Service for a male sales receptionist while the claimant was employed as a temporary sales receptionist. He also noted that when the claimant had been made redundant a few months earlier it had given her an excellent reference stating that it would be happy to re-employ her if trading conditions improved and had in fact re-employed her on a temporary basis.

The Equality Officer had no doubt that if the claimant had been a man the company would have offered the vacant post of sales receptionist to her instead of seeking nominations from the Service and, in that event, the question of appointing a sales receptionist/representative would not have arisen. The Equality Officer considered that the company had deliberately omitted to offer the claimant employment as a sales representative because of her sex and recommended that the company pay her £4,000 compensation. On appeal, the Labour Court upheld this recommendation.

8.3.6.2   Constructive dismissal

Garage Proprietor v. *A Worker* [2]

The Labour Court found that sexual harassment had occurred and that the claimant's decision to resign as a result of this harassment amounted to constructive dismissal.

---

[1]   EEO 1/1984; EE 5/1985; DEE 8/1985.
[2]   EE 2/1985. See §8.3.12 below.

8.3.6.3 Retaliatory dismissal

University College Dublin v. *A Female Worker* [1]

The claimant had been unsuccessful in her application for the position of permanent copying operator. Shortly after she advised the College that she thought she was discriminated against in respect of her job application, she was informed that no more work was available for her. The College appointed another temporary employee to her temporary position. She believed that she was dismissed for pursuing a claim under the Act.

The Equality Officer recommended that she be reinstated to the list of temporary employees and she was awarded £750.

8.3.7 EFFECTS OF PAST DISCRIMINATION

Eastern Health Board v. *79 Psychiatric Nurses* [2]

The claimants had to resign on marriage prior to 1973 because of the marriage bar then in existence. However, they came back to work and were given permanent employment in 1977. They maintained that they had lost out on their seniority in relation to conditions of employment. The Equality Officer recommended that there was discrimination and that discussions should take place to sort out their position. The Labour Court upheld the Equality Officer's Recommendation.

Problems arose in the implementation of the determination and the Court ordered that the claimants be given the benefit of their seniority, ignoring any short breaks in their service which might have arisen due to the fact that they were married or female.

Revenue Commissioners v. *Moran* [3]
appealed as
Minister for Finance v. *EEA* [4]

The claimant had been employed by the Revenue Commissioners as a Higher Tax Officer. On her marriage in 1969, she was obliged to resign from the civil service due to the operation of the marriage bar. The bar was later abolished by 1973 legislation which also extended the scope of reinstatement provision so as to permit married women to be re-admitted to their jobs (i) on grounds of hardship, or (ii) if they became widowed. A circular (No 50/79)

---

[1] EEO 5/1983. See *University College Dublin* v. *Chaney*, §8.3.2.4 above.
[2] EE 2/1979; DEE 4/1980; EEO 1/1981.
[3] EE 20/1991.
[4] EE 21/1991.

was issued by the Department of Finance describing the relevant provisions and prescribing conditions to be observed when making reinstatements.

The claimant applied for reinstatement on 8 January 1990. She was informed that this could only be granted on grounds of widowhood, and that if hardship was being argued, certain independent evidence of her means and circumstances would have to be supplied. As neither of the conditions applied for her case, she contacted the EEA which referred the dispute to the Labour Court on her behalf. The EEA also, on its own behalf, made a complaint to the Court against the Minister for allegedly procuring discrimination against the claimant by virtue of Circular 50/79. The Labour Court referred the matter to an Equality Officer.

The Equality Officer considered that the treatment of the claimant was less favourable than that accorded to widows and this constituted direct discrimination under s. 2(b) of the 1977 Act. Also, in directing the Revenue Commissioners to implement Circular 50/79, and to act in a manner now found to be discriminatory, the Minister for Finance had procured discrimination and contravened s. 9 of the Act.

The Equality Officer recommended that the claimant be reinstated in the civil service from the date on which she would have been reinstated had she been a widow, and that she should be paid with effect from that date. There should be no future discrimination, on grounds of sex or marital status, in relation to the eligibility for reinstatement of employees who resign from the civil service.

8.3.8   INDIRECT DISCRIMINATION

8.3.8.1   Age limits

North-Western Health Board v. *Martyn* [1]

The Equality Officer and the Labour Court accepted that the age limit requirement (27 years) for the clerical position was discriminatory because it adversely affected more married women than single women or men. The Health Board appealed to the High Court on a point of law.

The High Court overturned the Labour Court determination. It was stated by Barron J that at no stage was there any real statistical evidence given by either party. The Health Board had not disputed the allegations by the claimant with statistical evidence. The claimant had merely maintained that 27 years was too low for married women to be re-entering the workforce. Barron J said:

---

[1]   EE 14/1981; DEE 1/1982; [1985] ILRM 226 (HC); [1988] ILRM 519 (SC).

Discrimination within the meaning of s. 2(c) is a mixed question of law and fact. Where candidates for employment must comply with a requirement which is not essential for that employment it must be established as a matter of fact that the number of those of one sex who can comply is substantially higher than the number of those of the other sex who can also comply or the number of those of a particular marital status who can comply is substantially higher than the number of those of a different marital status but of the same sex who can also comply.

In the present case, accepting that there has been a finding that the age qualification is not essential for the post for which the respondent applied, no evidence was given to establish that a 'substantially higher' number of married women would have applied. It may or may not be self-evident that many married women under the age of 28 are not in the employment market because they are having their children and bringing them up. But even if it is self-evident, this represents only one category of persons who may be seeking employment at the age of 35 or 40 or above. There must be evidence and generally this evidence will be statistical. For example, if a condition is imposed which makes it difficult for women to comply, then two sets of statistics must be considered:

1. the actual statistics of the particular application for employment;
2. the actual statistics of an application for similar employment on the same conditions but without the impugned condition.

If it is found that the proportion of men to women applicants in the first set of statistics is 80/20 and in the second set of statistics 60/40, then as a matter of fact the particular requirement is one which discriminates against women. Obviously, it may be extremely difficult in practice to obtain the latter set of statistics, but that does not absolve the tribunal hearing the matter from seeking to obtain evidence which is as near as possible to such statistics.

The Supreme Court, however, considered that such requirement was discriminatory because the age was too low for many married women to re-enter the labour force after family responsibilities. However, that Court specifically stated that its judgment was on the narrow basis of unrefuted allegations and might not apply in every case.

8.3.8.2   Inessential requirements

Bailey Gibson v. *Nathan* [1]

The Labour Court held that a requirement to hold a union card for a particular post was not based on sex, and therefore a woman who did not have a card and was not appointed to the position was not the subject of indirect discrimination.

The claimant, who had 20 years' service with the printing company, had spent the last 10 years as an assistant to the operator on the carton folder/ gluer machine. In January 1988 the man operating this machine retired and the claimant applied for this position. The company had an agreement with the Irish Print Union (IPU) that operators of such machines must be members of the IPU. In April 1988 the company wrote to the IPU requesting it to consider training the claimant concerned for the post. In May 1988 the IPU advised the company that the normal practice must apply, i.e. that the

---

1   EE 1-2/1990; DEE 1/1991, [1990] ELR 191.

vacancy must be advertised and the IPU would have to be satisfied that there were no suitable IPU applicants available before it would consider the company's request. The company advertised the vacancy and subsequently interviewed a number of candidates, all of whom were male and members of the IPU. However, both the first and second preference IPU members rejected the company's job offer. In June the company wrote again to the IPU stating that it would again like to propose training for the claimant. The IPU requested the company to interview unemployed IPU members with a view to re-training one of them for the position. Seven male unemployed IPU members were interviewed and in September 1988 the vacancy was filled by one of them.

The claimant considered that the company had discriminated against her. The EEA referred the complaint under the 1977 Act in February 1989 to the Labour Court which in turn referred the matter to an Equality Officer. The Equality Officer considered that the company had indirectly discriminated against the claimant in terms of s. 2(c) of the 1977 Act and recommended that the company pay the claimant £700 in respect of distress and injury feelings.

The company appealed this recommendation to the Labour Court on the following grounds: no proper reference had been made under s. 2(c); the dispute (if any) was between the claimant and the IPU; the statistical evidence used by the Equality Officer relating to IPU membership applied equally to male and female workers; and there was no provision in the Act for the granting of compensation for injury to feelings.

The Labour Court determined that the IPU, although not a party to the proceedings, should be represented at these appeals. The IPU agreed and it argued that an IPU card was an essential requirement for the position because it was based on a collective agreement in a very structured industry. The sex of the member did not matter.

The Labour Court's determination stated that 'historical circumstances, which have resulted in more men than women in a craft industry, do not lead to the conclusion that the small number of woman in the industry now is an attribute of their sex'. Accordingly, there was no indirect discrimination.

Packard Electric Ltd v. *EEA* [1]

The requirement to have been laid off for 26 weeks was an 'inessential requirement'.

---

1   EE 14/1985. See §8.3.2.1 above and §8.3.9 below.

Our Lady's Hospital for Sick Children v. *A Worker* [1]

The question of whether or not a specific requirement relating to employment existed was central to the case. The Hospital decided to appoint a newly-qualified technician, because such person closely met the specifications for the post. The claimant maintained that the Hospital discriminated against her on the basis of marital status. She was not newly qualified.

The Equality Officer held in the claimant's favour. However, the Labour Court considered that in this case a preference did not amount to a requirement. Accordingly, there was no discrimination.

8.3.8.3   Other (excluding pregnancy)

CERT Ltd v. *Landy* [2]

The claimant was interviewed by CERT for the post of permanent food service instructor but following the interview a man was appointed to the post. The requirement relating to employment was the possession of certain City & Guild certificates and the reason why the claimant was not given the job was because she did not have such certificates, although she did have a higher qualification. At the Equality Officer stage, the claimant maintained that she was directly discriminated against and she lost her claim. She appealed to the Labour Court and the Court found that females were excluded from training for the specified City & Guild certificates. Thus, she was excluded from the post.

The Court stated that 'the company insistence on the lesser qualification, which on the evidence provided effectively excluded the female applicant, as the possibility of training did not exist in the past, was in this instance discriminatory'. As qualification was the key issue, she was discriminated against under s. 2(c) of the Act and was awarded £3,000.[3]

8.3.8.4   Pregnancy

An Foras Forbartha v. *Geraghty-Williams* [4]

The claimant was offered the position of biological technician subject to her furnishing a satisfactory medical report. The doctor's report said that she was pregnant but otherwise in good health. The offer of employment was withdrawn.

---

1   EE 25/1985; DEE 4/1985.
2   EE 20/1983; DEE 2/1984.
3   See also *Central Statistics Office* v. *O'Shea*, §8.3.2.2 above.
4   EE 6/1981; DEE 4/1982.

The Labour Court determined that this was indirect discrimination on the basis that 100 per cent of men could comply with the requirement of not being pregnant, but a similar proportion of women could not.

Southern Health Board v. *Cronin* [1]

The Equality Officer ruled that the Board's denial of benefit under the sick leave scheme in respect of pregnancy-related medical conditions constituted discrimination on grounds of sex.

Power Supermarkets Ltd v. *Long* [2]

The claimant had been employed as a full-time shop assistant with H. Williams Ltd. In October 1987 H. Williams went into receivership and she was made redundant. Power Supermarkets (trading as Quinnsworth) purchased four stores including the one in which she was working. Agreement was reached with her union that an interview list would consist of full-time and part-time staff who were in regular employment at that time. In November 1987 she was interviewed and was subsequently advised that she had been selected for employment and was told to contact the personnel officer. The claimant called to the company on 29 December 1987 and advised them that she was due to give birth in January 1988. She was then advised that if she came back to the company when the baby was born they would re-consider her for employment.

The claimant issued a questionnaire under s. 28 of the Act stating that she was denied access to employment and requesting the company's response. The company did not respond in writing. She then referred the dispute to the Equality Officer maintaining she was directly discriminated against. The Equality Officer recommended that she was not directly discriminated against. The Equality Officer considered that she had not referred an indirect discrimination case under the Act. The claimant appealed the recommendation to the Labour Court where it was upheld. She referred the Labour Court determination to the High Court for judicial review. Johnson J (in summary) considered that both the Equality Officer's and the Labour Court's findings, that they had no jurisdiction to hear a claim of indirect discrimination, were null and void. The case was remitted to the Equality Officer to consider the issue of indirect discrimination.

The Equality Officer considered that the company had imposed a requirement not to be pregnant and close to confinement in order to obtain employment; this requirement affected a higher proportion of females than males and such affect was due to an attribute of the female sex. Such a

---

1   EE 10-12/1984.
2   EE 5/1988; DEE 1/1990; 1991, unreported (HC); EE 15/1991; DEE 2/1993.

requirement was inessential for employment in terms of the Act. Accordingly there was indirect discrimination.

The claimant was appointed to a full-time position with continuity back to January 1988.

8.3.9 PROCUREMENT OF DISCRIMINATION

Packard Electric Ltd v. *EEA* [1]

The issue arose from a collective agreement between the parties. The practice continued because of widespread opposition from the full-time workforce to it being amended. The EEA specifically referred to the fact that one of the trade unions involved had continued to issue membership cards to persons recruited as full-time workers to the positions to which the twilight workers wanted access. There was a closed shop arrangement with the unions. The Equality Officer considered the granting of membership cards may have facilitated the continued operation of the discriminatory practice but this did not constitute procurement of discrimination.

8.3.10 PROMOTION

Model School, Limerick v. *Culloo* [2]

The school consisted of a girls' school and a boys' school. The claimant was principal of the girls' school. Both schools were amalgamated and the position of principal was available. The female claimant was unsuccessful.

The Equality Officer considered that the interview board discriminated against the claimant as in summary she had additional qualifications, had co-educational teaching experience and the interview board were unable to provide good objective reasons for her non-appointment. Furthermore a member of the board, subsequent to the interview, said to the claimant that 'it seems an injustice has been done but we've never thought of women for these positions before'.

The claimant did not seek the remedy of appointment as principal due to the disruption that could take place as the male had been in the job for a year at that stage. She was awarded £11,000. The Labour Court considered that the appeal against this recommendation was not in order; and the High Court upheld the Labour Court's view in May 1989.

---

[1]   EE 14/1985. See §8.3.2.1 above and §8.3.13 below.
[2]   EE 8/1987; (1989) 8 JISLL 119 (HC).

8.3.11   PROTECTIVE LEGISLATION

Tayto Ltd v. *O'Keeffe* [1]

The dispute concerned whether the company had discriminated against the seven female claimants in relation to access to employment as night-shift cleaners. The company argued that it was necessary to employ only male cleaners to comply with s. 67(1) of the Factories Act 1955 and reg. 3(2) of the Factories Act 1955 (Manual Labour)(Maximum Weights and Transport) Regulations 1972. The company maintained that an integral part of the job consisted of lifting weights in excess of 35.2 lb (the maximum weight that a female can lift) and other duties which may cause an injury to females. Accordingly, to exclude females from such work was not discriminatory as s. 14 of the 1977 Act provides that nothing done by an employer in compliance with any requirement of or under the Factories Act 1955 will constitute discrimination in contravention of the 1977 Act.

The Equality Officer accepted the company's arguments. However, an employer must take reasonable steps to provide for the employment of persons of either sex without being in breach of any requirement of such safety legislation.

In the circumstances of this case, the claims failed on the grounds that it was not reasonable to accept the claimants' arguments that two females could do each job.

8.3.12   SEXUAL HARASSMENT

Garage Proprietor v. *A Worker* [2]

The claimant was a 15-year-old girl working as a shop assistant/petrol pump attendant. She commenced employment on 15 July 1984 and ceased her employment on 7 January 1985. She claimed that during this period she had been sexually harassed by her employer. She resigned and referred this matter to the Labour Court.

The Court determined that inappropriate conduct took place during the claimant's employment and that her decision to resign from her employment amounted to constructive dismissal. The Court stated that '... freedom from sexual harassment is a condition of work which an employee of either sex is entitled to expect ... any denial of that freedom (is) discrimination within the terms of the Employment Equality Act 1977'. The claimant was awarded £1,000 compensation.

---

1   EE 13/1985.
2   EE0 2/1985.

A Company v. A Worker [1]

The claimant maintained that during the period of her employment she was subjected to continuous sexual harassment by the husband of the company's managing director (who was engaged by the company to act as an independent contractor) and that her dismissal was directly attributable to this sexual harassment. The company denied sexual harassment and said her dismissal was attributable to the company's financial and economic circumstances. The claimant asked the Court to:

- find that her dismissal was directly due to sexual harassment and was, therefore, discriminatory;
- find that the claimant was sexually harassed at work and this harassment was sex discrimination within the meaning of the Act;
- award suitable compensation; and
- direct this employer and all employers to take steps to prevent sexual harassment in the workplace.

The Court determined that no evidence was produced by the claimant to show that the employer was aware of the alleged sexual harassment or that this was the reason the claimant was dismissed. The claimant admitted that she did not at any stage inform her employer or any other member of staff of the alleged incidents. All the incidents were categorically denied. In the face of such completely contradictory evidence, which on balance did not support the allegations made, the Court did not find the claim sustainable.

A Company v. A Female Worker [2]

The claimant had been employed as a bookkeeper for approximately 10 years. She maintained that she had been sexually harassed by a man who was not an employee of the company but who was on the company premises with the agreement of the employer. The Labour Court decided that the behaviour of the company's female manager, after banning from the premises the man alleged to have harassing the claimant, amounted to constructive dismissal of the claimant. The man who harassed the claimant was excluded from company premises during working hours by the general manager after the entire female staff of the company stopped work, walked out and warned that they would not return until the man was 'removed or controlled'. Following this the claimant maintained that there was a deliberate strategy to undermine her and that she was removed from her more responsible duties. The general manager attended the Court but stated that the company would not 'involve itself in any matter which has as its origin allegations against a person who is not and never was an employee of the company'.

---

1   DEE 2/1988.
2   EEO 3/1991.

The Court determined that the company was 'aware of the harassment and chose to ignore it until industrial action forced it to act. It is irrelevant that the perpetrator of the harassment was not an employee of the company'. The claimant was awarded £7,500.

A Limited Co. v. 1 *Female Employee* [1]

In three further cases, the claimants were unsuccessful in proving sexual harassment which amounted to discrimination on the grounds of sex within the meaning of the Act. However, in January 1989 the Labour Court awarded £1,500 in compensation for sexual harassment to a woman executive whose hotel bedroom had been ransacked and suggestively re-arranged during a residential company training programme. The men involved were three senior members of management, including the firm's managing director. This was the first case in which it was established that sexual harassment may be a matter of intention and psychological effect; and may be symbolic in form as well as verbal or physical.

8.3.13 STATISTICAL EVIDENCE

Revenue Commissioners v. *Irish Tax Officials' Union* [2]

This case involved a dispute as to whether or not the Commissioners discriminated on the basis of sex, against four named female clerical assistants who were in competition for promotion to the grade of tax officer. Very briefly, the facts were that in November 1984 a competition was announced. 654 clerical assistants applied: 26 per cent male and 74 per cent female. Four boards were set up on a regional basis, i.e. A, B, C, and D. A total of 120 candidates from all boards (29 per cent male and 15 per cent female) were placed on a promotional panel. The four claimants, who were not selected, were based in the Cork tax office and were interviewed by Board D. This Board placed in order of merit 21 males and 97 females. The first 27 persons were placed on the promotional panel. This 27 included 14 males (52 per cent) and 13 females (48 per cent). From the Cork office alone, there were 15 male and 54 female applicants; 73 per cent of the males and 7 per cent of the females were successful in obtaining a place on the panel.

The Equality Officer considered that discrimination occurred as the Revenue Commissioners could not show any reason for not placing the four female claimants on the panel. It was recommended that the four female clerical assistants be placed on the panel in order of merit. Both parties appealed to the Labour Court.

---

1   January 1989, confidential recommendation: EE 4/1988, EE 5/1988 and EE 10/1988.
2   EE 6/1986; DEE 2/1987.

The Labour Court assumed that in a group as large as 100 the abilities of the female applicants, on average, would be equal to the abilities of the male applicants, and thus the same proportion could be successful. However, it could not be expected that the proportion would be exactly equal. The Court applied the statistical Chi-square test, such application showing that discrimination did occur. The Court then had to consider whether the discrimination had any detrimental effect on the promotional prospects of the four claimants in this case. It was considered that if the Board had shown no bias, only two of the four claimants would have been placed on the panel. Accordingly, the two claimants should be placed back in the position as if they had been awarded 20th and 25th place on the panel respectively.[1]

Department of Industry and Commerce v. Kearns [2]

The claimant, a married woman with four children, alleged that the Department of Industry and Commerce in denying her access to promotion discriminated against her on grounds of sex and marital status. In 1974, she was appointed executive officer and she became eligible for promotion to higher executive officer after 5 years. In 1989, the Department selected a male Executive Officer to fill an 'acting-up' position as a higher executive officer; he was considerably junior in service. Then Department stated that the policy of promotion was based on merit with due regard to seniority.

The claimant argued (*inter alia*) that the Department had shown on previous occasions that it preferred to promote men and its record on promotion indicated that it treated women less favourably than men. The Department argued that statistics were not proof of discrimination but merely reflected trends over a particular period of time, and that it could produce statistics which totally changed the trend shown by the claimant's union. On the basis of the Department statistics the 'failure' rate (i.e. where more senior persons were passed over) for males was 42 per cent and for females 83 per cent. In other words, males assessed on a criterion of merit, with due regard to seniority, had a success rate of 58 per cent while females had a success rate of 17 per cent.

The Equality Officer applied the Chi-square test to the actual results, and it clearly showed that more women should have been promoted, and accordingly fewer 'passed over'. She said this raised a strong inference of unlawful discrimination. She found the decision not to promote the claimant discriminatory and recommended a retrospective promotion, with compensation of £600.

---

1   See §8.3.2.2 above.
2   EE 3/1991.

North-Western Health Board v. Martyn [1]

The Equality Officer and Labour Court had accepted the claimant's argument that an upper age limit for the post in question was indirectly discriminatory. However, the High Court overturned them on the grounds that insufficient statistical evidence had been provided. The Supreme Court then overturned the High Court judgment.

8.3.14   PRACTICE AND PROCEDURE

8.3.14.1 Time-limits

Aer Lingus Teo. v. 24 Air Hostesses
Aer Lingus Teo. v. Labour Court [2]

The claimants had alleged discrimination in relation to job seniority because they had been forced to resign on marriage and had later been refused permanent employment; although other women, who had married later than they (i.e. after the removal of the 'marriage bar' in 1970) had either been re-employed or had never been forced to resign. Also, in the calculation of seniority, the claimants had been refused recognition for their past service and experience; whereas the other married women had been given full recognition.

However, at no stage prior to the 1988 High Court hearing had there been a decision on the merit of these women's claims, due to the emergence of procedural issues requiring prior resolution. In 1982 the Labour Court had found that the complaint was outside the six-month time-limit laid down in s. 19(5) of the 1977 Act and that there was no reasonable cause for the delay. The Employment Equality Agency then made a referral of the same basic issue under s. 20 of the 1977 Act; and in November 1988 the High Court found that s. 19(5) was not intended to debar references by the EEA to the Labour Court under s. 20. This judgment was appealed to the Supreme Court, which ruled in July 1986 that once a reference was made under s. 20, it must be dealt with as if it were a reference under s. 19 and the procedures therein must be followed. The High Court then ruled on the case in February 1988.

On the procedural issue, Carroll J held that the Labour Court was not obliged to determine first of all that a complaint was admissible before making a decision as to whether it should refer it to an Equality Officer for investigation (or to an Industrial Relations Officer), or deal with the matter itself. Time limits were an entirely separate matter: they could be invoked by

---

[1]   EE 14/1981; DEE 1/1982; [1985] ILRM 226 (HC); [1988] ILRM 519 (SC). See §8.3.8.1 above.

[2]   [1990] ELR 113 (HC); and 125 (SC).

the employer; were part of the dispute; and could be investigated as such by the Equality Officer. They did not restrict the Labour Court's jurisdiction to refer a case under s. 19(2).

This judgment clarified the High Court's view on appropriate procedures and granted the claimants the right to have the Labour Court investigate their (very long-standing) claim. Incidentally, while noting that she was not obliged to do so, Carroll J in her judgment also commented on the question of whether the claimants had suffered discrimination and stated that in her view they had. She also stated that while existing work practices based on seniority might now prove unchallengeable due to the time bar, this could not be used as a licence for the company to discriminate indefinitely or to introduce new forms of discrimination against the claimants.

The Supreme Court allowed the appeal of Aer Lingus to the extent of prohibiting the Labour Court from proceeding further with the investigation of the dispute alleged to have been referred by the claimants. The Employment Equality Act did not have retrospective effect and consequently a difference in treatment occurring before the coming into force of the Act was not capable of constituting discrimination within the meaning of the Act.

Aer Rianta v. Labour Court [1]

The original claim was by 37 male employees who sought an equal entitlement to adoptive leave with female staff. One of the company's four arguments was that the claim was 'out of time' and should not be heard, since s. 19(5) of the 1977 Act provided that referrals should be made within six months of the first act of alleged discrimination - and adoptive leave for women had applied since 1984. The Labour Court, in a preliminary ruling on the time-limits issue, found that there had been reasonable cause for the delay and referred the claim back to the Equality Officer for investigation. The issue of time-limits was raised again by the company, but the Equality Officer felt he had no jurisdiction to deal with this issue, as it had already been decided upon by the Labour Court. He found on the facts of the case that the adoptive leave scheme discriminated against the men; and recommended its extension to them. The company appealed this to the Labour Court, again raising the time-limits argument. The Labour Court refused to hear the appeal unless the company deleted this reference, since time-limits had already been the subject of an earlier Labour Court ruling; whereupon the company referred the matter to the High Court for judicial review. Barrington J disagreed with the procedure adopted by the Labour Court, and said it could not refuse to hear an appeal merely because it had already decided on some of the issues. Section 19(5) of the 1977 Act did not deprive the Labour Court of its jurisdiction to hear the case; under that section, the Labour Court was a court of appeal and once it was satisfied that

---

1   EE 11/1987; 16 March 1989, unreported (HC). See also §8.3.5.7 above.

a dispute on discrimination existed, its function was to refer the matter to the appropriate officer. The initial error had been for the Labour Court to act as a court of first instance rather than a court of appeal. Because of this, the original proceedings were nullified and the case would have to proceed on that basis. The appeal was therefore sent back to the Labour Court for determination.

8.3.14.2 Application of legislation

St Patrick's College, Maynooth v. *ITGWU* [1]

The female part-time employees were claiming equal pay with a male comparator engaged in full-time general operative duties.

The Equality Officer stated:

> In considering whether the College's practice of paying the claimants a lower rate of pay is actually indirectly discriminatory on the basis of sex, it seems relevant to the Equality Officer to consider whether the practice is essential for some reason which is objectively justifiable on grounds which do not discriminate in any way on the basis of sex ... . The Equality Officer is satisfied that this is not the case. Therefore, the Equality Officer considers that he cannot but conclude that the claimants are being paid less (than the male comparator) on the basis of a practice which is indirectly discriminatory on grounds of sex and that the College's argument under s. 2(3) of the Act is not a valid one.
>
> In rejecting the College's argument under s. 2(3) of the ... 1974 Act, the Equality Officer has had regard to s. 56(2) of the ... 1977 Act which provides that the two Acts shall be construed together as one Act, and to those provisions of ss 2(c) and 3(2) of the 1977 Act which in conjunction with each other effectively prohibit any practice by an employer which results or would be likely to result in indirect discrimination on the basis of sex, even where there is no intention to discriminate on that basis.

---

[1]   EP 4/1984.

8.4   DECISIONS ON SOCIAL SECURITY

8.4.1   RETROSPECTION

McDermott and Cotter v. Minister for Social Welfare [1]
Cotter and McDermott v. Minister for Social Welfare [2]

This was, *inter alia*, a claim for arrears of unemployment benefit, arising from the 17-month delay in implementing the Directive. Hamilton J initially referred the issue to the ECJ for a preliminary ruling, asking, essentially, whether the Directive had direct effect in Ireland since 23 December 1984, so that it could be relied on by the claimants even in the absence of implementing legislation. The ECJ replied that it did and could (following its earlier decisions in the *Drake* [3] and *FNV* [4] cases). The matter was then referred back to the Irish High Court for a decision on its application to the facts of the particular cases in question.

As part of this reference (in July 1987), a number of other issues affecting the applicants were also raised, namely, their entitlement to unemployment assistance, to adult and child dependant allowances, to the various transitional payments, and to damages, in addition to the retrospection on their unemployment benefit.

In an unreported judgment dated 10 June 1988, Hamilton J decided in favour of the claim for retrospection in relation to the amount and duration of unemployment benefit; however, he disallowed the claims relating to unemployment assistance, adult and child dependent allowances and transitional payments. In disallowing the claim for an adult dependent allowance (which would have been payable, at the time concerned, had the claimant been a man), Hamilton J referred to 'the equity of the case' and said that because Mrs Cotter's husband had been engaged in full-time employment and had not been financially dependent on her at that time, 'it would be unjust and inequitable to pay [her] an adult dependant increase ... and it would be unjust and inequitable to require the people of Ireland to pay her such increase'. He concluded the judgment by limiting claims relying on the 'direct effect' principle to periods after the ECJ ruling of 24 March 1987 and to proceedings brought before that date; and made no reference whatsoever to the question of damages.

---

1   Case 286/85, [1987] ECR 1453, [1987] 2 CMLR 607, [1987] ILRM 324 (HC and ECJ).

2   Case 377/89, [1991] ECR I-1155 (ECJ).

3   *Drake v. Chief Adjudication Officer*, Case 150/85, [1986] ECR 1995, [1986] 3 CMLR 43 (ECJ).

4   *Netherlands v. Federatie Nederlandse Vakbeweging*, Case 71/85, [1986] ECR 3855, [1987] 3 CMLR 767 (ECJ).

The claimants were dissatisfied with the negative aspects of this judgment and announced their intention to appeal them to the Supreme Court. A further cause for dissatisfaction was that although the ruling favoured the payment of retrospection; and although the Minister for Social Welfare was not appealing this part of the judgment; and although the parties had agreed on the amounts which were due to the claimants; payment of the agreed amounts had not yet been permitted by the Court. This was because Hamilton J, on hearing that the other aspects of the judgment were to be appealed, refused to issue the court order enabling the payments to be made, pending a final resolution of the other issues. Thus payment of the amounts in question, having already been delayed for four years, were again further delayed, pending resolution of the remaining issues.

The claims rejected by the High Court were for increases in adult and child dependant allowances and the payment of transitional compensatory payments. The High Court considered that it would be unfair and inequitable to pay these sums to the applicants when their spouses were not financially dependent upon them.

On appeal to Supreme Court, it was argued that to concede the applicants' claims would offend against a principle prohibiting 'unjust enrichment', a principle which, under Irish law, could constitute grounds for refusing or restricting the payments. The Supreme Court was uncertain as to whether this principle of national law was compatible with the direct effect of art. 4(1) of Directive 79/7/EEC and therefore referred two questions to the ECJ. The first question was whether the Directive required the payment to married women of dependants' allowances, without proof of actual dependency, as had been the case for married men at the time in question, even if this could result in some double payments. The ECJ ruled on 13 March 1991 that the Directive did so require. It also ruled, in reply to a second question, that the transitional payments awarded to certain married men should be paid to married women in similar family circumstances, i.e. irrespective of actual dependency, even if this infringed the prohibition on 'unjust enrichment' laid down by national law.

On 6 June 1991 the Supreme Court was told that the outstanding issues in this case had been settled between the parties, on terms which included payments to Ms Cotter and Ms McDermott, without admission of liability.

8.4.2   TIME-LIMITS

Emmott v. *Minister for Social Welfare* [1]

The claimant was a married woman with two dependant children and had been in receipt of disability benefit, at the reduced rate then applying to

---

[1]   [1991] ECR I-4269 (ECJ).

married women, from December 1983 until May 1986. After the ECJ's judgment in the *McDermott and Cotter* case, Ms Emmott sought payment of the higher rate, which had applied to married men in similar circumstances, as from 23 December 1984 (the date on which Directive 79/7/EEC should have been implemented). The Minister for Social Welfare replied in June 1987 stating that no decision could be made on her claim as the Directive was the subject of High Court litigation. However, her claim would be examined as soon as that court had given judgment, and this happened in June 1988.

In July 1988 the High Court granted Ms Emmott leave to institute proceedings for judicial review in order to recover the benefits in question, but without prejudice to the defendant's right to raise the issue of her non-observance of normal time-limits for initiating proceedings. Under 1986 Rules of the Superior Courts, such applications should normally be made 'within three months from the date when grounds for the application first arose, or six months where the relief sought certiorari, unless the Court considers that there is good reason for extending the period'. Since the Minister pleaded that the applicant's delay in initiating proceedings now constituted a bar to her claim, the High Court decided to refer the matter to the ECJ.

On 25 July 1991 the ECJ ruled that Community law precluded the reliance by Member States, in such cases, on national procedural rules relating to time-limits for bringing such proceedings, where the Member State concerned had not properly implemented the Directive.

8.4.3   TRANSITIONAL PAYMENTS

Carberry v. *Minister for Social Welfare* [1]

The claimant was a married woman who had been receiving disability benefit since July 1986. Her husband became unemployed in January 1987 but because he had not been unemployed and receiving benefit on 17 November 1986, the family did not qualify for transitional payments, although it would have done so if the claimant had been a man.

Barron J accepted that Mrs Carberry was entitled to receive the transitional payments, since her circumstances were such that had she been a man, she would have been entitled to receive them. He then dealt with the question of retrospection and whether the amounts should be payable to her in respect of the period from 23 December 1984 to 17 November 1986.

Stating that the law in relation to retrospective claims had been altered since the judgment of Hamilton P in *McDermott and Cotter* (by the ECJ's

---

[1]   28 April 1989, unreported (HC).

decision in *Barra* [1]), Barron J found in favour of the applicant's claim for arrears. He pointed out that in the *Barra* case, the ECJ had stated that it was for that Court alone to decide on any time limitations on the principle of 'direct effect'. No such limitation had been laid down by the Court in the case of *McDermott and Cotter*. He therefore saw no reason to grant the plaintiffs' request for a reference to the ECJ, since essentially the same question was at issue; and said that they were 'entitled to rely retrospectively upon the ruling of the ECJ in those cases' (i.e. *Barra* and *Gravier* [2]).

Since this judgment conflicted with the earlier one by Hamilton P on the question of retrospection and 'direct effect', the subsequent ruling in *McDermott and Cotter* was awaited with interest. The subsequent cases referred to above appeared to clarify all issues and an appeal to the Supreme Court seemed unnecessary. However, like all other women whose claims had been 'frozen' pending the outcome of these cases, Ms Carberry had still received no settlement at the time of writing.

8.4.4   ADULT DEPENDANT'S ALLOWANCE

Healy v. *Eastern Health Board* [3]

In this case, the applicant was a married woman who had been receiving a disabled person's maintenance allowance (a means-tested payment) from March 1986. Her husband had been claiming unemployment assistance (also a means-tested payment) until November 1986. Following the changes in the definition of 'adult dependant' in November 1986, the combined family income fell because she was no longer regarded as her husband's dependent and his payment was correspondingly reduced. Despite this reduction, the Health Board did not allow any increase in the claimant's means-tested payment. In an unreported judgment Keane J said that the regulations had been applied in an unconstitutional manner, because if the couple had not been married, the husband's entitlements would not have been taken into account in determining the claimant's payments. The case was therefore won on the basis of the Constitution, rather than by reference to Directive 79/7/EEC.

8.4.5   MARRIED COUPLES' ENTITLEMENTS

Hyland v. *Minister for Social Welfare* [4]

Indirect discrimination, based on marital status, was also at issue in the *Hyland* case, in which the validity of s. 12 of the 1985 Act was challenged.

---

1   *Barra* v. *Belgium* Case 309/85, [1988] ECR 355, [1988] 2 CMLR 409 (ECJ).
2   *Gravier* v. *City of Liege*, Case 293/83, [1985] ECR 593, [1985] 3 CMLR 1 (ECJ).
3   11 March 1988, unreported (HC).
4   [1989] ILRM 196 (HC); [1990] ILRM 213 (SC).

This section of the Act limited the amount of unemployment assistance payable to married couples, where each partner was entitled to a payment in his/her own right, to the total amount which would have been payable to them prior to the November 1986 changes (i.e. the amount payable to one 'breadwinner' with a dependent spouse). Counsel for Hyland argued that s. 12 constituted indirect discrimination, but in his judgment Barrington J held that since s. 12 applied equally to married men as to married women, and since, in his view, art. 4 of the Directive only proscribed marital discrimination where it was sex discrimination in disguise, there was no issue of indirect sex discrimination in this case. However, as in the *Healy* case, the provision was held to be contrary to art. 41 of the Irish Constitution as it constituted an attack on the institution of marriage. The claim therefore succeeded on the basis of the Constitution rather than the Directive.

The Supreme Court affirmed this order, agreeing that the provisions of s. 12 of the 1985 Act penalized the married state in a manner similar to those of ss 192 to 198 of the Income Tax Act 1967 and s. 21 of the Act of 1980, which had been deemed unconstitutional in the *Murphy* case.[1] It rejected the respondents' contention that the differences in objectives between taxation statutes and social welfare statutes could affect the constitutional effect of s. 12(4) of the 1985 Act; and said that if a statutory provision breached a constitutional right, it was irrelevant what the legislature's purpose in enacting it had been.

After this ruling, the Oireachtas enacted the Social Welfare (No 2) Act 1989,[2] which amended s. 12 of the 1985 Act, by reducing the entitlements of cohabiting unmarried couples to the same level as those of cohabiting married couples; and removed the right to retrospective claims by all married couples who had not initiated proceedings prior to 9 May 1989 (the date of the Supreme Court's ruling).

---

[1] *Murphy* v. *AG* [1982] IR 241 (SC).
[2] See §7.4.3.2 above.

9. DOCUMENTATION

9.1   BIBLIOGRAPHY

9.1.1   BOOKS AND REPORTS

CURTIN, Deirdre, *Irish Employment Equality Law*, Dublin, Round Hall Press, 1989.

EMPLOYMENT EQUALITY AGENCY, *Annual Reports*, Dublin.

SECOND COMMISSION ON THE STATUS OF WOMEN, *Report to Government*, Dublin, Stationery Office, 1993.

VON PRONDZYNSKI, Ferdinand (ed.), *Women and the Completion of the Internal Market*, Dublin, Department of Labour, 1990.

VON PRONDZYNSKI, Ferdinand, and McCARTHY, Charles, *Employment Law in Ireland*, London, Sweet & Maxwell, 1989.

WHYTE, Gerry, *Sex Equality, Community Rights and Irish Social Welfare Law*, Dublin, Irish Centre for European Law, 1988.

9.1.2   ARTICLES AND REVIEWS

CURTIN, Deirdre
— 'Birds of Passage and Pension Schemes', *Journal of the Irish Society for Labour Law*, Vol. 5, 1986, p. 37.
— 'Effective Sanctions and Equal Treatment Cases', *Common Market Law Review*, Vol. 22, 1985, p. 505.

9.2   INFORMATION

9.2.1   USEFUL ADDRESSES

Department of Equality and Law Reform
    43-49 Mespil Road
    Dublin 4

Employment Equality Agency
    36 Upper Mount Street
    Dublin 2

Labour Court/Labour Relations Commission
    Haddington Road
    Dublin 4

INDEX